FACING THE EXTREME

ALSO BY TZVETAN TODOROV

A French Tragedy: Scenes of Civil War, Summer 1944

The Morals of History

On Human Diversity: Nationalism, Racism,
and Exoticism in French Thought

Genres of Discourse

Literature and Its Theorists

The Conquest of America

Theories of the Symbol

Mikhail Bakhtin

Symbolism and Interpretation

An Introduction to Poetics

Encyclopedic Dictionary of the Sciences of Language

The Poetics of Prose

The Fantastic: A Structural Approach
to a Literary Genre

FACING THE EXTREME

Moral Life in the Concentration Camps

TZVETAN TODOROV

Translated by Arthur Denner
and Abigail Pollack

Weidenfeld & Nicolson

LONDON

First published in Great Britain in 1999
by Weidenfeld & Nicolson

Originally published in France in 1991 under the title
Face à l'extrême by Editions du Seuil

Published in the US in 1997 by Henry Holt and Company, Inc.

© 1996 Tzvetan Todorov
English translation copyright © 1996 by Metropolitan Books

A CIP catalogue record for this book
is available from the British Library.

ISBN 0 297 64306 1

Printed in Great Britain by Clays Ltd, St Ives plc

Weidenfeld & Nicolson
The Orion Publishing Group Ltd
Orion House
5 Upper Saint Martin's Lane
London, WC2H 9EA

FOR MY WIFE

Contents

PROLOGUE
A Trip to Warsaw 3
A Place for Moral Life? 31

NEITHER HEROES NOR SAINTS
Heroism and Saintliness 47
Dignity 59
Caring 71
The Life of the Mind 91

NEITHER MONSTERS NOR BEASTS
Ordinary People 121
Fragmentation 141
Depersonalization 158
The Enjoyment of Power 179

FACING EVIL
Nonviolence and Resignation 197
Forms of Combat 213
The Perils of Judgment 229
Telling, Judging, Understanding 254

EPILOGUE
Notes on Morality 285

Works Cited 297

Index 303

PROLOGUE

A Trip to Warsaw

SUNDAY VISITS

It began very simply, in November of 1987. A friend had offered to show us some sights that were not on the official tour of Warsaw. We had accepted eagerly, glad for the opportunity to escape the program to which we had been bound by the conference, our reason for being in this city. So it was that we arrived on a Sunday around noon at the church where Father Popieluszko—the priest who had been killed by the secret police for his ties to the Solidarity movement—had officiated and where he now lay buried. It was a striking scene. Merely on entering the courtyard of the church, it seemed, we were in a different world, overflowing with banners and posters we had seen nowhere else in the city. Inside, in the semicircle of the choir, was an exhibit documenting the life of the martyred priest, each of the glass cases—like so many personal stations of the cross—illustrating a moment in his career. There were pictures of him in private meetings and pictures of him in crowds; there was a map that traced the route of his last journey, and then a photograph of the bridge from which he had been thrown into the river. A little further on, a crucifix with Popieluszko in place of Christ. Outside was the tombstone itself, around which a heavy chain, riveted to stones, formed the outline of a map of greater Poland (reaching into Lithuania and the Ukraine). All in all, there was an intensity here that stuck in your throat. And everywhere around us the crowd, endless: the service had just concluded, and we waited a long time for the flood of people leaving the building to subside so that we could enter, but when we finally did we found that the church, miraculously, was still full.

I could not help thinking then of the visit we had made that same morning to the Jewish cemetery in Warsaw. We were alone. A step or two off the central path and we were plunged into indescribable chaos: trees had grown up between the graves; weeds and wild grasses had crowded in, erasing all the boundaries between them, and the tombstones themselves had gone the way of the coffins and sunk into the earth. We suddenly understood that, by contrast, other cemeteries were full of life, because in them the past remained present, whereas here even the tombstones—those petrifications of memory—were dying. The extermination of the Jews during the war, marked by a few monuments at the entrance to the graveyard, had had this further effect: it had killed a second time those who had died the century before, for it had killed the memories in which they might have lived on. There was total silence around us, and yet our voices seemed not to carry. Hardly had we entered the cemetery when we lost one another. The trees that had pushed up between the graves blocked our view, and our shouts went unanswered. And then, just as suddenly, we found one another again and began to wander about silently, pausing here and there before the funerary monuments that sprang out at us from this fantastic forest.

There was an emotional connection between these two parts of the morning, but also a difference I could not define. Several days later, back in Paris, I continued to feel unsettled by my inability to understand. I thought that by reading some books on Polish history I could put an end to my confusion and overcome my feeling of uneasiness. During my stay in Warsaw I had been told, on separate occasions, of two books that might interest me. Perhaps, I thought, these books contained the key to this feeling that puzzled me. And so I bought them and began to read, immersing myself in them. As it happens, they dealt with two events in recent history—the Warsaw ghetto uprising of 1943 and the Warsaw Rising of 1944. I felt that they did indeed shed some light on the present; I wanted to know more and looked for other books on these events. This is what I found.

WARSAW, 1944

The first of the two books, *Varsovie 44*, contains interviews that Jean-François Steiner conducted with people who either had taken part in the Warsaw Rising or had witnessed it or were experts on Polish history. (The revolt took place in the summer of 1944 when the Red Army had reached the eastern suburbs of Warsaw; the Polish resisters hoped to bring down the German occupation force on their own, thereby confirming Poland's independence from Russia. They fought heroically for months but failed.) These interviews, interspersed with various documents from the period as well as excerpts from literary works, form a long montage of texts, all revolving around the question of how the decision to revolt was reached. In the detailed accounts describing the rising fervor, I realized I was actually reading a reflection on heroism. Certainly the rebels were heroes, but, more than that, the hold that heroic values had on their spirit seemed to have played a decisive role in the outbreak of the revolt and in its progress. This heroic spirit had acted as a kind of drug; it kept the fighters in a state of exaltation that helped them withstand even the most difficult ordeals.

But what exactly *is* heroism, I asked myself as I read. With respect to the great antinomy underlying human actions—necessity versus freedom, or impersonal law versus individual will—heroism clearly falls on the side of freedom and free will. Where, to the eyes of ordinary people, the situation seems to offer no alternative, where it seems that one must bow to circumstances, the hero fights the odds and, through some extraordinary deed, manages to bend destiny to his own ends. The hero is the opposite of the fatalist; he is on the side of the revolutionary, never the conservative, for he has no particular respect for the status quo and believes people can attain any goal they choose, provided they have the will to do so.

The leaders of the Warsaw Rising, those who gave the orders for it to begin, plainly acted in this heroic spirit. Colonel Okulicki was the chief of operations for the Polish Home Army (the Armia Krajowa, the underground organization that spearheaded the revolt and that, unlike the smaller Armia Ludowa, the Communist People's Army, had links to London, not Moscow); his fate was especially tragic—he died not from Hitler's bullets, as he would have wished, but in Stalin's prisons, which he feared above all else. According to recollections of survivors, Okulicki embraced a heroic outlook from the start. "He wanted things to be the way he thought they ought to be," states a witness, "and he refused to accept their being otherwise" (Steiner 101). Okulicki's concern for what ought to be far outweighed his attention to what was. The same was true of Brigadier-General Tadeusz Pelczynski, the chief of staff. In his interview with Steiner thirty years later, he recalls, "We knew Poland was doomed, but we could not accept that verdict" (241). Similarly, General Tadeusz Bor-Komorowski, the commander in chief, remembers that on the eve of the uprising he simply "discounted the possibility that it might fail," believing that things would turn out just as they should (Ciechanowski 247). When, after the fighting had begun, someone told Colonel Antoni Monter, the Home Army region commander for Warsaw, that a certain neighborhood had fallen into German hands, he shot back, "I do not accept this information" (Zawodny 22). That attitude is typical of the hero: he may know that his ideal is unrealizable (in this case, both Poland's position on the map and the Red Army's military potential made Soviet occupation a foregone conclusion), but because he desires it above all else, he pursues it with all his might.

Pelczynski turns this heroic principle into something like a military code of honor. "For a soldier," he asserts, "there is no order that cannot be carried out if he has the will to do so" (Steiner 112). There is no distinguishing between reasonable and unreasonable orders, between those that do and those that do not take account of the situation as it really is. All that matters, according to this code, is whether or not there is a sufficient measure of will. This, it seems, was the Polish military tradition. Steiner cites a prewar general who explains to his subordinates that material shortages can always be compensated for by an effort of will, by the soldiers' capacity for self-sacrifice. "Let there be an inverse relation between your munitions and Polish blood," he admonishes them. "Anytime you lack some of the former, make up for it with some of the latter" (122). Okulicki's position was identical: in the hands of people with sufficient determination, sticks and bottles would be perfectly adequate against German tanks. Later, Pelczynski would say the same: "We saw their material superiority over us. But . . . the Polish people had the advantage of better morale." The Poles, moreover, were not alone in their choice. As another Polish official put it, "When the people of Paris were marching on the Bastille, they did not count their clubs" (Ciechanowski 261).

Heroes, then, prefer the ideal to the real—that much is certain. During the Warsaw Rising, the ideal went by several names. Clearly the rebels were fighting for the freedom of Warsaw (and, if possible, its survival); more often, however, they spoke in terms of a loftier ideal, that of "the nation." "We must fight," says Okulicki, "without regard for anything or anyone, and in our heart of hearts there can be only one thought—Poland" (Steiner 108). To claim that one's ideal is "the nation" is not enough, however, for the nation can be many things: a group of human beings—my family and friends or my compatriots, for instance—or a certain number of places and houses and roads. These interpretations Okulicki rejects: the uprising, he argues, must not be postponed "under the pretext of saving a few lives or a few houses" (108). It is a question of saving not the people of Warsaw but the idea of Warsaw, not individual Poles or Polish territory but an abstraction called Poland. "For us, Poland was the object of a genuine cult," another rebel commander declares. "We loved her not simply as a country; we loved her as a mother, a queen, a virgin" (10). Thus the country was deified (and feminized); in the process many of its real characteristics were simply ignored.

And so it was not the Polish people who had to be saved but, rather, certain qualities of theirs: their will to freedom, their desire for independence, their national pride. "If we do not fight," Pelczynski warns, "the Polish nation risks a terrible moral collapse" (121). And as it was becoming impossible to defend material values, he states on another occasion, the Polish people had to content themselves with moral values (Ciechanowski 277). Kazimierz Sosnkowski, the Polish supreme commander in chief in London, writes the following in a letter to Prime Minister Stanislaw Mikolajczyk: "Acts of despair are sometimes unavoidable in the lives of nations, in view of the common feelings of the population, the political symbolism of such acts, and their moral significance for posterity" (158). In other words, people must die so that moral and political values can survive. A further implication, of course, is that there must be someone to define what is moral and what is not and to determine—with an eye to history and to the future—what course of action to take in the present.

But even Poland the abstraction is not always enough; Poland must itself be offered up to an even more distant ideal—that of the West, which, in its turn, comes to stand for civilization, or even "humanity." The Russians are the forces of barbarism and Poland the last line of defense against them. Thus it becomes possible to sacrifice the lives of any number of people in the name of defending humanity. In a letter to Bor-Komorowski, Sosnkowski reveals his desire to make the Polish question "a problem for the conscience of the world, a test-case for the future of European nations" (185). Bor himself recalls, "We felt that the battle for Warsaw would have to call for a response from the world" (269). Okulicki justifies the revolt in a similar fashion: "An effort was needed which would stir the conscience of the world" (211). The insurrection becomes a sacrificial act in the name of a series of increasingly remote and always impersonal beneficiaries or audiences—Warsaw, Poland, the West, the world. Lives are sacrificed not for other human beings but for ideas. In the final analysis, nothing less than the absolute can satisfy these heroic spirits.

In the lives of the heroes, certain human qualities are more highly prized than others. Foremost among them is loyalty to an ideal— loyalty that is valued in and of itself, independent of the nature of the ideal. (That is why we can admire a heroic enemy.) The hero, in this sense, is the opposite of the traitor: whatever the circumstances, he never betrays (behavior that is no doubt a vestige of the chivalric code of honor). Thus when Okulicki was arrested and interrogated by the Soviet secret police, he remained silent; of course, such restraint also requires a great capacity to withstand physical suffering. The hero is a solitary figure, in fact, doubly so: not only does he fight for abstractions rather than for individuals, but family and friends, by their very existence, make him vulnerable. The hero's education is an apprenticeship in isolation; it is also, of course, the time when his courage hardens and grows strong. The courageous act is, in fact, the most direct manifestation of heroism. Once again, Okulicki serves as example: in the heat of battle, he volunteers to attack an enemy machine-gun nest; his pockets stuffed with hand grenades, he races alone across the open field. Here, courage is simply the willingness to risk one's life to attain a goal. Life is not the supreme value; indeed, it can be sacrificed at any time. When a clear goal is absent, however, or when the goal is an insignificant one, what we have is no longer heroism and bravery but bravado: one risks one's life for no particular reason. Okulicki, for example, hated to hide. "Bombs and shells were falling all around us," a witness reports. "The few people we came upon were dashing from one shelter to the next, and there was Oku-licki strolling calmly down the middle of the street as though unaware of the danger" (Steiner 98). Conversely, a lack of courage is what the hero most despises in others.

The hero, then, is prepared to sacrifice his own life as well as the lives of others, provided the sacrifice advances the chosen goal. But even this stipulation ceases to matter—and here we are not speaking of bravado—the instant the hero decides to act on behalf of a benefi-ciary as remote as history or humanity: there is little risk of abstrac-tions like these ever disappointing heroic expectations. That is why the leaders of the Warsaw Rising decided that it should take place "whatever the cost" (215). When the battle is fought for the benefit of no real, concrete individual, or particular group of individuals, it be-comes an end in itself, irrefutable proof of the heroic spirit of those who wage it. We must fight, Stefan Grot-Rowecki, who preceded Bor-Komorowski as commander of the Home Army, used to say, "even if a hopeless struggle awaits us" (Ciechanowski 137). "We shall all be massacred," predicts one of the rebels as events begin to unfold, "but at least we will have fought" (Steiner 190). Similarly, though in hind-sight, Pelczynski declares, "It was our duty to fight; as far as I was concerned, nothing else mattered" (241).

Okulicki's reasoning is more elaborate. If the insurrection begins and the Russians come to our aid, he argues, the wager is won, but if they don't intervene, if they let the Germans massacre us, all is still not lost: Warsaw will be destroyed, many Poles will die, but the Soviet perfidy will be obvious to everyone; the Western powers will fight the Russians in a Third World War, and out of the ashes a new Poland will arise. . . . His predictions, of course, proved only partially correct: the Soviet forces did not support the Warsaw Rising, which, it bears repeating, was not only directed against the Germans, but also had the Russians in mind. The Germans put down the insurrection, killing 200,000 people, deporting 700,000, and leveling Warsaw. But World War III did not take place, and Poland became a satellite of the Soviet Union much as if the insurrection had never taken place. The goal, then, was not attained, yet if it had been, would it have been justified at such a price? What kinds of acts are those that must be done "whatever the cost"?

The leaders of the Warsaw Rising often seemed to be following the slogan "Better dead than Red." They felt their choice was either to revolt and die or to surrender and live. They preferred the first solution. "For a Pole," Okulicki declares, "it is better to die than to be a coward," and it was said of Pelczynski that "when he suddenly understood that he had no choice but to surrender or die, he chose to die" (107, 238). Bor-Komorowski also preferred action, however futile, to inaction. And Monter's order to the commanders of the Mokotow sector of Warsaw on the fifty-sixth day of the fighting reflects a similar outlook: "You are forbidden to withdraw," he said (Zawodny 22). This kind of heroic stance commands respect. Still, one wonders if the choice set out above reflected the real possibilities. "Red" is the opposite not of "dead" but of "white" or "brown" or "black," and in the final analysis it is only the living who have a color. One of the fighters who opposed the uprising put it this way: "If all of us continue trying to die for Poland, one day soon there won't be any Poles left to live here" (Steiner 108). And when the heroes of the Warsaw Rising were dead, Warsaw went Red all the same.

To the hero, death has more value than life. Only through death—whether one's own or that of others—is it possible to attain the absolute: by dying for an ideal one proves that one holds it dearer than life itself. "Despair had driven them to aspire to the absolute," one witness says, "and at that level there was no solution but to die" (230). Measured against aspirations for the absolute, real life necessarily seems an unsatisfactory compromise. As another witness observes, "Heroes are not made to live" (11).

Perhaps life and death are opposites in another sense as well. In certain exceptional circumstances like the Warsaw Rising dying is easy, particularly if one believes in the resurrection of the soul. But even if one does not, death remains an unknown, and that is its fascination. To sacrifice one's life is to put all one's courage into a single definitive act, whereas staying alive can require a daily, moment-by-moment kind of courage. Life, too, is sometimes a sacrifice, but it is not a flamboyant one: to sacrifice my time and energy, if that is what is demanded of me, I have to stay alive. In this sense, it can be more difficult to live than to die.

Those who opposed the plans for the Warsaw Rising did not do so in the name of some slogan that would have merely stood the heroic principle on its head; they did not say, "Better Red than dead" or "It is better to surrender than to die." That was what their adversaries wanted people to believe. After Okulicki had heard the objections, he "started calling us cowards, telling us we were dragging our feet on the decision because we weren't brave enough to fight" (248). As a result, there was no way to protest. "We hardly dared criticize the slightest proposal for fear of making ourselves seem like cowards or traitors" (171). This last comment is revealing: one can act like a hero for fear of seeming a coward. The hero is not necessarily intrepid. It is simply that he feels a particular kind of fear, the fear of being afraid, and that feeling takes priority over all others and finally eclipses them.

Those who disagreed with Okulicki chose not the other alternative but rather a different set of options entirely. According to one dissenter whom Steiner interviewed, the real choice was between "a serious political and military action" and "a suicide perpetrated by irresponsible leaders who sought refuge in a glorious death because they didn't have the courage to face the difficulties of life" (221). For this man, the courage to live is rarer and more precious than the courage to die. Another of Okulicki's opponents uses the term *responsibility* (249). Politics and war must not be carried out in the name of what Weber calls the ethics of conviction, because these things are not matters of principle. The fact that I hold a belief does not guarantee that the community as a whole will benefit if I go ahead and act on it. One needs to anticipate the consequences of one's decisions while keeping in mind the actual course of events, not merely what one wishes would happen. Here, the word *responsibility* recovers its original meaning—a leader *is responsible for* the lives and well-being of those he commands; at the same time, he *responds to* appeals from many different sources.

The hero's world—and perhaps herein lies his weakness—is one-dimensional; it is composed of pairs of opposites: us and them, friend and foe, courage and cowardice, hero and traitor, black and white. That outlook best befits situations in which the orientation is death, not life. In Warsaw of 1944, it was not simply the forces of good and evil that confronted each other but the Russians and the Germans, the Home Army and the People's Army, the government in exile and the civilian population. In circumstances this complex, reaching the best solution—in this instance, unfortunately, merely the lesser evil—requires a careful consideration of all sides rather than unswerving loyalty to an ideal. The values of life are not absolute values: life is diverse, and every situation is heterogeneous. Choices are made not out of concession or cowardly compromise but from a recognition of this multiplicity.

There is, however, a drawback to the nonheroic attitude: it does not lend itself well to stories, at least not to those in the traditional mold. Narratives, however, are indispensable for any society; in fact, heroes are themselves invariably inspired by literary or legendary example, usually impressed upon them in childhood. Even in the heat of the moment, the hero already foresees the effect his deed will produce once translated into words: the future story, the story that will one day be told, shapes the present. Okulicki, for example, criticizes other plans for the revolt as "not being spectacular enough," while his own plan is one of which "the whole world will speak" (106, 107). The insurgents' bulletin of October 3, 1944, declares, "Nobody in Poland, or in Warsaw, or in the whole world can . . . say that we surrendered too soon" (Zawodny 194). Concern for what will later be said is present at the very moment of action. The rebels understood themselves to be writing, as the time-honored formula has it, "one of the most glorious pages in the history of Poland." Thus, when Pelczynski realizes that Steiner, his interviewer, has no compelling interest in glorifying heroes, he becomes indignant: "If this is how you plan to write your book," he complains, "we might as well end this conversation right now" (Steiner 260). Beautiful tales need unblemished heroes. Spirits of a more practical bent, who take the constraints of reality into account, do not make particularly good narrative subjects. Prime Minister Mikolajczyk seems to have been such a man. "He didn't see himself as Christ or Saint George or the Virgin Mary," a witness says (58). How, then, is someone like him to be made into the hero of a tale?

THE GHETTO, 1943

The relation between heroism and narrative is also one of the main themes in *Shielding the Flame,* the second book that had been recommended to me in Poland. Written in the 1970s, this book, too, is constructed around a series of interviews, but between just two people, Hanna Krall and Marek Edelman, a leader of the other uprising in Warsaw, the ghetto revolt of 1943. And whereas *Varsovie 44* presents a montage in which the author does not appear, Krall decided that she herself should figure in the text.

The Warsaw ghetto uprising is another of the most glorious pages of history, in this case, the history of Jewish heroism; this has been said a thousand times. But it so happens that Edelman could not produce a truly heroic account of the events, at least not until some time after they had occurred. Krall describes Edelman's very first attempt to do so, three days after escaping from the ghetto, as he delivers a report to the representatives of various underground political parties. He gives a neutral account, flat and colorless, a simple description of what had just taken place. We lacked weapons and experience, he says. The Germans fought well. Deeply disappointed by the mediocre quality of the narrative, Edelman's audience attributed it to the state of shock its author must have been in at the time. "He was not talking the way he was supposed to talk. 'How is one supposed to talk?' Edelman asked me. One is supposed to talk with hatred and grandiloquence—one is supposed to scream. There's no other way to express all this except by screaming. And so, from the very beginning, he was no good at talking about it because he was unable to scream. He was no good as a hero because he lacked grandiloquence" (Krall and Edelman 14–15).

Hatred of the enemy, high emotion (pathos), a feverish tone (shouting, screaming): these are the ingredients missing from Edelman's report. On the other hand, they are not entirely absent from his text of 1945, a sober account (included in the French edition of the book) that nonetheless seeks to bring out the rebels' heroism. Thirty years later, when Edelman looks back on these events in his interview with Krall, he sees himself as a young man who wanted to imitate the conventional hero. Back then, he says, his dream was to run around "with two guns strapped to [his] body; the guns completed the outfit, very *de rigueur*. You figured in those days if you had two guns, you had everything" (1–2). He realizes now to what extent this desire to see himself as a hero figured in his attraction to firearms, in the very act of pulling the trigger. "People have always thought that shooting is the highest form of heroism," Edelman says. "So we shot" (3).

But now he sees things very differently. What actually took place seems to him to belie the official, heroic version of events. "Can you even call that an uprising?" he asks. "All it was about, finally, was our not letting them slaughter us when our turn came. It was only a choice as to the manner of dying" (10). Mordechai Anielewicz, the principal leader of the uprising, whose "heroic posture" Edelman had celebrated thirty years before, now appears in a different light: he is no less sympathetic a character, of course, but neither is he so completely an object of idolatry. If Anielewicz was elected to lead the uprising, Edelman says, it was "because he very much wanted to be a commander." And, he adds, "he was a little childish in this ambition" (22). Edelman also tells how Anielewicz, as a young boy, would apply red dye to the gills of the fish his mother sold, so that the fish would look fresh. This anecdote, translated into several languages, "angered many people," for Edelman "had stripped everything of its magnitude" (4, 10). The public—like Pelczynski, in his interview with Steiner—wants its heroes heroic.

Edelman insists on telling his story exactly as he remembers it, however, and not according to the conventions of heroic narrative. The desire for absolute accuracy leads him to observations like "In the Ghetto, there should only have been martyrs and Joan of Arcs, right? But if you want to know, in the bunker on Mila Street, together with Anielewicz's group, there were some prostitutes and even a pimp. A big tattooed guy, with huge biceps . . ." (42). Edelman claims, moreover, that he survived not because of some act of heroism but because the SS man who shot at him must have had an uncorrected astigmatism: all the bullets fell a little too far to the right (43).

This is not to say, of course, that the ghetto uprising did not give rise to acts of heroism like those of Okulicki. There was Michal Klepfisz, for instance, who threw himself onto a German machine gun so that his comrades could escape. While Edelman clearly admires acts of this sort, they do not truly capture his imagination. What interests him are actions of a different sort, equally virtuous but distinct enough from those with which we have been dealing that we need a different term to describe them. Let us then use the term *heroic virtues* in speaking of Okulicki and the term *ordinary virtues* to describe the cases that Edelman reports.

Like heroic virtues, the ordinary virtues are acts of will, individual efforts of refusal to accept what seems an implacable necessity. But such willful determination does not lead to the conclusion that "there is no order that cannot be carried out." In truth, it doesn't *lead* anywhere at all, because it provides its own justification. Edelman describes how he decided one day to become a resistance fighter. Walking down Zelazna Street in the ghetto, he saw an old man who had been hoisted up onto a barrel by two German officers; they were cutting off his beard with a huge pair of tailor's scissors and were doubled over with laughter. "At that moment, I realized that the most important thing was never letting myself be pushed onto the top of that barrel. Never, by anybody" (38). What Edelman understood is, first, that there is no qualitative difference between great and small humiliations and, second, that one can always express one's will, choose one's actions—and refuse to follow orders. The uprising may have been nothing more than a way for us to choose our death, he says. But the difference between choosing death and submitting to it is enormous; it is this difference that separates human beings from animals. In choosing one's death, one performs an act of will and thereby affirms one's membership in the human race. The Jews of Warsaw took no pride in the fact that Jews in some of the other Polish cities had let themselves be slaughtered; they decided that they, for their part, would act. In so doing, they had already achieved their goal: they had affirmed their humanity.

"To choose between life and death is the last chance to hold onto one's dignity," Hanna Krall observes (46). *Dignity:* this, then, is the first ordinary virtue, and it simply means the capacity of the individual to remain a subject with a will; that fact, by itself, is enough to ensure membership in the human race. To choose death means something very different from what it means in the context of the heroic virtues. For the hero, death eventually becomes a value and a goal, because it embodies the absolute better than life does. From the standpoint of the ordinary virtues, however, death is a means, not an end: it is the ultimate recourse of the individual who seeks to affirm his dignity.

Thus, suicide is valued not in itself but rather as an expression of will. Yet even the suicide that has the assertion of dignity as its goal is not always, from the perspective of the ordinary virtues, a truly admirable act. Dignity is a necessary but not a sufficient condition, as Edelman's description of two very famous suicides suggests. The first is that of Adam Czerniakow, president of the Jewish Council set up by the Germans, who killed himself in his office on learning of the decision to deport the residents of the ghetto to Treblinka. "We reproached him for having made his death his own private business. We were convinced that it was necessary to die publicly, in the eyes of the world" (9–10). In *Notes from the Warsaw Ghetto,* Emmanuel Ringelblum, the great historian of the ghetto, echoes that opinion: "The suicide of Czerniakow—too late, a sign of weakness—should have called for resistance—a weak man" (327). In choosing to take his own life without revealing to the community the fate that awaited it, without exhorting the people to fight back, Czerniakow acted with dignity but without real concern for others. It's not that he was oblivious to his community; the journal in which he set down his thoughts and impressions makes that clear. And in his suicide note, he writes, "I am powerless, my heart trembles in sorrow and compassion. I can no longer bear all this. My act will show everyone the right thing to do" (Hilberg et al. 344). Czerniakow means to address his contemporaries, but he chooses to do so in such a way that they cannot hear him. Was suicide really his only option?

The second suicide (which in fact may not have been a suicide at all) is that of Mordechai Anielewicz, the young commander of the ghetto rebels. "He should never have done it," Edelman says. "Even though it was a very good symbol. You don't sacrifice your life for a symbol" (6). (Sosnkowski says the exact opposite, that the symbol is precisely the thing one should die for.) Two suicides, in many ways different—one too private, the other too symbolic—but with much in common nevertheless: each takes into consideration the remote beneficiary of the act, history, and each neglects those who are most directly affected, the other inhabitants of the ghetto. Thus, instead of serving as a means of helping others, the suicides were acts that began and ended with themselves.

This further requirement of virtuous acts, that they not only demonstrate the dignity of their authors but also contribute to the welfare of others, might be called *caring*. Caring, or concern, is the second ordinary virtue: acts of ordinary virtue are undertaken not in behalf of humanity or the nation but always for the sake of an individual human being. Concern for others carries with it certain rewards. There are things we can do for others that we are incapable of doing solely for ourselves, and so concern for others can keep us from giving up. "Everybody had to have somebody to act for, somebody to be the center of his life," Edelman recounts. "To be with someone was the only way to survive in the ghetto. . . . So if someone, somehow, by some miracle escaped and was still alive, he had to stick to some other human being" (42–43, 48).

On the subject of those who died because they cared for someone else, Edelman is no longer reticent at all; on the contrary, it is precisely these acts of ordinary virtue that make the strongest impression on him. And so we learn of a young girl named Pola Lifszyc and what she did as the transport convoys began to leave for Treblinka. "She went to her house and . . . saw that her mother wasn't there," Edelman says. "Her mother was already in a column marching toward the *Umschlagplatz*. Pola ran after the column alone, from Leszno Street to Stawki Street. Her fiancé gave her a lift in his *riksa* so that she could catch up—and she made it. At the last minute, she managed to merge into the crowd so as to be able to get on the train with her mother" (45). (The train, of course, was one of those whose passengers never returned to their point of departure.) Why was Pola in such a hurry? Did her fiancé have any idea what his bicycle was being used for?

Edelman tells us of a nurse named Mrs. Tenenbaum who had obtained a pass that permitted its bearer to avoid deportation—temporarily. Her daughter did not have one, and so Mrs. Tenenbaum handed the pass to her, asking her to hold it for a moment, then went upstairs and swallowed a fatal dose of Luminal, thereby avoiding any and all discussion. During the three months following what amounted to a temporary stay of execution, the time afforded her by the pass, Mrs. Tenenbaum's daughter fell in love and knew real happiness. Edelman tells another story, of a niece of Tosia Goliborska, one of his colleagues, who, immediately after her wedding ceremony, found the barrel of a soldier's rifle shoved up against her belly. Her new husband put out his hand to protect her, only to have it blown off. "But this was precisely what mattered," Edelman says, "that there be someone ready to cover your belly with his hand should it prove necessary" (48–49).

Most often, the beneficiary of such concern was a family member— a mother or daughter, brother or sister, husband or wife. But with so many loved ones gone, other "relatives" were found, people who acted as "surrogates." And even when the surrogate beneficiary was not one person but many—like the children whom Dr. Janusz Korczak accompanied from his orphanage to Treblinka so that they would not go alone or the fellow Jews whom Abraham Gepner, a rich industrialist, chose to remain with—the beneficiaries were never an abstraction but individuals of flesh and blood, personally known to the subject. To fall short of such concern was not necessarily cause for blame, but it did mean a tacit breach of the human contract, as an episode related by one of Steiner's eyewitnesses illustrates. After the uprising of 1943 and before the Warsaw Rising of 1944, this witness came upon the Christian husband of a Jewish woman in the ruins of the ghetto. Like Pola, this woman had made the decision to go with her relatives on the transport train; her husband chose to stay behind. Although she did not reproach him for his decision, something between them had been severed nonetheless. "What she wanted," said the husband, "was for me to have gone to die with her. Instead, I let her go and I let her die. And I've been atoning ever since" (Steiner 202).

Sometimes caring can lead people to take not their own lives but, paradoxically, the lives of others. A doctor poisons the children in the hospital where she works, before the SS has a chance to take them away. "She saved these children from the gas chamber," Edelman says. But in order to do so, she had to sacrifice her own poison. "[The nurses] were saving this poison for their closest relatives. And this doctor had given her *own* cyanide to kids who were complete strangers!" (9). It is precisely in this sense that to live can be more difficult than to die. Edelman also tells of the nurse who was attending a woman in childbirth on the second floor of a hospital as the Germans were clearing out the first. When the baby was born, "the doctor handed it to the nurse, and the nurse laid it on one pillow, then smothered it with another one. The baby whimpered a little, and then fell silent" (47). The nurse did what had to be done; no one reproached her for it. Nevertheless, forty-five years later this nurse, Adina Blady Szwajger, now a pediatrician, cannot forget that she began her medical career by taking a life.

Ordinary virtues, then, have distinct characteristics very much in evidence even after the end of the war. Edelman's circumstances are less dramatic now, and he is no longer called upon to risk his life; his earlier choices, however, have steered him toward a new profession: he has become a cardiologist. "As a doctor, I can now be responsible for human lives," he declares. "But why would I want this responsibility? Doubtless because everything else seems unimportant to me" (126). Responsibility is a particular form of caring, the form incumbent on people in privileged positions, like doctors or leaders. Indeed, it is for not having seen their responsibilities through that Anielewicz and Czerniakow fell short—although in different ways—of what caring demanded.

These two kinds of virtue—the ordinary and the heroic—differ with respect to the beneficiaries of the acts they inspire: acts of ordinary virtue benefit individuals, a Miss Tenenbaum, for example, whereas acts of heroism can be undertaken for the benefit of something as abstract as a certain concept of Poland. Both kinds of virtue, however, demand courage and the sacrifice of energy or life. And both can call for a split-second decision—whether Okulicki's attack on an enemy machine-gun nest or Pola's leap onto her fiancé's bicycle. Heroic virtues tend to be the province of men, while ordinary virtues are equally if not more characteristic of women (but it is true that the physical abilities required are different). Yet the real difference comes down to the question of whether it is for people or ideas that one has chosen to die (or live).

This opposition is not to be confused with the opposition between the particular and the general, that is, between loyalty to one's own group and a love of humanity as a whole. To be loyal to one's compatriots alone means not to care about foreigners; but foreigners are individuals like everyone else. And "humanity" need not be interpreted as a mere abstraction, the way the leaders of the 1944 Warsaw Rising understood it; it can also mean the community of all concrete human beings. Moral obligation—to care for a person—can be universal without being abstract. Therefore, those who prefer their own kind exclusively, who act out of blind loyalty, do not necessarily value people more than ideas; they value certain individuals more than others. Yet by the same token, those who see humanity as an abstraction can also commit crimes in its name—and all the more easily in that, depending on the moment and the people involved, ideas can mask very different realities. Indeed, those ideas that seem the purest and most generous and disinterested are often made to serve the most tragic ventures. After all, Hitler used to say that he was fighting the Russians in order to halt barbarism and rescue civilization. With human beings, however, there is no such danger: they represent only themselves.

Let us return for a moment to Mordechai Anielewicz. In many ways he appears to be a hero in the traditional mold, like Okulicki. He was a man of great physical strength and personal courage, both of which spurred him to action; loyal beyond reproach, he was prepared to leap into the flames to save a comrade's life. He was driven by a completely selfless idealism. His life had but one goal, to fight the Nazis, which explains why, when the uprising began, he could write in a letter, "The dream of my life was realized. . . . The armed Jewish struggle and the revenge became a reality" (Suhl 109). Something of the same spirit is evident in a letter written in 1940 by Anielewicz's friend Mira Fuchrer while she lived in the ghetto: "I have never been so happy," she confides (Kurzman 15). All other preoccupations are cast aside. Anielewicz's organization was run with the kind of austerity characteristic of political or religious militants: the men were forbidden to smoke, drink, or have sexual relations. As his friend Ringelblum wrote after Anielewicz's death, "The moment Mordechai decided on struggle, no other question existed for him. The scientific circles and the seminars came to an end; the manifold cultural and educational work was interrupted. Now he and his comrades concentrated only on the area of struggle" (Suhl 89). Like the leaders of the 1944 Warsaw Rising, Anielewicz wanted his death to be charged with symbolic meaning, to bear a message for those who were not there: "We will give our death a historical meaning," he wrote in a letter smuggled out to a friend in Palestine, "and full significance for future generations" (Kurzman 98).

A true hero, Anielewicz fully accepted the idea of his own death. According to Ringelblum, the situation in the ghetto, for Anielewicz, came down to a single question: "What kind of death will the Polish Jews select for themselves? Will it be the death of sheep led to the slaughter without resistance, or of people with honour who want the enemy to pay for their death with his own blood?" (Suhl 89). The choice was not between life and death but between two types of death, that of honorable men or that of sheep. Like Okulicki, Anielewicz reduced the future to a set of alternatives that in fact left no choice. But did his formulation of the options really exhaust all the possibilities? In Anielewicz's framing of the alternatives, death with honor is clearly the preferred solution. Unwilling to accept compromise, Anielewicz wanted victory or death, which, under the circumstances, meant the latter. This would explain his suicide (if indeed that is what it was): the bunker in which he was barricaded had an exit that was not being watched by the SS, but survival not being Anielewicz's ultimate goal, he did not use that exit. As Aryeh Wilner, one of his comrades, explains, "We did not want to save our lives. . . . We wanted to save our dignity" (Borwicz 69). While some of Anielewicz's comrades may have shared that point of view, others, including Marek Edelman, did not.

Anielewicz gave secondary importance not only to his own life but to the lives of others around him (even if he was prepared to sacrifice himself for them). In the months preceding the uprising, the ZOB (Zydowska Organizacja Bojowa, or Jewish Combat Organization), led by Anielewicz, refused to build hideouts or dig tunnels to the "Aryan side," as members of the other resistance organization, the right-wing ZZW (Zydowski Zwiazek Wojskowy, or Jewish Military Union), did; Anielewicz feared that preparations of this kind would weaken the rebels' fighting spirit. At one point it had become possible—for a price, naturally—to hide a few people in houses beyond the ghetto walls. Anielewicz opposed this plan for the same reason: whatever money there was should be used to finance the struggle, not to save individual lives. "For him," Ringelblum writes, "there existed now only one goal, and he was sacrificing all for that particular goal: the struggle with the enemy" (90). Anielewicz was equally opposed to another proposal, this one from the National Committee, of which he himself was a member. In February and March 1943, the committee wanted to transfer certain cultural and communal activities to the "other side" to ensure their continued operation. In Anielewicz's eyes, however, this meant once again favoring survival over struggle.

Ringelblum observes that within the ghetto the conflict over the most effective way to counter Nazi persecution divided the community along generational lines. The older people hoped for survival, their own as well as their families'. But the young, "whose hands and feet were not bound by family ties," preferred honor to life. "The youth—the best, the most beautiful, the finest that the Jewish people possessed—spoke and thought only about an honorable death. They did not think about surviving the war. They did not procure for themselves Aryan papers. They had no dwellings on the other side. Their only concern was to discover the most dignified, most honorable death, as befits an ancient people with a history of several thousand years" (90). The young people, with Anielewicz (and also Ringelblum) in the lead, favored the heroic virtues above all others, whereas married men and women, bound by the love they felt for each other, for their children, and for their aging parents, opted for the ordinary virtues.

To return to the project undertaken by Edelman and Krall, their aim was not to rewrite history; the story of the uprising had by then become a matter of record. But history—like the hero—tends not to be concerned with individuals, whereas individuals and details are precisely what interest Edelman and Krall. "We are not writing History, after all," Krall says. "We are writing about remembering" (68). But even when speaking about individuals, one must be careful: beyond a certain threshold, they become a mass, and that mass an abstraction. As Edelman tells Krall of a comrade who was burned alive in the fighting, he stops to asks her, "Do you think that will impress anybody—one burning guy, after four hundred thousand burned people?" (That was the number of ghetto residents who died.) "I think that one burned guy makes a bigger impression than four hundred thousand," Krall replies. "And four hundred thousand a bigger impression than six million" (4–5).

A death can be beautiful, or not. Edelman describes the death of a young girl as she runs through a field of sunflowers, and he cannot help calling it "a truly beautiful death" (16). Having taken part in both Warsaw uprisings, Edelman finds the second one aesthetically superior to the first: for one thing, the rebels were armed; they could meet the enemy in hand-to-hand combat, face to face. "What a terrific congenial fight that was!" Edelman recalls (71). But even in the earlier uprising, the question of beauty was not altogether extraneous to the decision to take up weapons and begin the fight. As Edelman remarks with resignation, "After all, humanity had agreed that dying with arms was more beautiful than dying empty-handed. Therefore, we followed that consensus" (37). One can argue about whether it is more beautiful to race across rooftops than to remain hidden in a cellar, whether, in other words, the consensus should or should not be accepted, but at least one thing is certain: it is no less worthy to suffocate in a hole in the ground than it is to die scaling a wall. Today, however, caught up as we are in the pleasures of spectatorship, we have come to prefer beauty over such values as dignity. As Krall suggests, "It's easier to see someone die in battle than to watch Pola Lifszyc's mother climb into a railroad car" (37).

This is what Edelman refuses to accept. "He begins to shout," Hanna Krall recounts. "He shouts that I probably consider the people . . . surging into the cars of the train to have been worse than

the ones who were shooting. . . . To die in a gas chamber is by no
means worse than to die in battle. . . . After all, it's much easier to
die firing" (37). Shouting, however, doesn't do much good. History
ultimately triumphs over remembering, and history needs heroes. On
the graves of Michal Klepfisz and others killed in Zielonka, there
stands a monument: "An upright man with a rifle in one hand, a
grenade upraised in the other one; he has a cartridge pouch sashed
about his waist, a bag with maps at his side, and a belt across his
chest." None of the fighters from the ghetto looked like this; they had
no guns, they had no equipment, they were grimy and dirty. "But on
the monument, they look the way they were ideally supposed to. On
the monument, everything is bright and beautiful" (77). Monuments
obey the conventions of their genre; they do not try to speak the
truth. Weeds grow rampant in Warsaw's Jewish cemetery, crowding
out the tombs, while white monuments and heroic sagas conceal by
their imposing eloquence the words and actions of the inhabitants of
the ghetto.

QUESTIONS

By the time I had finished reading these two books, it had become
clear to me that, whatever the differences between the uprisings of
1944 and 1943, these differences had nothing to do with the spirit
that drove their leaders. Posters in the ghetto exhorted people to die
with honor, and the same notion held sway among the militants of the
Home Army. It was "national dignity," writes Emmanuel Ringelblum,
that led the Jews to fight (Suhl 94); eighteen months later, national
dignity would lead the Poles to rise up as well. Colonel Okulicki saw
the Warsaw Rising as "a message to the world"; the leaders of the
ghetto uprising spoke in similar terms. They were fighting "to awaken
the world" (Suhl 117), to "let the world see the hopelessness of our
battle—as a demonstration and a reproach" (Kurzman 52). For many
in Poland, the Warsaw Rising has come to symbolize, more than any
other event in the country's history, the selfless heroism of the Polish
people. Similarly, in Israel, the twenty-seventh of Nissan, the date in
the Jewish calendar on which the Warsaw ghetto uprising began, is a

national holiday to commemorate the heroic spirit of the Jewish people.

The differences between the two uprisings have little to do with the sequence of the events that took place. When the Jews rose, the members of the Home Army who were stationed close by declined to intervene; the immediate reason for this refusal was not just the anti-Semitism of the Poles or the traditional isolation of the two communities from each other but also the pro-Soviet position of the Jews (into which that same anti-Semitism may perhaps have forced them). In any case, as Ringelblum writes, "The orientation of Hashomer [the organization out of which Anielewicz himself had come] was a pro-Soviet one—faith in the victory of the Soviet Union and in its heroic army" (Suhl 87). As for the Home Army, it was just as hostile to Stalin as it was to Hitler. However understandable that position, the Home Army drew seriously wrong conclusions from it and simply saw no reason to help those who appeared to be the allies of its worst enemy. Similarly, when the Poles revolted the following year, the Russians nearby did not intervene; they knew that the uprising was directed as much against them as against the Germans. Why go help those who not only hated them but were fighting against them? History repeats itself, tragically; again and again the logic of resentment prevails. And yet, in 1943, the anti-Soviet Polish forces were not really threatened by the Jewish rebels; nor, in 1944, were the Soviets by the Polish rebels. Both times ideological conviction took precedence over concern for protecting human lives.

Nonetheless, there was a difference between the two uprisings, and that difference has to do with the contexts in which they occurred; it is for this reason, moreover, that they do not have the same historical significance. The revolt of the Warsaw ghetto was a sane reaction to a policy of systematic extermination; every day, the Nazi occupiers of Warsaw sent a trainload of victims to Treblinka to be killed on arrival. With or without the uprising, the ghetto's days were numbered. And even if it was a futile heroism that drove some people to act, the revolt nevertheless took place when there was no other possible outcome but death. It may not have saved any lives, but the fact that it happened at all may well have helped others to live by showing them the possibility of active resistance. The Warsaw Rising, too, was the product of multiple motivations, not the least of which was the sheer despair caused by the political stalemate. Yet this revolt was not really inevitable; rather, it resulted from a calculation that proved errone-ous, in a situation that offered other possibilities. The love of abstrac-tions took precedence over the interests of individual human beings; the revolt helped no one, neither then nor afterward, neither there nor anywhere else.

The ghetto uprising deserves respect. Why exactly? It inspired no like actions during the war itself; much later, in Israel, it would even come to be used as a moral warrant for actions that may have been heroic but that were not necessarily just. Of course, it demonstrated the dignity of the ghetto inhabitants, but so did many other actions. In *Life and Fate,* the great Soviet Jewish writer Vasily Grossman, having first deplored the passivity of the Jewish victims in general, goes on to insist that "the great rising in the Warsaw ghetto, the uprisings in Treblinka and Sobibor . . . bear witness to the indestructibility of man's yearning for freedom" (216). That sentiment is echoed by Auschwitz survivor Jean Améry. "For a short time in those days," he writes, "I was able to foster the illusion that my dignity was totally restored through my own, no matter how modest, activity in the resis-tance movement, through the heroic uprising in the Warsaw ghetto" (*Mind* 91). He also writes, "Thanks to the insurgent Jews in some of the camps, above all in the Warsaw ghetto, today the Jew can look at his own human face, as a human being" (*Humanism* 34). But it seems clear to me that people can preserve their humanity and affirm their dignity or desire for freedom without rising up, weapons in hand, against the enemy; one does not need a ghetto uprising to reassure oneself that these qualities live on. If the uprising was a courageous reaction to a hopeless situation, so was Pola's act one of freedom, dignity, and humanity. For dignity is always and exclusively the dig-nity of an individual, not of a group or a nation, and honor need not always be soaked in the enemy's blood. The uprising in the Warsaw ghetto must be respected not so much because of its display of heroic virtues but because it was the right political answer to desperate cir-cumstances.

·   ·   ·

I closed my books. The uneasiness that led me to them in the first place had dissipated by now. Yet in its place came a new and more tenacious anxiety, and it could not be reduced to a purely intellectual question about the nature of heroism. I began to wonder how people in general react in extreme circumstances, how they *should* react, how *I* would react. But before I go any further, I need to clarify how I believe we should understand this central term of my investigation and where my interests and intentions lie.

Today, as we near the end of this, the twentieth century, we are tempted to ask what its place will be in history, how it will be remembered. Although I can't answer these questions with any more assurance than can the next person, of this I am fairly certain: one invention that this century has witnessed will long be included among its defining attributes. That invention, of course, is the concentration camp, along with its frequent antechamber, the ghetto.

Concentration camps, by which I mean both the Nazi lagers and the Soviet gulags, clearly epitomize extreme circumstances, but I am interested in them as much for themselves as for the truths they reveal about ordinary situations. I am assuming, then, that they indeed can reveal such truths, but the legitimacy of this assumption will surely be questioned by those who maintain that the camps and ordinary situations are incommensurable, that there are no valid comparisons to draw between them. If that is the case, my interest in extremity might be written off as a penchant for, if not a capitulation to, sensationalism. Needless to say, I do not see it that way. My intent is to use the extreme as an instrument, a sort of magnifying glass that can bring into better focus certain things that in the normal course of human affairs remain blurry. I hope that in carrying out that intention I will not betray the facts themselves.

It was Bruno Bettelheim, in the very first articles he wrote on his arrival in America in 1942, after his internment, who formulated the idea that the concentration camps are an extremity that can teach us about the human condition. For my part, I think the camps and the experiences of those interned in them represent a double extremity, which is to say, they are extreme in two distinct senses of the word:

the camps are the extreme manifestation of the totalitarian regime, itself the extreme form of modern political life. Let me explain.

Totalitarianism is the extreme of our political life in the same way that for Horace death is the limit to all things, and hence to life: a negation and a foil, the limiting case; totalitarianism in this sense is the opposite of democracy. It is in an altogether different sense of the word that the camps represent the extreme of the totalitarian regime: they are its quintessence, its most intense and concentrated manifestation; the camps are thus a central, so to speak, rather than peripheral (limiting) extreme. If one considers totalitarianism from a political or a philosophical point of view, one is hard pressed to decide which of its attributes most accurately defines it. Is it the single-party system? The conflation of state and ideology? The revolutionary project? From the standpoint of the individual's experience, however, the pertinent trait is incontestably terror, and this terror the camps both distill and amplify. Hannah Arendt is correct in seeing terror as the essence of totalitarian government, even if to characterize it in such a way ignores other important attributes of the totalitarian system.

To be sure, the camp distorts the image of the society it reflects, for of the various aspects of the totalitarian system it retains only repression and terror; the camp need not concern itself with ideology (indeed, as Solzhenitsyn liked to point out, the camps were the only place in Russia where one could think as one wished). Many characteristics specific to both the camps and the society—enforced confinement under pain of death (the usual penalty for defying prohibition); the reign of secrecy; a strict hierarchy of social strata (totalitarianism is in no sense egalitarian); the implication of everyone in the functioning of the machine; the corruption of the soul under constraint; the constant presence of violence and death—are traceable to that terror.

The camps are the culmination of the principle of terror; by the same token, totalitarian countries are merely camps with a milder regime. Vasily Grossman, writing about the Soviet system, says, "Life inside the camps could be seen as an exaggerated, magnified reflection of life outside. Far from being contradictory, these two realities were symmetrical" (*Life and Fate* 845). And Primo Levi, reflecting on the phenomenon of Nazism, finds that "the Lager, on a smaller scale but with amplified characteristics, reproduced the hierarchical structure of the totalitarian state" (*Drowned* 47). The concentration camp, then, is neither an exaggeration nor an anomaly but rather the logical outcome of the totalitarian project. It would seem to follow that if a society has no camps, it is not truly totalitarian.

We must be careful, however, when we assert that the camps by their extremity reveal truths about our own lives. Totalitarianism, as I have said, is the opposite of democracy, not its essence. One cannot compare totalitarian terror to the legitimate violence of the lawful state, which, by common consent, sets limits that designate certain acts—murder, assault and battery, theft, rape, and so on—as punishable. The citizen of a democracy, the democratic subject, if you will, can act in accordance with his own will, whatever the pressures acting on him; he can conduct his personal affairs as he sees fit and retains his freedom of opinion; he enjoys certain guarantees, or freedoms, backed by the state itself. The world is not a ghetto; nor is it one vast concentration camp. Nor is Auschwitz, therefore, the ineluctable—if somewhat premature—outcome of modernity, whose truth is at last revealed. Moreover, if the term *modernity* can encompass realities as divergent as democracy and totalitarianism, one must wonder how useful the term really is. Yet precisely by virtue of being the opposite of democracy, by marking its extreme limit, totalitarianism can teach us a great deal about it.

Primo Levi understood the necessity of this dual perspective. On the one hand, he was repelled by comparisons of the free world with the world of the camps. "No," he stated flatly, "that's not the way it is, it's not true that the Fiat factory is a concentration camp, or that the psychiatric hospital is a concentration camp. There's no gas chamber at Fiat. You can be very badly off in the psychiatric hospital, but there's no oven, there's an exit, and your family can come to visit" (*Camon* 19–20). On the other hand, he sought in Auschwitz a lesson for the world, not just that part of it which created the camps. No human experience, no matter how exceptional, is without meaning, he writes: "fundamental values, even if they are not positive, can be deduced from this particular world" (*Auschwitz* 79). My book, then, is simply an attempt to follow Levi's precept. My goal is to reach a better understanding of our own moral life, and although I focus on life inside the camps to achieve that goal, this does not mean I believe the two worlds to be identical.

One other thing became clear to me at the outset: any reflection of mine on the subject of the extreme that did not implicate me personally and draw on my own experiences was likely to be a futile exercise. Although I was never in a concentration camp or even close to one, apart from those that have been converted into museums, I did live in a totalitarian state until the age of twenty-four, and it is through that experience that I have sought to understand the inmates of the camps, to the extent possible for someone who was not there himself. That experience also gave me my first intimate encounter with political evil, but as something done by me, not to me. Nothing spectacular, merely the common lot—docile participation in various public demonstrations, acceptance of the code of social behavior without protest, mute acquiescence to the status quo.

The years that have slipped by have not made me forget that experience. If I feel I must return to it here, it is not just because there are places where totalitarianism is still alive and well; the real reason is my conviction that if we fail to master the past it may master us. It is not the past as such that preoccupies me but rather my belief that the past contains a lesson for all of us today. The problem is—what lesson? Facts are not transparent, and events never reveal their meaning all by themselves. If they are to teach us something, they must be interpreted, and for this interpretation of the lessons of totalitarianism and the camps, I alone will be responsible.

A Place for Moral Life?

There are various perspectives from which the accounts of life in the camps can be read. One can ponder the precise chain of events that led to the creation of the camps and then to their extinction; one can debate the political significance of the camps; one can extract sociological or psychological lessons from them. Yet even though I cannot ignore those perspectives altogether, I would like to take a different approach. I want to look at the camps from the perspective of moral life and, like Edelman and Krall, to concern myself with individual destinies rather than with numbers and dates. But already I hear an objection: Wasn't that question settled a long time ago? Haven't we learned only too well the sad and simple truth the camps revealed, namely, that in extreme situations all traces of moral life evaporate as men become beasts locked in a merciless struggle for survival?

That opinion is not only a commonplace of popularized presentations of these events but also crops up frequently in the accounts of survivors themselves. We became indifferent to the misfortune of others, they say; if we wanted to survive, we had to think only of ourselves. That is the lesson brought out of Auschwitz by Tadeusz Borowski, who committed suicide in 1951: "In this war," he writes, "morality, national solidarity, patriotism and the ideals of freedom, justice and human dignity had all slid off man like a rotten rag. . . .

There is no crime that a man will not commit in order to save himself" (*This Way* 168). In other words, moral behavior is not innate in us. Another Auschwitz survivor, Jean Améry, who committed suicide in 1978, reached the same conclusion. "There are no natural rights," he writes, "and moral categories come and go like fashions" (*Mind* 11). A third Auschwitz survivor, Primo Levi, who took his life in 1987, says that the hardships of the camps rendered any kind of moral position impossible. "Here [in the lager] the struggle to survive is without respite, because everyone is desperately and ferociously alone." To survive, it was necessary "to throttle all dignity and kill all conscience, to climb down into the arena as a beast against other beasts, to let oneself be guided by those unsuspected subterranean forces which sustain families and individuals in cruel times" (*Survival* 80, 84). "It was a Hobbesian life," Levi writes, "a continuous war of everyone against everyone" (*Drowned* 134).

The lessons brought out from the gulags are not all that different. Varlam Shalamov, imprisoned for twenty-five years, seventeen of them in Kolyma, is particularly pessimistic: "All human emotions—of love, friendship, envy, concern for one's fellowman, compassion, a longing for fame, honesty—had left us with the flesh that had melted from our bodies during our long fasts," he writes. "The camp was a great test of our moral strength, of our everyday morality, and 99% of us failed it. . . . Conditions in the camps do not permit men to remain men; that is not what camps were created for" (56). Eugenia Ginzburg, who spent twenty years in Kolyma, agrees that a moral life was impossible in the camps: "It is hard to describe the way in which someone ground down by inhuman forms of life loses bit by bit all hold on normal notions of good and evil, of what is permissible and what is not. . . . Perhaps we ourselves [intellectuals] were as morally dead as the rest" (*Within* 13, 144). When one is thinking only of one's own survival, one no longer recognizes any law other than the law of the jungle, which means the total *absence* of law and its replacement by brute force.

When the survival instinct totally dominates moral life, one loses a sense of compassion for the suffering of others and no longer offers the help one normally would. Rather than aid the next person, one might instead further his decline if it meant relief from one's own

suffering. Even without committing hostile acts, the prisoners sometimes fail to carry out even the most basic obligations of human solidarity. In a chapter of *My Testimony* entitled "Hard to Stay Human,"
Anatoly Marchenko, who was deported to Mordovia, tells how his
cellmates calmly finished their breakfast while a fellow prisoner
slashed his wrists and collapsed in a pool of blood. "A man pours out
blood before my very eyes and I lick my soup bowl clean and think
only about how long it is till the next meal. Did anything human
remain in me, or in any of us, in that prison?" (154). The members of
the work groups whose job it was to clean the trains that arrived at
Auschwitz did not feel the slightest remorse when they made off with
food or other objects that the new deportees had brought with them
and that now lay in piles on the platform. "We all had only one
thought: why not take advantage of the last moments of life since
everything else already belongs to the land of dreams," write Szymon
Laks and R. Coudy (87). Richard Glazar, who had the job at Treblinka and took similar advantage of the situation, recalls how he felt
when the trainloads of prisoners became less frequent and then suddenly picked up again. "Do you know what we did? We shouted
'Hurrah, hurrah!' It seems impossible now. Every time I think of it, I
die a small death. . . . The fact that the death of others—whoever
they might be—meant our life, was no longer relevant" (Sereny 213).
Even the closest family ties were vulnerable in this fight for survival.
Borowski, for example, tells how a mother, to save her own life, pre-
tends not to know her child. And Elie Wiesel, another Auschwitz
survivor, describes in *Night* how a son snatches a piece of bread from
the hands of his father, and he speaks of the relief he felt when his
own father died, because it increased his own chances for survival.

If an individual's every action is determined by the orders of those
above him and the need to survive, then he has no freedom left at all;
no longer can he truly exercise his will and choose one behavior over
another. And where there is no choice, there is also no place for any
kind of moral life whatsoever.

DOUBTS

In reading the testimonies of survivors, however, I come away with the impression that the situation is not as bleak as it may have seemed. Alongside examples illustrating the disappearance of all moral sensibilities, one finds examples that have a different lesson to teach. Primo Levi, who saw in the camps only an attenuated struggle of all against all, has barely finished writing, "All are enemies or rivals," when he stops and realizes how excessive that statement really is. "No," he declares, "I honestly do not feel my companion of today . . . to be either enemy or rival" (*Survival* 37). There are numerous stories in Levi's *Survival in Auschwitz* (originally entitled *If This Is a Man*) that contradict his grim generalization. His good friend Alberto, for instance, who perished during the forced marches after the evacuation of the camps, struggles to survive yet does not become a cynic. He knows how to be both strong and tender. Another friend, Jean, who was the Pikolo, or messenger-clerk, of Levi's work unit and who did survive, also strove to stay alive but "did not neglect his human relationships with less privileged comrades" (100). If there were so many exceptions, can the rule still be said to hold?

The same Tadeusz Borowski whose stories about life at Auschwitz are among the most pitiless has also written, "I think that man will never cease to rediscover man—through love. And to rediscover that love is the most important and most durable thing there is" (*This Way* 135). We know, moreover, that at Auschwitz Borowski behaved totally differently from the characters he writes about; his devotion to others was beyond measure. But he understood just how far human degradation could go and did not try to exempt himself from the corruption around him. His central character, also named Tadeusz, is a cynical and pitiless kapo, and his story is told in the first person. Borowski suggests a rule for all who write about Auschwitz: Do not write unless you are willing to take responsibility for the worst humiliation that the camp inflicted on its inmates. In making this rule, he has also, of course, made another choice and committed another moral act.

Varlam Shalamov, who narrates the despair and degradation experienced by all the prisoners at Kolyma, writes, "I couldn't denounce a fellow convict, no matter what he did. And I refused to seek the job of foreman, which provided a chance to remain alive, for the worst thing in a camp was the forcing of one's own or anyone else's will on another person who was a convict just like oneself" (57). As Aleksandr Solzhenitsyn observes, a decision of this kind proves that not all choice was forbidden and that Shalamov was at least himself an exception to his own rule. Laks and Coudy, Auschwitz survivors who chronicled the progressive loss of their human identity, nonetheless point out that without the help of others survival was impossible. Was help given? Thirty years after the publication of his original account, Laks confirms that it was: he owes his survival, he writes, "to my encounters with a few countrymen with a human face and a human heart" (19). And Eugenia Ginzburg describes innumerable acts of solidarity that the principle she herself formulates has no way of accounting for. If there were sons who snatched bread from the hands of their fathers, Robert Antelme, a Buchenwald survivor, saw ones, too. He describes "the hungry old man who'd steal in front of his son, so the son could eat. Father and son . . . hungry together, offering their bread to each other with loving eyes" (262).

Ella Lingens-Reiner, an Austrian prisoner, reports in her recollections of Auschwitz that she met another Jewish doctor there, Ena Weiss, who defined her philosophy of life this way: "How do I keep alive in Auschwitz? My principle is—myself first, second, and third. Then nothing. Then myself again—and then all the others" (118). This formula has often been cited as the most accurate expression of moral law—or rather, of its absence—at Auschwitz. And yet Lingens-Reiner is quick to point out that this woman violated her own law every day, helping tens, indeed hundreds, of other prisoners. Lingens-Reiner goes on to describe the transformations that moral life underwent in the camp, and in so doing she mirrors the kind of contradiction she finds in Weiss. "We camp prisoners had only one yardstick," she writes, "whatever helped our survival was good, whatever threatened our survival was bad and to be avoided" (142). Yet this characterization comes directly after a detailed account of a conflict of conscience that greatly tormented her: should she intervene in behalf of a sick woman, thereby compromising her own chances of getting out alive, or should she think only of herself and decline to help her fellow prisoner? In the end, Lingens-Reiner choses the former, but even if she hadn't, her hesitation alone would have been sufficient proof that the moral sense within her was still very much alive.

Matters of conscience are not at all rare in extreme situations, and their very existence attests to the possibility of choice, and thus of moral life. One might flee such dilemmas because they entail that one freely choose an evil, albeit a lesser one perhaps than might have existed in the absence of choice. They cannot always be avoided, however. Lingens-Reiner is a doctor. Should she or should she not choose to kill newborn babies to give their mothers a better chance of surviving? Should her only medicine be used to ease the suffering of one person who is gravely ill or of two people who are not so sick? A terrible dilemma confronted the Vilno resistance fighters: they were told to deliver their leader, Isaac Wittenberg, to the Gestapo or see the ghetto destroyed by Nazi tanks. Any kind of negotiation with an occupying power brings with it wrenching moral conflicts.

It is not true that life in the camps obeyed only the law of the jungle. The rules of camp society may have been different but they still existed. Stealing from the administration was not merely licit but admirable; on the other hand, stealing from a fellow prisoner—especially bread—was an abomination and most of the time was severely punished. This law functioned as rigorously in the gulags as it did in the concentration camps. In both places informers were detested and punished. As Anna Pawelczynska, an Auschwitz survivor, observes, the Ten Commandments did not disappear; they were simply reinterpreted. Murder, for example, could be a moral act if it kept an assassin from carrying out cruel and vicious assignments. Bearing false witness could become a virtuous act if it helped save human lives. To love one's neighbor as one loved oneself was perhaps an excessive demand, but to avoid harming him was not. Germaine Tillion, a survivor of Ravensbrück, renders a subtle and, as far as I can determine, accurate judgment of moral life in the camps when she concludes, "This tenuous web of friendship was, in a way, submerged by the stark brutality of selfishness and the struggle for survival, but somehow everyone in the camp was invisibly woven into it" (xxii).

So numerous are the counterexamples to the principles of immorality expressed by the survivors that the presence of such principles in their accounts calls for some explanation. Why do the survivors draw general conclusions that are not borne out by the particular cases that they themselves report? Terrence Des Pres, the author of a study on concentration camp survivors, proposes an answer: former prisoners insist on the negative aspect of their experience because it is precisely this aspect that renders their experience unique and that must be underlined at every opportunity. "As a witness," Des Pres writes, "the survivor aims above all to convey the otherness of the camps, their specific inhumanity" (99). The particular examples the survivors cite, on the other hand, reflect a more complex situation. I would add another reason for some survivors' reluctance to qualify their conclusions: if they paint the bleakest picture possible, it is because they still suffer remorse for not having come to the aid of others, who were left to a horrible fate—this despite the fact that nonintervention was a perfectly understandable and justifiable response under the circumstances. While Germaine Tillion lies ill in the Ravensbrück infirmary, a "selection" snatches away her mother, a prisoner in the same camp. Tillion herself tells us nothing more, but through the account of her friend Margarete Buber-Neumann, we learn that Tillion suffered unbearably for having let her mother be taken away. "[Germaine] sprang down from her bed, her face contorted with sudden emotion," Buber-Neumann writes. " 'My God!' she sobbed. 'My God! How could I have thought only of myself! My mother! My mother!' " (*Ravensbrück* 201). In her own eyes she may be guilty, but no humane court of justice could ever pronounce such a verdict against her.

There is yet another, I am tempted to say cultural, reason this idea of unmitigated immorality appears in the survivors' accounts. The camps, it is often said, illustrate the principle that the behavior of the individual depends not on his own will but on the conditions surrounding him, that life is a war of all against all, that morality is no more than a superficial convention. Statements like these are abundantly present not only in the literature of the survivors but throughout the last two centuries of European thought, especially in the dominant ideology of the totalitarian countries; we can find such statements as readily in Marx as in Nietzsche. It may well be that the camps are an indirect outcome of these ideologies; this does not, however, prove that every single aspect of life in the camps illustrates them.

And so when Tadeusz Borowski declares that "the whole world is really like the concentration camp. . . . The world is ruled by neither justice nor morality. . . . The world is ruled by power" (*This Way* 168), he is not simply drawing a conclusion from his own experience; he is also reformulating a commonplace of European thought that the Nazi regime, as it happened, adapted to its own ends. Czeslaw Milosz, who knew Borowski before Auschwitz and put him into his book *The Captive Mind* as the character Beta, writes that as early as 1942 Borowski saw the world as nothing more than a battleground where brute force contended with brute force. His protagonists personify the belief that success is the ultimate test of quality—in his narratives it is the fittest who survive. He intends his stories as an illustration of social Darwinism, which is why acts of goodness have no place in them, or scarcely any. Borowski's joining the Polish Communist Party after the war is revealing: he needs the world to be every bit as ugly as the one he depicts in his fiction for his attitude of hatred and intolerance to be justified, and he has found in Communism an ideology to suit his outlook. But it is an ideology not very different from that of the Nazis, who believed, after all, that certain human beings, their fine manners aside, are scarcely more worthy of respect than animals are.

Borowski also professes a determinism shared by both the Communists and the Nazis, according to which human actions are dictated by social conditions or racial heritage, not by the will of the individual. The camps, crucibles designed to transform the human substance, are the ultimate fulfillment of those doctrines. Under the appropriate conditions—those of maximum pressure—the intended result is inevitable. Hunger, cold, beatings, slave labor—all of these will transform human beings into whatever those wielding power desire. This is the philosophy underlying the creation of the camps, yet it cannot be deduced from the conduct of the prisoners.

It is necessary, however, to introduce a certain distinction here, for there may exist a threshold of suffering beyond which an individual's actions teach us nothing more about the individual but only about the reactions that unbearable suffering elicits from the human mechanism. One can be brought to that threshold by prolonged starvation, or by the imminent threat of death, or even—as in the Nazi camps—by the initial encounter with an atmosphere of terror and menace. "Hunger proves an insuperable ordeal," Anatoly Marchenko writes. "When he reaches this ultimate degree of degradation, a man is prepared for anything" (122). Twenty years earlier, Gustaw Herling, another prisoner of the gulag, concluded, "There is nothing . . . a man cannot be forced to do by hunger and pain" (131). Indeed, these extreme means make it possible to destroy the social contract at its very foundations and to obtain from human beings purely animal reactions.

But what exactly does that observation mean? Does it reflect the fundamental truth about human nature, that morality is but a superficial convention jettisoned at the first opportunity? On the contrary, what it demonstrates is that moral reactions are spontaneous, omnipresent, and eradicable only with the greatest violence. Plants can be forced to grow horizontally, Rousseau says, but unconstrained they will nevertheless grow upward. It is not under torture that human beings reveal their true identity. Suppressing the usual components of human social life creates a completely artificial situation that tells us only about itself. Herling is right: "I became convinced that a man can be human only under human conditions and I believe that it is fantastic nonsense to judge him by actions which he commits under inhuman conditions" (132). It is for this reason, too, that I will not dwell at length on situations where that threshold has been crossed.

Even before considering the details of moral life in the camps, one can see that the hypothesis that individuals behave as wolves toward one another is not supported by observation. Des Pres's readings of survivors' accounts come to the same conclusion: "The 'state of nature,' it turns out, is not natural. A war of everyone against everyone must be imposed by force" (142). The popular version of Hobbes's doctrine is wrong: except under extreme constraint, human beings are prompted, among other things, to communicate with one another, to help one another, and to distinguish good from evil.

ONE AND THE SAME WORLD

This conclusion should not be understood as an expression of complacent optimism. In affirming the continuity between ordinary experience and that of the camps (except where the latter crosses beyond the threshold of the bearable) and thus the pertinence of the same moral questions to both worlds, I am not saying that good reigns supreme, everywhere and at all times. Far from it: I would say instead that this continuity between the ordinary and the extreme points to conclusions that are hardly encouraging.

In everyday life as well as in the camps, one can observe an opposition between two types of behavior and two types of values, what could be called vital values and moral values. Vital values dictate that saving my own life and furthering my well-being are what matter most; moral values tell me that there is something more precious than life itself, that staying human is more important than staying alive. To choose moral values (whether "heroic" or "ordinary") over vital values does not necessarily imply that life is somehow a less worthy goal; survival remains a perfectly respectable objective—particularly where the ordinary virtues are concerned—but not at any price.

Let there be no mistake. I do not mean that moral values are somehow external to life, that they are a foreign element that stifles and suppresses life. Rather I believe that moral values and behaviors are a constitutive dimension of life. The difference between moral values and vital values might be got at in the following way: for the vital values it is my life that is sacred; for moral values it is the life of someone else that is. What extreme situations teach us is that both kinds of values are always active. As Jorge Semprun, a Buchenwald survivor, writes, "In the camps, man becomes that animal capable of stealing a mate's bread, of propelling him toward death. But in the camps, man also becomes that invincible being capable of sharing his last cigarette butt, his last piece of bread, his last breath, to sustain his fellowman" (60). And Anatoly Marchenko says, "People here vary, just as they do everywhere. You have marvelous people, and you have rotten ones, you have brave men and cowards, you have honest men with principles and you have unprincipled swine who are prepared for any kind of betrayal" (305). This observation, of course, is as true of the ordinary lives that all of us lead as it is of the situations described by Marchenko and Semprun.

In the camps, such diversity appears not only between people but also within the course of each individual life. Even the most admirable persons typically passed through several phases. During the first, often corresponding to the initial few months in the camp, previously held moral values collapse beneath the weight of the new and brutal circumstances. The prisoner discovers a world without pity and finds that he can actually live in such a world. If the prisoner survives this first stage, however, he may reach a second, in which he once again discovers a set of moral values, although perhaps not the same as he held before. The embers have not been extinguished, and it takes only the smallest relief from brutality for the flames of conscience to flare up anew. "Even in the jungle of Birkenau," writes Olga Lengyel, a doctor at Auschwitz, "all were not necessarily inhuman to their fellowmen" (212).

Furthermore, when I note that moral qualities existed in the camps, I am not extolling suffering, holding it out as the source of virtue. That notion appears in the writings of certain survivors, influenced perhaps by the Christian tradition. Solzhenitsyn, for example, emphasizes the beneficial effects of being in prison, which he believed led to a deepening of the self; he maintains—the testimony of other survivors to the contrary—that the same was true of the concentration camps. Irina Ratushinskaya, who was deported to the Mordovia camps in Russia, remembers hearing this song behind the barbed-wire fences:

> I thank you, rusty prison grating,
> And you, sharp glinting bayonet blades,
> For you have given me more wisdom
> Than learning over long decades.

And she herself exclaims, "Thank you, O Lord, that it fell to my lot to endure the rigors of prison transports, . . . to languish in punishment cells and to starve" (135, 148).

Of course, one cannot help but admire the moral courage of people like Solzhenitsyn and Ratushinskaya, but their proposition seems to me a dangerous generalization from their own experience. From what I have seen and read, it seems to me that the virtues of suffering are far more ambiguous: it makes some people better while it degrades others. Moreover, all suffering is not alike. It is probably true, though, that an experience like the prison camps forces some people to mature more rapidly than they might have otherwise, teaching them lessons they would not have learned on the outside. Survivors often feel as if they came closer to the truth during their captivity than at any other point in their lives. But this spiritual growth or emotional enrichment, assuming it does take place, is not a moral virtue. And finally, even if there were some discernible relation between suffering and morality, I do not see what sort of precept one might extrapolate from it: no one has the right to tell others that they should seek unhappiness so as to become more virtuous. Twenty years in a camp made Eugenia Ginzburg a wiser and more complete human being than she would have been had she remained the high-handed, dogmatic Communist she was in the 1930s, but what merciless God would dare ask that she choose, of her own free will, to suffer?

The difference between life in the camps and ordinary life does not lie in the presence or absence of moral life. In everyday life the contrasts of which I have been speaking are not clearly apparent. Egocentric acts pass themselves off as ordinary and routine behavior, and furthermore, less is at stake because human lives don't depend on them. In the camps, however, where it is sometimes necessary to choose between holding on to one's bread and holding on to one's dignity, between starving physically and starving morally, everything is out in the open. "Camps," Semprun writes, "are extreme situations in which the cleavage between 'the men' and 'the others' is more pronounced" (72). The depravation of some is hastened and is there for all to see; but the betterment of others is also intensified. "Camp either cleanses your conscience or destroys it forever," Ratushinskaya writes. "People emerge either much better than they were or much worse, depending on how they were predisposed" (198). Of course, both depravation and elevation occur outside the camps, but not so visibly. Life inside the camps projects, magnifies, and renders eloquent what can easily escape notice in the humdrum of our daily lives.

What extreme and ordinary situations also share is that, in both, most people choose what I call vital values and only a few choose the other path. Or perhaps it is this: most of the time individuals opt for vital values without necessarily losing a sense of morality. Once again, the choices are far more visible in the camps, which is why the camps are often thought to offer some sort of general lesson in immorality. The fact is, however, that selfishness is just as prevalent in ordinary times. To put it simply, the most optimistic conclusion we can draw from life in (and outside) the camps is that evil is not unavoidable. The actual numbers are not important; what matters is that the possibility of choosing moral values continues to exist. "Of the prisoners, only a few kept their full inner liberty," Viktor Frankl, an Auschwitz survivor, concludes, "but even one such example is sufficient proof that man's inner strength may raise him above his outward fate" (107).

It is therefore possible—and this book rests on the wager that it is —to take the extreme experience of the camps as a basis from which to reflect on moral life, not because moral life was superior in the camps but because it was more visible and thus more telling there. In the pages that follow, I examine both sides of moral life—the virtues, ordinary and heroic, and the vices, ordinary and monstrous. Finally, I attempt to analyze our responses in the face of evil.

NEITHER HEROES
NOR SAINTS

Heroism and Saintliness

THE MODEL AND ITS TRANSFORMATIONS

The accounts of the Warsaw uprisings revealed two kinds of virtues, one heroic, and the other ordinary. I would now like to draw on the broader range of material from the camps, and try to arrive at a better understanding of both. But first I propose to cast a brief look at the tradition of heroism and saintliness as it has existed in Europe for nearly three thousand years. Obviously, it is impossible to reconstruct that tradition in its entirety here; we can, however, examine a few of its aspects and establish a context for our discussion.

The point of departure for the hero, as this figure has come down to us from Greek epic, is his decision to attain, whatever the cost, the ideal of *excellence,* an ideal of which he is himself the measure. Achilles, the prototypical hero, does not serve a cause (or if he does, then he serves it badly) and fights for no purpose that could be situated in time and space. He is a hero because he pursues a model of heroic perfection which he has interiorized; he becomes an embodiment of strength—physical strength, of course, but also courage, energy, and moral fortitude. The outward manifestation of this internal criterion of excellence is glory, and hence the accounts that tell of it. Without a story to exalt him, the hero ceases to be heroic.

Whatever the cost: the classical hero, in other words, always values something above his own life (namely, his excellence—he thus stands on the side of the moral values, not the vital ones); but more specifically, he is linked to the domain of death. For him the choice is between a life without glory and a glorious death. The hero chooses death, not because he values it in itself—he is not, after all, morbid—but because, unlike life, death is an absolute. (The symmetry of the two terms is misleading.) Death is inscribed in the hero's very destiny. These things make the hero different from other men. Endowed with exceptional strength, he already stands apart from ordinary people, and in choosing death over life, he separates himself from them even further.

Achilles is the pure hero, the very embodiment of classical heroism. Other heroes, including his contemporaries, share only certain facets of this model or recast it in their own ways. Hector, for example, generally conforms to the model; at the same time, his goal is not simply heroic perfection, for he also wants to protect his country. Thus he inaugurates a long tradition of heroes who serve not the heroic ideal alone but an external authority as well—king, country, the people, or some noble cause. This tradition, which continues into the present century, is not the exclusive province of soldiers. Think of Hans Brinker, the little Dutch boy who plugged a hole in the dyke with his thumb and thereby saved his village from inundation.

Another strain of heroism retains this loftiness of soul without calling on physical strength. Socrates, through his death, provides the best example of this variant: he would rather die for the cause of justice than survive through an injustice. Socrates is on solid ground when he invokes the example of Achilles to explain his conduct. He is also like a saint or a religious hero, even though these figures belong to a different tradition entirely, the biblical and not the Homeric. (Homer's moralizing commentaries anticipate the assimilation of the two, however.) There are obvious differences between the saint and the hero, but a sage like Socrates has qualities in common with both.

Consider the example of Eleazar, the Old Testament saint and martyr. He is subjected to an ordeal to make him violate the laws of his religion: he is forced to "open his mouth and eat pork." Yet, like Achilles, he prefers "an honorable death to an unclean life," and like Socrates, he rejects any attempt to escape the death sentence by means he judges dishonest. He chooses instead to serve the glory of God and His Holy Writ: "I shall leave the young a fine example, to teach them how to die a good death, gladly and nobly, for our revered and holy laws." No sooner said than the deed is done; Eleazar is beaten to death, the narrator tells us, but by that death "he left a heroic example and a glorious memory, not only for the young but also for the great body of the nation" (2 Maccabees 6.18–31). Here we are truly in the Socratic tradition, any differences between the idea of justice and obedience to dietary regulations notwithstanding.

Like the hero, the saint is an exceptional being. He neither submits to the laws of his society nor has the same reactions as other people. His extraordinary qualities, in particular his spiritual strength, make him a solitary figure who cares little about the effect of his actions on those close to him. It might even be said that the true saint knows neither internal struggle nor even, when all is said and done, suffering. Like the hero, he rejects compromise; consequently, he is always ready to die for his faith, which is not true of his compatriots, however pious they may be.

The love of God fills the saint's heart, leaving no room there for a comparable love of his fellowman: to love men as one loves God smacks of idolatry, for men are of this world, not of the kingdom of God. The story of Perpetua tells how her judges, in an attempt to force the future saint to deny her faith, confront her with her elderly parents, her husband, and her young child. If you insist on clinging to your faith, the judges tell her, your child will become an orphan and your husband a widower, and your parents will be condemned to end their days in loneliness and poverty. "Have pity on us, my daughter," her father cries. "Stay and live with us." But Perpetua pushes them all away, including her son. "Get away from me!" she tells them. "You are the enemies of God. For I do not know you" (Voragine 400). Perpetua loves God more than she loves her family and so she chooses death, thereby achieving her sainthood. For the saint, God alone is an end and thus is to be chosen over any particular human beings, to their detriment if need be.

This model of heroism and saintliness, already multiform to begin with, did not remain intact, not even as an idealized image (to say nothing of actual behavior). Already in the *Odyssey*, the hero has come to embody a different ideal—not strength but cunning and reason. The *Odyssey* gives currency to Odysseus' victory, which is not to have to choose, as Achilles did, between long life and glory. Odysseus represents the possibility of reaping the benefits of both. He achieves glory (the mere existence of the epic is proof enough), but he also grows old peacefully, in the bosom of his family.

To the traditional categories of saints—the martyr and the ascetic—should now be added that of the saint of charity who devotes his or her life to the poor and downtrodden. Even if their devotion entails abnegation, saints of this type do not live in the shadow of death. Saint Vincent de Paul, in the seventeenth century, seems more like a social worker than someone destined for a glorious death; the same might be said today of Mother Teresa, who has ministered to the poor of Calcutta and elsewhere. Saints of charity devote themselves to other human beings, but through them they continue to seek God. Human beings are a means by which God's law may reign on the earth.

An avatar of the heroic ideal persisted into the Middle Ages, giving rise to the code of chivalry (a very different model from that of Achilles), and at least as far as the seventeenth century, where it can be found in the aristocratic virtues and in the concept of honor. But with the triumph in Europe of the ideology of individualism toward the end of the eighteenth century, the heroic model falls rapidly out of favor. People no longer dream of glory and adventure but aspire to personal happiness or even, quite simply, to a life of pleasure. By the mid–nineteenth century, such perspicacious observers as de Tocqueville, Heine, and Renan, even if they do not criticize the general direction in which society seems to be evolving, cannot help but deplore the passing of the heroic spirit and its replacement by a taste for the personal comforts of bourgeois life. Fictional heroes become eminently unheroic: Julien Sorel and Emma Bovary have little in common with Achilles and Antigone. Certainly Achilles was, in his own way, very much an individualist; he fought not for the good of the community or in defense of a social ideal but to meet his own standards of excellence. Still, the resemblance is merely superficial, for the world of the Greek heroes is the opposite of modern democracy. The degradation of the heroic model continues into the twentieth century, culminating in Chaplin's tramp and Beckett's hoboes; today the vanquished command more sympathy than do their victors. It would seem that we have turned the page on heroism for good.

War—the setting of choice for the classical hero—is, at least in this part of the world, almost universally condemned. If countenanced at all, it is as an unavoidable evil, a fatal calamity. Military virtues are hardly held in high esteem; dying for one's country, the most common variant of the classical model of heroism, no longer seems to tempt many people. Obviously, modern warfare has little to do with the Achillean model of single combat; today, it is the development of weaponry, not the fighters' courage or strength, that determines the outcome of the battle, and credit for the victory goes to the engineer sitting quietly in his office rather than to the soldier on the front lines. Besides, there are no front lines anymore, or direct contact between adversaries; the pilot who drops his bombs from a plane never sees his victims. The very notion of the professional soldier has been called into question, since in situations of total warfare the destruction of industrial potential or the extermination of civilian populations is just as effective as any other act of war, if not more so (witness the capitulation of Japan after Hiroshima). Heroes seem to have no place in the modern world.

I doubt, however, that the disappearance of the heroic model is quite this complete. More likely, the model has undergone yet another transformation without our being aware of it and may still govern some parts of our lives, though not all. Tolerant of ideological diversity, the societies to which we belong permit the coexistence of a number of models whose mutual antagonism surfaces only sporadically. I am not referring here to such admired but relatively marginal figures as sports heroes—our modern Herculeses—or those saintly heads of charitable agencies who risk their lives among lepers and the most destitute. I have in mind something much more ubiquitous. I can't help thinking in this regard of an image at the beginning of Hans Christian Andersen's "The Snow Queen." The devil has fabricated an enormous looking glass, the Mirror of Evil, and along with his fellow demons, is carrying it to God, who causes it to slip from its bearers' hands. The mirror falls and breaks into trillions of pieces, thus doing far more evil than it had before, since many of the fragments, being no bigger than grains of sand, now fly everywhere, all across the world. Heroism, of course, is not the same thing as evil, but like Andersen's looking glass, once it ceases to exist as a single entity, it reappears in ever more minuscule forms in every sort of human activity.

Today at least two ideological models preside over the sphere of human interactions. The first model, a modern version of classical heroism, dominates and suffuses the *public* sphere—the worlds of politics, business, and, to a certain extent, scientific and artistic endeavor. The other model (or, rather, models) governs the *private* sphere—that of personal relationships, everyday life, and moral aspirations. These two models account for the simultaneous presence of heroic virtues (valued in the public sphere) and ordinary virtues (appreciated in the private realm).

How, then, has the heroic model changed? First, the threat of death no longer hovers over the actions of the modern hero; he is not prepared to risk his life to be seen as heroic. The modern hero is no longer an exceptional being of miraculous birth, in privileged contact with the world of gods or beasts. He is an ordinary person, like any other, part of the social fabric. Nevertheless, there is continuity between the classical heroic ideal and the modern one. Take the cult of power, which today seems a matter not of physical power but rather of political, economic, or intellectual power. All the domains where such power is exercised—politics, business, science, art—place a premium on qualities that call to mind the martial virtues: toughness and competitiveness (in negotiations with allies as in conflicts with adversaries), tactical and strategic skill (in concealing objectives, shifting alliances, and predicting others' moves), efficiency (in quickly making the right decisions), and, above all, the capacity to win, to be the best, to see one's way to success. Germany "no longer cites its heroism on the battlefield," writes Jean Améry, "but the productivity that has no like in the entire world" (*Mind* 81). The good politician is the one who wins. This same competitiveness can be found in the arts and sciences. In contrast to the hero who gives his life for his country or for an ideal, his modern descendant does not serve goals that are external to him (in this he resembles his original model, the proud Achilles). The appetite for power is not transitive; it does not lead to anything beyond itself. The quest for power today is not a way of doing good or of serving some ideal. Power is sought for its own sake; it is an end, not a means.

The ways in which modern society, through its symbolic practices, represents human relations illustrates the opposition of the two models, the public (heroic) and the private (ordinary). Just as the heroes of antiquity could not do without glory or without the stories that recorded their exploits, their contemporary counterparts, the heroes of modern political, economic, and intellectual life, would not be what they are without the press, the radio, and, of course, television. Today's fictional narratives tend to choose one model or the other and so fall into two groups, the difference between them roughly corresponding to the distinction commonly made between popular culture and high culture. The first group comprises adventure films, spy novels, and the countless TV cops-and-robbers series; novels and films of the second group reject those thematic standbys. When a war movie glorifies the victors ("our side"), it resorts to the first model; when it explores the experience of a deserter, for instance, or the sufferings of civilians, it relies on the second.

I am not particularly drawn to the heroic virtues, and yet when I think of actual situations of war, I find that my opinion changes. Here I differ from the radical pacifist: if all war were by definition evil, then martial virtues could never be considered good. I believe, however, that these virtues are in fact sometimes good, because some wars are just. From the minute it became clear that there was no other way to contain Hitler, going to war against him became the right choice; in circumstances like these, martial virtues and classical heroism seem to me entirely appropriate. I expect my military commander to be decisive, not hesitant or defeatist (I prefer Churchill to Chamberlain, de Gaulle to Daladier). I expect the soldier fighting beside me in the trenches to cover me to the end and not desert his post out of fear or indifference. Loyalty, courage, tenacity, and endurance are valued here; they are indispensable qualities.

But war is not the continuation of peace by other means. The fact that many people believe otherwise is one of the major proofs that the history of the world does not obey the laws of progress; so too is the shift from professional armies to total war, from laws of war to the logic of "victory at any price." New situations demand new qualities: sending heroes into retirement once the war is over may be less an expression of ingratitude than a mark of lucidity. After the Second

World War, Churchill and de Gaulle were no longer needed; left in power, they might have become dangerous. In normal times, democracy does quite well without these "great men." As Brecht's Galileo says in a burst of true democratic spirit, "Woe to the country that needs heroes."

IN EXTREME SITUATIONS

Let us now return to the extreme situations that are the primary concern of this book. In the camps, acts of heroism and saintliness did occur, but survivors all seem to agree that they were extremely rare. To be a hero or a saint, one needs exceptional qualities; by definition, then, very few people had them. Moreover, the guards did everything they could to make acts of heroism or martyrdom impossible—or at least to make sure they went unrecognized, which amounts to the same thing. Nonetheless, such acts did take place, and it is worth mentioning some of the exemplary individuals who performed them.

One of the most unmistakable heroes was surely Sasha Pechersky, the leader of the Sobibor rebellion. Nothing in his background seems to have destined him for such a role. Before the war, he was a student of music and director of several groups of amateur musicians. Mobilized on the first day of hostilities, he was captured in October 1941; it was in captivity that he began to show his heroic potential. Not only did Pechersky manage to survive in difficult circumstances, but he tried to escape, was recaptured, and still survived. Eventually, in September 1943, he was sent to Sobibor. Ten days later, his decision to revolt and to escape from the camp was made. First he had to find people he could trust, people who thought as he did: one's choice of confederates is clearly critical. He surrounded himself with prisoners who had already fought in the war and whose physical and moral condition was still relatively undamaged; with others, he pretended to know nothing of what was going on. His serenity, good humor, dignity, and attentiveness to those around him endeared him to everyone. In the meantime, he was putting the finishing touches on his plan, and on October 14 at four o'clock in the afternoon, the revolt began. First, some Soviet POWs quietly killed several isolated guards and made off with their weapons. Then, while Pechersky led an abortive attack on the camp arsenal, other prisoners cut a passage through the barbed wire to allow a mass escape. Ten SS men were killed, about four hundred prisoners escaped, and of these, one hundred survived. Shortly thereafter, Sobibor was shut down; Pechersky, who was among the survivors, joined up with a group of resisters and lived to see the end of the war.

Sacha Pechersky is the kind of hero one wants every hero in an extreme situation to be: decisive and effective but, at the same time, affectionate and temperate; he is not driven by ideology. Without him or someone like him, the Sobibor rebellion could not have happened. He took great risks to ensure the survival of at least a part of his community, but he saw to it that those risks were kept at a minimum. Forceful and courageous, he was also a man of good judgment; the classical hero he resembles most is Odysseus, leading his companions out of the cave of the Cyclops. And like Odysseus, Pechersky returned home and lived to a ripe old age, the one obstacle to his becoming a hero for popular consumption. (In 1993, I saw him in a documentary directed by Lily van der Bergh. There he was with his wartime companions fifty years later; he was hardly able to move on his own, but his quiet dignity made an unforgettable impression on me.)

The priest Maximilian Kolbe, a prisoner in Auschwitz, achieved even greater renown and was canonized by the Catholic Church. His deed is famous: one day, following an escape, fifteen inmates from his lager were singled out for death by starvation. Kolbe knew that one of them had a wife and children, so he stepped forward and offered to die in the man's place. His offer, which stunned everyone, was nonetheless accepted. And so Kolbe died, and the prisoner whose place he took survived the war. We will doubtless never know what ultimately motivated this sacrifice, but it seems inseparable from Kolbe's faith in God. He died less for Franciszek Gajowniczek, perhaps, than to fulfill his Christian duty; there is something of the severity of the saints of antiquity in Kolbe. Before the war, he was an active anti-Semite, in charge of a number of publications that excoriated the Jews for controlling the world's economy.

Rudi Massarek took part in the Treblinka revolt, although he did not share Pechersky's good fortune (or his desire to live). This half-

Jew from Prague could have escaped deportation, especially since he was as tall and blond as a Viking. But he married a Jewish woman and followed her, first into the ghetto of Terezin, then to Treblinka. As soon as they arrived there, his wife was killed. After a period of complete inertia, Massarek joined a group that was planning a rebellion; when it began, he chose to remain behind to cover his comrades' flight. "He died, deliberately, for us," says one of the survivors. "No one at all could have got out of Treblinka . . . if it hadn't been for the real heroes; those who, having lost their wives and children there, elected to fight it out so as to give others a chance" (Sereny 246). Massarek's behavior calls to mind that of Michal Klepfisz in the Warsaw ghetto. He acted, I believe, out of motives different from Father Kolbe's: Massarek became a hero not out of love for God but because his wife's death made it impossible for him to live. His action also has a meaning that is different from that of Pechersky's, for Massarek chose to die and Pechersky to live.

Those who died as heroes in the camps were believers for the most part, Christians or Communists. Their faith was obviously of enormous help to them when it came time to die. Those for whom risking their lives came most easily were not like Pechersky; they acted in the name of an ideology, not out of a love of life. Like the heroes of antiquity who took to the battlefield in order to show their worth, the heroes of the camps sometimes rejoiced at being thrown into such situations of trial, for there they could prove their heroism. Solzhenitsyn tells the story of a woman condemned to death whose last week seemed to her the most luminous of her entire life. "That is the kind of ecstasy," Solzhenitsyn writes, "that descends upon the soul as a reward when you have cast aside all hopes for impossible salvation and have steadfastly given yourself over to a great deed" (659–60). Charlotte Delbo, an Auschwitz survivor, tells of a fellow inmate who remembers writing, "I'm being deported. This is the greatest day of my life." Later the woman recalls, "I was insane, insane. The heroine crowned with her halo, the martyr going to her death singing. Undoubtedly, we needed this exaltation to maintain our clandestine way of life" (Auschwitz 259).

The farewell letters of Marcel Raiman, shot to death on Mont Valérien in February 1944, contain dramatic testimony of the conflict between heroic exaltation and a love of life. A Jewish militant from the ranks of the Communist Youth Party, Raiman became a terrorist of great audacity under the German occupation. He killed German soldiers and officers on the streets of Paris, shooting them at point-blank range or lobbing grenades at them. He was arrested in November 1943 and tortured for several months. On the eve of his execution, he wrote to his family. "I am completely tranquil and at peace," he told his aunt. "And I am sure that all this is more painful for you than for us." He enclosed other letters, for his mother and brother (who had already been deported and would not return). "Forgive me for not writing a longer letter," he wrote to his mother, "but we are all so happy that I cannot bear to think of the pain you will feel." And to his brother, Simon, he wrote, "I send you a big hug, I adore you, I am happy. . . . Pay no attention if my letter seems crazy. I just can't stay serious." Marcel Raiman could not seem to stop writing these elated letters, as if the act itself assured him that he was still alive, still in touch with his family. When all three letters were finished, he added postscripts. "I love everyone," he wrote, "and hurrah for life! Let everyone be happy. Marcel." And then, suddenly, like a child: "Mama and Simon, I love you and wish I could see you again. Marcel" (Diamant 163–64).

Marcel Raiman was a hero who loved people. Yet the true believer, as we have seen, can so love God (or Communism: "Stalin, I love you!" shouts one militant in her delirium) that he or she forgets to love people. Margarete Buber-Neumann, deported first to Kazakhstan, then to Ravensbrück, describes the Jehovah's Witnesses whose *Blockälteste* she was for two years. Deported to Ravensbrück because they believed that Hitler was the devil incarnate, the women refused to do any work that might contribute to the war effort. They had only to renounce their faith and they could leave the camp, but not one of them did. Of all the groups in the camp, they were the most tightly knit (and the most highly regarded by the SS); their love for Jehovah was so great that they refused all compromise.

None of their fellow prisoners, however, benefited from that love. Buber-Neumann reports her conversation with a woman named Ella Hempel, who, with what would seem to be the single-mindedness of Saint Perpetua, had left her husband and four young children rather than renounce her faith. The letters she received from home could not weaken her resolve; she preferred to stay in Ravensbrück and live her faith. The Jehovah's Witnesses had no more sympathy for the other prisoners than for their own families. "If they took any risks at all," writes Buber-Neumann, "it was only in the service of Jehovah . . . and never of their fellow prisoners" (*Ravensbrück* 147). Buber-Neumann encountered this attitude firsthand, as none of these women offered help during her period of solitary confinement.

Like other fervent believers, the Jehovah's Witnesses had no love to spare, not even for themselves; they were ready to suffer and—like Eleazer—to die rather than violate a dietary taboo, not caring that they were participating in their own annihilation and thus helping to further the Nazis' criminal projects. "To refuse a piece of sausage because it isn't kosher is heroic when one is starving to death. . . . In the camps, practicing the Jewish religion very quickly became a form of suicide" (Fénelon, *Sursis* 255). But heroes do not necessarily love people, even when they themselves are those people.

What the actions of all these heroes and saints suggest is that there is perhaps a distinction to be made within the category of the heroic itself. Heroism always implies courage, strength, and self-abnegation, as well as the belief in some abstract ideal; sometimes, however, heroic behavior was subordinated to the welfare of real human beings (even if the hero did not know them), while other times it was not. Kolbe may have sacrificed himself because of his religion, but by doing so he saved the life of another human being. Ella Hempel's action was also religiously motivated, but no particular individual benefited from it; in this instance heroism becomes an act without a human end. The Warsaw uprisings showed that these two varieties of heroism can exist side by side, and often in the same person. Yet we cannot judge them in the same way. Even in the exceptional circumstances of war and revolt, when heroism is a necessary virtue, not all heroes are equally deserving of praise.

Dignity

Acts of ordinary virtue, I believe, are infinitely more numerous than acts of heroism. I have said that dignity is the first of the ordinary virtues; now we must ask what exactly it is. The answer is not self-evident.

Jean Améry, born Hans Mayer, an Austrian Jewish intellectual who settled in Belgium after his liberation from Auschwitz, is one of those survivors who deeply pondered their experience and left us ample trace of their reflections in their writings. Améry's understanding of dignity changes several times in the course of his inquiries. His first conclusions, based on his recollections of what he saw and heard, are those of a skeptic: everyone has a different notion of dignity, he argues, and in the end this lack of agreement makes the word itself nearly useless. For one person, dignity is a daily bath; for another, it is the possibility of communicating in his native tongue; for a third, it means freedom of expression; and for a fourth, it is the right to sexual partners of his choice. Among the philosophers, one finds even less agreement. Pascal, for instance, writes that all man's dignity lies in thought, while Kant says that dignity amounts to treating others not as a mere means but always as an end. For Camus, human dignity resides wholly in a perpetual revolt against the human condition. What are we to make, Améry asks, of this chaos of divergent opinions?

Subsequently, Améry analyzes his own attitudes and offers a more personal interpretation. Dignity, he now argues, is a form of social recognition. Society is the arbiter of individual worth, and we delude ourselves if we think we can substitute our own opinions of ourselves for those that others have of us. An individual can claim whatever dignity he wants, but such claims are futile if society declines to acknowledge them. And what happens if society not only refuses to recognize your dignity but actually declares you not worthy of life, as Nazi Germany did the Jews? The nonconsenting individual seems to have only one choice, and that is violent revolt: every blow must be answered in kind. If society condemns you, then dignity consists of fighting that society. If it strikes you down, you must strike back. Améry relates the following episode: One day in Auschwitz, he is assaulted by another prisoner, a Polish common-law criminal by the name of Juszek. To maintain his dignity, Améry returns his attacker's blow, punching this huge man in the face, as a result of which Améry is beaten even more cruelly. But he has no regrets. "My body, when it tensed to strike, was my physical and metaphysical dignity. . . . In the punch, I was myself. . . . I gave concrete social form to my dignity by punching a human face" (*Mind* 91). Améry's position is very nearly that expressed by Franz Fanon in his argument for the necessity of counterviolence.

This position does not, however, satisfy Améry for very long. He finds the situation of the Jews in the ghettos and the camps even more hopeless than that of the Algerian peasants who are the subject of Fanon's reflections. For the Jews, the possibilities of response were more limited, and the remedies Fanon advocates do not apply. Does this mean, then, that these people could never have any dignity? Améry's intuitive response is to reject the idea that it is only by striking back with one's fists that one can recover one's dignity. He leaves one wondering, though, whether, in his desire to give social sanction to dignity, he has not confused it with something that might better be called honor. For honor is a form of recognition that society bestows according to its codes, whereas dignity can be experienced even by the isolated individual.

Bruno Bettelheim, who, having survived Buchenwald and Dachau, spent years studying the moral problems posed by life in the camps, discusses dignity in the context of autonomy, which he defines not as the isolation of the individual within society but rather as "man's internal ability to regulate his own life" (*Heart* 102). For Bettelheim, the human will mediates between consciousness and deed. The aim of the camps is to destroy autonomy, "to break the prisoners as individuals" (109). To prevent this destruction is to maintain one's dignity, however limited the autonomy one has managed to win back. The important thing is to act out of the strength of one's will, to exert through one's initiative some influence, however minimal, on one's surroundings. The prisoners realized, writes Bettelheim, "that they still retained the last, if not the greatest, of the human freedoms: to choose their own attitude in any given circumstance. Prisoners who understood this fully came to know that this, and only this, formed the crucial difference between retaining one's humanity (and often life itself) and accepting death (often their real death) as human beings: whether one retained the freedom to choose autonomously one's attitude to extreme conditions, even when they seemed totally beyond one's ability to influence them" (158). Here, the terms *freedom, will, autonomy,* and *dignity* are more or less synonymous.

No power can take away this ultimate choice or can deprive a human being of this freedom, the very freedom that defines his humanity and that permits him to remain human. No constraint, not even that of social determinism, is ever total: "Everything can be taken from a man but one thing," Viktor Frankl declares, "the last of the human freedoms—to choose one's attitude in any given set of circumstances, to choose one's own way" (104). But Améry, who eventually came to agree, was also correct in rejecting a purely subjective and internal definition of dignity. As Améry suggests, it is not enough simply to decide to acquire dignity; that decision must give rise to an act that is visible to others (even if they are not actually there to see it). This can be one definition of dignity.

THE EXERCISE OF WILL

The preservation of dignity requires transforming a situation of constraint into one of freedom; where the constraint is extreme, such a transformation can amount to choosing to do something one is forced to do. Améry arrived at the same conclusion: minimum dignity, the only dignity possible in situations in which one no longer has any choice, means going of one's own accord to the death that others have prepared for you; it is, for example, the suicide of one who awaits execution—the difference between the two is infinitesimal yet sufficient. In *This Way for the Gas, Ladies and Gentlemen*, Borowski tells of a young woman who, having understood the fate in store for her, decides to jump into the truck ferrying new arrivals to the gas chambers. It is acts of this sort that inspire the admiration of Zalmen Gradowski, a member of the Auschwitz *Sonderkommando* (the special unit of Jewish slave laborers assigned to drag the corpses from the gas chambers to the crematoriums). Before he was killed, he buried his diary near the crematoriums in Birkenau, where it was found after the war. "The victims walked proudly, boldly, with firm steps," he writes, "as though they were marching toward life" (Roskies 557). Filip Müller, another member of the *Sonderkommando*, observes the same response in the "family camp" on the part of men and women who had just learned, by public announcement, that they were about to be killed. Rather than protest, they sang the Czech national anthem, followed by "Hatikvah." Others, too, sang in the trucks that carried them to the gas chambers.

Gustaw Herling's account of "Stalin's assassin" offers another example of the way adapting the will to reality allows a feeling of dignity. According to Herling, this man, a high-ranking Soviet official who loved to boast about his marksmanship, made a bet that with one shot he could put a bullet through the eye of the photograph of Stalin hanging on the wall. He won the bet, but within a matter of months he found himself in prison and, later, in the gulag. The whole affair was absurd: he had absolutely nothing against Stalin. Once sentenced, however, he began to reinterpret his deed and eventually took responsibility for it as an act of will, as an intended aggression against Stalin, which was not at all what it was to begin with. To anyone who would listen, he cried, " 'I killed Stalin! . . . I shot him down like a dog!' Before he died, as a last rite, he wanted to take responsibility for a crime he had not committed" (55). By accepting the "crime," he also accepts the punishment; it was the only way for him to regain his dignity.

Even in places where murder is a daily occurrence, suicide, in and of itself, implies greater freedom. By committing suicide, one alters the course of events—if only for the last time in one's life—instead of simply reacting to them. Suicides of this kind are acts of defiance, not of desperation; they are a final freedom, as Olga Lengyel makes clear when she describes the solace she finds in the knowledge that, come what may, she always has her capsule of poison: "There is some comfort in knowing that as a last resort, one is master of his own life or death! In a sense, this represents the ultimate in liberty" (18). Contemplating the body of a friend in Kolyma who has committed suicide, Eugenia Ginzburg, too, finds comfort in recognizing that this ultimate freedom is still available. "If I should so want," she writes, "I could dispose of my own life just like that" (*Within* 100).

The camp guards understood full well that to choose the moment and the means of one's death is to affirm one's freedom; indeed it is precisely to destroy this freedom—and the dignity that stems from it—that the camps were created. Thus, even though the guards killed with such apparent ease, they did everything in their power to prevent people from putting an end to their own lives. When Filip Müller entered the gas chamber voluntarily, the guards found him and yanked him back. "You bloody shit!" they shouted. "Get it into your stupid head: *we* decide how long you stay alive and when you die, and not you!" (114). It is less important that the inmates die than that they be alienated from their wills, for it is this alienation that enables the guards to experience fully their power over others. Hence, Bettelheim explains, the guards' irritation when confronted with a suicide, even though it spared them a "dirty job": any act of self-determination is a threat and must be severely punished.

The success of any such defiant suicide enrages the guards. Mala Zimetbaum escapes from Auschwitz but then is recaptured and tortured by her guards. She refuses to reveal the names of her accomplices, remaining silent throughout. Finally, she is brought to the gallows in the main square of the camp before all the inmates, who have been assembled to witness her execution. Mala briefly addresses her comrades, then turns and slashes her wrists with a razor blade she has managed to conceal. The guards, who in another minute were going to hang her, are furious. "You want to be a heroine! You want to kill yourself! That's what we are here for. That's our job!" (Suhl 188).

Inmates who carry out hunger strikes provoke this same rage, though to a somewhat lesser degree, as they draw nearer to a death that would normally leave their guards indifferent. These inmates, like those who commit suicide, choose starvation rather than submit to it. Irina Ratushinskaya describes how the hunger strikers in the Soviet gulags of the 1980s were force-fed, even though hunger was a constant problem and their usual daily rations barely enough to keep them alive. The process of force-feeding—her hands tied behind her back while liquid is poured through a tube directly into her body—reminds her of nothing so much as rape.

A relatively common way of exercising one's will is to refuse to obey an order. In a sense, this is a purely passive mode of resistance (one is not actually doing anything), but still it could easily cost an inmate his or her life. In Auschwitz, there were doctors who refused to discriminate between Jews and Aryans; others declined to participate in medical experiments. These doctors, it is true, risked censure, not death. On the other hand, when members of the *Sonderkommando* refused to obey orders, it was they who were killed in place of their victims. Hermann Langbein describes a German Communist named Hiasl Neumeier, who, imprisoned at Dachau, "became famous there for refusing to participate in the beating of his comrades, preferring to be beaten in their stead" (157)—a modern exemplar of the Socratic precept that it is better to submit to injustice than to inflict it. The fate of Else Krug at Ravensbrück is more tragic: a former prostitute who had catered to a masochistic clientele—and who thus had great expertise in the practices of sadism—she refused to beat another prisoner. Her act of defiance led directly to her execution (Buber-Neumann, *Ravensbrück* 34).

The refusal to obey orders was also the principle of dignified conduct for the extraordinary Milena Jesenska, the Czech journalist who had been a friend of Kafka and was interned at Ravensbrück after the Germans occupied her country. There she met Margarete Buber-Neumann, who became a great friend and, eventually, her biographer. Milena managed to affirm her dignity through innocuous acts that nevertheless demonstrated her contempt for the arbitrary order to which all aspects of life in the camp were subject. "She didn't march right in rows of five, she didn't stand right in roll call, she didn't hurry when ordered to, she didn't toady to those in command. Every word Milena said was an infringement of the regulations" (*Milena* 9).

Waving a handkerchief or whistling a tune became an act of autonomy and defiance that provoked the ire not only of the guards but also of inmates who had internalized the existing order. On one occasion, Milena, for no apparent reason, activated the camp siren. "Just once she wanted to be 'the flounder,' as in the fairy tale of the fisherman and his wife," Buber-Neumann writes, "just once she wanted to be the one who had all the power" (163). This seemingly gratuitous act allowed Milena to affirm her dignity, a goal that no practical gesture, voluntary or not, could have accomplished. Finding water to quench one's thirst certainly requires an intervention of the will, but the utilitarian nature of the act makes it difficult to harvest its moral fruits. Setting off the camp siren, on the other hand, is a disinterested act, and it is for this very reason that Milena can affirm her dignity through it. That said, it is important to note that the kind of acts at issue here are not those that harm others. Milena has nothing in common with Raskolnikov or Lafcadio.

SELF-RESPECT

To exercise one's will is one way, but not the only way, to affirm one's dignity. When one acts of one's own accord (for example, by committing suicide) one demonstrates both that free will exists and that it is possible to establish an adequation between the internal and the external: purely internal decisions, as we have seen, do not lead to dignity. When I make a decision and also act in accordance with that decision, that is dignity. The exercise of will is thus one ingredient; the agreement of the internal with the external is the other. Dignity then becomes the capacity to satisfy, through one's actions, criteria that one has internalized. Dignity in this sense is synonymous with self-respect: I want my actions to find favor in my own eyes.

One example of dignity so defined might be simply staying clean in circumstances where everything conspires to prevent it—where water is scarce, dirty, or frozen, the latrines far away, the climate severe. An abundance of testimony confirms that inmates who managed to stay clean, who found a way to pay even minimal attention to their clothing, inspired their fellow prisoners' respect (and also increased their chances of survival—virtue, in this case, is more than its own reward). Primo Levi insists that he owes his own survival to a lesson he learned early in his confinement from Steinlauf, a fellow inmate and one-time sergeant in the Austro-Hungarian army: stay clean in order not to debase yourself in your own eyes. "So we must certainly wash our faces without soap in dirty water," Levi writes, "and dry ourselves on our jackets. We must polish our shoes, not because the regulation states it, but for dignity and propriety" (*Survival* 36).

Another example of this type of dignity is the refusal to behave according to the logic of personal interest and short-term advantage. To have concern for others and not just for oneself, for those absent as well as for those present, is to take a first step toward dignity. To refuse to humble oneself before one's superiors is dignified behavior. To decline a privilege one deems undeserved—a scrap of food proffered to underscore one's inferiority or a reward for something one has done not for material gain but because it was the right thing to do —is to give evidence of one's dignity. Herling tells the story of Eugenia Fyodorovna, a nurse in the Vologda gulag who, as the head doctor's mistress, enjoyed numerous privileges. It happened, however, that she fell in love with one of the prisoners. To behave in accordance with her feelings and not with her material interests was, in these circumstances, an act of dignity. It cost her dearly: as punishment, her lover was moved to another camp, and when she asked to be transferred herself, so as not to have to be near the head doctor, she forfeited all her privileges. "In January of 1942, Eugenia Feodorovna died giving birth to her lover's child, thus paying with her life for her short resurrection" (112). Dignity does not always ensure survival.

Yet another form of dignity is the satisfaction derived from a job well done. Using one's skill or expertise to the best of one's ability can enable one to preserve a measure of self-respect. Solzhenitsyn describes the pleasure and pride the prisoner feels when he has built a wall correctly. "You need that wall like you need a hole in the head," he writes, "nor do you believe it is going to bring closer the happy future of the people, but, pitiful tattered slave that you are, you smile at this creation of your own hands" (610). Primo Levi makes several similar observations from his experience in Auschwitz: Lorenzo, the mason who saves Levi's life, manages to preserve his dignity by doing a good job of the work he is ordered to do. "When they set him to build protective walls against the aerial bombs he built them straight, solid, with well-staggered bricks and as much mortar as was required, not in deference to orders but out of professional dignity" (*Drowned* 122). (This is why meaningless work, such as carrying sand back and forth, or digging a hole and then filling it up again, is particularly degrading. It is impossible to do it well, and impossible therefore to keep one's self-respect.) Similarly, Ratushinskaya and her friends try to work as carefully as they can when they have to produce useful goods. "We turn out first-class gloves as a point of honor," she says. "We do not sabotage the equipment, and see nothing demeaning in our job" (69).

MORAL AMBIGUITIES

It is debatable, however, whether doing a job well always constitutes a virtue. As George Orwell noted during the war, "The first thing that we demand of a wall is that it shall stand up. If it stands up, it is a good wall, and the question of what purpose it serves is separable from that. And yet even the best wall in the world deserves to be pulled down if it surrounds a concentration camp" (161). Was it walls of this kind that Levi's benefactor Lorenzo and Solzhenitsyn's prisoner built? Acts and works must be judged not only for what they are but also by what they do; one must keep in mind their function as well as their quality. It is precisely because dignity depends not on social approbation but only on a coherence between consciousness and action that its being a virtue is open to question. Not all dignity is moral. In the final analysis, its moral nature must come from without; dignity commands respect only when it works for the good. Bettelheim recalls disputes among prisoners over this question. "When erecting buildings for the Gestapo," he writes, "controversies would begin over whether one should build well. New prisoners were for sabotaging, a majority of the old prisoners for building well" (*Heart* 205). If the wall surrounds a camp, it is not good; a wall built badly and in the spirit of defiance is far preferable.

The accounts given by the camp guards, too, abound with examples of love for the job well done. Rudolf Höss, the commandant of Auschwitz, describes himself as "obsessed with his work"; he neglects to mention that his work was that of a mass murderer. "I invested my whole being in the accomplishment of my task," he states. "I used to think of nothing but my work, and I put all human feeling aside" (139, 140, 142). It is easy to see how those two components of his life might eventually find themselves in conflict with each other. Even his wife lectures him: "Stop thinking always of your duties," she tells him, "think of us, too!" (216). A little less dignity of this sort would have been a good thing. Thirty years later, survivors still recall the "obvious pleasure" that Franz Stangl, the commandant of Sobibor and Treblinka, took in his work. Stangl's answer to an interviewer's question corroborates his victims' recollections. "Everything I did of my own free will," he says sharply. "I had to do as well as I could. That is how I am." The son of another camp guard likewise declares, "Yes . . . I can quite imagine that [my father] would have approached Treblinka with the same thoroughness with which he approached his work at home: it was his principal quality as a craftsman" (Sereny 131, 229, 225). What makes for a good craftsman, it seems, does not necessarily make for a good man.

The dubious moral status of the job well done is even more apparent in the case of people whose work may have involved them somewhat less directly in the destruction of human lives. Before and during the war, Professor Ferdinand Porsche did his job as best he could, which is to say he designed tanks that were more and more powerful and deadly. Albert Speer put his organizational genius into the service of the arms industry; out of love for his work, he produced ever more numerous and efficient weapons. And at the other end of the spectrum, Alma Rose, the famed violinist and conductor of the women's orchestra at Auschwitz, was prepared to sacrifice the welfare of her musicians in the interest of making beautiful music. "We must do our work properly," she says. "Whatever we do, whether here or anywhere else, we must do it well, if only for our self-respect" (Fénelon, *Sursis* 178, 184). She does not shrink from brutality; like Höss, she has repressed her human feelings in the name of professional perfection. Such behavior, of course, is not alien to our everyday lives, far from the world of the concentration camps and the gulags. As Bruno Bettelheim observes, "Although the concentration camps and the crematoriums are no longer here, this kind of pride still remains with us; it is characteristic of a modern society in which fascination with technical competence has dulled concern for human feelings" (*Surviving* 257).

All forms of dignity are stamped with this same ambiguity, for they all depend on standards that do not transcend the perspective of the individual but instead remain immanent in him or her. Keeping himself clean and polishing his shoes helped Primo Levi maintain his self-respect, but the same was true for Levi's guards. As Fania Fénelon, a member of Alma Rose's orchestra, says, "I don't know whether this concern for appearance was part of Nazi ideology but it certainly occupied a key position in their lives. Furthermore, their shoes and boots always shone and smelled; I shall never forget the smell of German leather" (*Playing* 96). Distinguishing between the two situations requires a broader sense of context: the lives of Levi and his comrades were in grave danger, which was not exactly true for their guards.

The kind of coherence between internal standards and external behaviors that leads to self-respect is no less common among the guards than among their prisoners and gave rise in both to the same feeling of dignity. Höss was a confirmed Nazi who acted on his convictions. So was Mengele, who apparently did not suffer from the split personality characteristic of so many others. Himmler had a reputation, even among the Nazis, of acting with glacial rigor. Göring, of all the Nuremburg defendants, was the one who remained truest to himself. Must we therefore admire these men? If we do not, it is because we have made a distinction between a dignity that is moral and one that is not, between a self-respect we can admire and one that leaves us cold. The Nazi who always acts in accordance with his convictions may deserve some sort of respect, but that does not make his behavior moral. Moral behavior requires more than harmony between acts and ideals; it requires also that those ideals not work against the good of humanity.

Caring

The second ordinary virtue is the one that I have called caring. Here again, it is necessary to distinguish between two types of situations, between those that lie on this side of the ultimate threshold and those that lie beyond it, by which I mean situations in which one finds oneself faced with imminent death. What can one do for others in such situations, how can one express one's concern for them? One can choose, as Pola Lifszyc did in Warsaw, to die with them. Borowski tells a story of another young woman who went to Auschwitz to die with her mother. J. Kosciuszkowa, who survived her internment at Auschwitz, tells of a mother who gave birth there and managed to hide her baby for five months; when the child was discovered and taken from her, she chose to go with him. "Clutching her son to her breast, she carried him into the gas chamber" (Langbein 231). Then there is the young man who grew too weak to work and whose father lay down beside him so that they might await death together (107). There is also the Dutch woman who, when her husband was selected for the gas chamber at Sobibor, took his arm and walked with him to their deaths (Suhl 31). Another Dutch woman in Sobibor chose to die with her Polish lover, one of ten hostages executed in reprisal for another prisoner's escape (Trunk 280).

These people knew that they were doomed no matter what they did, but they preferred to take control of their destiny rather than submit to it passively. In this sense they resemble those who commit suicide to retain their dignity, the only difference being that here the action is directed beyond the self toward other human beings who are the object of their attachment. There is no one to tell us if the beneficiaries of these acts—Pola's mother, for example, or the Dutch woman's Polish lover—were happy to receive these testimonies of love or if they felt guilty for having drawn their loved ones with them to their deaths.

In the Warsaw ghetto it was sometimes necessary to kill people precisely because one cared about them. In Auschwitz a young man killed his brother "to spare him the truck ride to the gas chambers" (Langbein 108). Children born in the camps were routinely killed by nurses—poisoned, strangled, dropped into cisterns, smothered with pillows (231–32). As Olga Lengyel writes, "The fate of the baby always had to be the same. . . . After taking every precaution, we pinched and closed the little tyke's nostrils and when it opened its mouth to breathe, we gave it a dose of a lethal product. An injection might have been quicker, but that would have left a trace and we dared not let the Germans suspect the truth" (100). Because children were fated to die in any case, acts like these allowed at least the mother's life to be saved. And yet, as we have seen, this kind of decision still presented those who carried out the task with a cruel and complicated moral choice.

These cases, however, are exceptional ones, and if we limit ourselves to them, we may not understand caring as an ordinary virtue. On this side of the threshold, though, there are numerous acts of caring, beginning with the simplest and, in the camps, perhaps most important: the sharing of food. Here again, we find a limit beyond which sharing was impossible simply because hunger and thirst were too great. Once these were even minimally satisfied, however, it seems that some people shared and others did not. Eugenia Ginzburg remembers the day she discovered cranberries growing in the forest. "I ate the first two clusters all by myself; only on finding a third one did I remember my fellow creatures" (*Journey* 412). Ginzburg also remembers being on the receiving end, when an old convict brought her some oat jelly that he had lovingly prepared but would not eat himself; he was happy just to watch her enjoyment. "He looked at me," Ginzburg writes, "his eyes alive with kindness and happiness" (*Within* 48).

Irina Ratushinskaya and her companions received a gift not of food but of clothing that had been stitched together from rags and scraps of cloth by the old women who had occupied their barracks before them. "How much human warmth is stored up in these beggar-like witnesses to the ingenuity of our *babushki?*" Irina marvels (55). Mended countless times, the tattered clothes had become the repository of previous acts of caring. In the end, there is not a single prisoner, male or female, who does not remember being cared for, counseled, or protected at least once by someone else—the person in the next bed, perhaps, or another laborer. Sometimes a look sufficed: forty years after being marched to a forced-labor camp in Poland, David Rodman recalls that, as the convoy of prisoners passed, a young man came out of his house and looked on with a "noble face [that] expressed deep sorrow and compassion. . . . I know exactly the house next to which he stood. I still can see the look of suffering on the young man's face, the exact color of his shirt. . . . It impressed me that someone felt for me and cared because I suffered" (Tec 72).

Other people performed riskier deeds. One person might offer to send your letter to a friend or a relative. Someone else might hide you: Margarete Buber-Neumann, flat on her back in the infirmary, used her body to cover the tiny Germaine Tillion, whose name had been called for the next selection; had their ruse been discovered, both would have been sent to the gas chambers. Sasha Pechersky and Rudolf Vrba, escapees from Sobibor and Auschwitz, were hidden by Polish peasants. Another person might refuse to denounce you and, in solidarity with you, would endure the punishment for the theft you committed. Yet another person would save you from being raped, even though by doing so he lost his job under the shelter of a roof, which in the camps often meant the difference between life and death (Ginzburg, *Journey* 394).

Survivors of the camps brought out with them descriptions of a few individuals they felt were true incarnations of this virtue of caring for others. For Primo Levi, it is Lorenzo the mason, the non-Jewish Italian conscript laborer who every day brings him and another Italian prisoner an extra bowl of soup. Lorenzo refuses to take anything in return and almost never speaks, not even to the people he helps, who are more numerous than any of them realizes. For Robert Antelme, it is Jo, another quiet sort. On the train carrying them to an unknown destination during the final evacuation of the camps, Antelme cannot find anywhere to sit or lie down. "I lie down on top of Jo," he writes, "who fends me off but doesn't shout." Later, still without speaking, Jo holds out his hand to Antelme; in his palm lie a few soybean seeds, not only edible but actually nourishing. In the end, when everyone has to keep moving, "Jo helps me to walk. Jo's silent fraternity: my head against his back, in the car; the seeds in his hand; now his arm that I lean on" (267, 275).

Ginzburg's bright angel was a German doctor named Anton Walter, who would eventually become her second husband. She calls him her "jolly saint" (a rare combination) and remembers how he "used to run around the village [of Tascan], hunting for spirits for a tramp who longed for a drink before he died," she writes (*Within* 115, 138). For Ratushinskaya, it was Tatyana Mikhailovna Velikanova, a human-rights activist and longtime prisoner who patiently endured the intolerance and belligerence of her fellow inmates and made a permanent place in the camp for "the honorable practices of dignity and care for others" (73). For many Auschwitz survivors, it was Mala Zimetbaum, the same Mala Zimetbaum who enraged her guards by committing suicide before they could execute her. An interpreter and a runner, or messenger, Mala was very popular within the camp. "She utilized this privilege," a fellow inmate recalls, "to help establish contact between members of separated families, and frequently risked her life by carrying messages and medicine. . . . One of Mala's functions was to assign the sick released from the hospital to various work details. She always tried to send the women still weak from their illness to the lightest type of work. And she always warned the patients of the coming selections, urging them to leave the hospital as quickly as possible" (Suhl 184). Fania Fénelon recalls that whenever inmates had difficulties, whenever a problem came up, they would go to Mala (*Playing* 161).

For Margarete Buber-Neumann and for many other women at Ravensbrück, it was Milena Jesenska who most personified the caring attitude. While Milena refused to follow orders, she forged strong bonds with those she loved and knew how to make a gift of her radiant personality. In the infirmary, where she was responsible for keeping files on venereal diseases, she would alter the test results of patients with syphilis in order to protect them from the selections. Each time she changed an entry, she put her life on the line. She took personal interest in these patients, even though, as prostitutes and "misfits," they belonged to a very different world from hers: she knew how to find the "spark of humanity" within them. Milena and Buber-Neumann shared the kind of deep friendship in which giving is more pleasurable than receiving. It hardly mattered what was given: Milena once brought her a cup of real coffee, with real milk and real sugar, an "impossible treasure" acquired only after exhaustive bargaining and at the risk of severe punishment, for prisoners were forbidden to move about the camp. On another occasion, the undertaking was even more dangerous: when Buber-Neumann was in solitary confinement, Milena requested to speak with the highest-ranking Gestapo officer in Ravensbrück and not only persuaded him to listen to her but got him to let her visit her friend in prison, an absolutely unheard-of favor. On her deathbed, Milena was surrounded by friends; after her death, Buber-Neumann found that "life had lost all meaning for me." And she says something remarkable: "I was thankful for having been sent to Ravensbrück because it was there I had met Milena" (*Milena* 204; *Ravensbrück* 73).

(*Margarete Buber-Neumann has died—she died the same day the Berlin Wall came down. Born at the beginning of the century, in the same year as my mother, like her, she became senile a few years before her death. There is perhaps no better symbol of this century than her life: arrested by the KGB, she spent two years in the gulags, after which, in 1940, she was turned over to the Gestapo, only to spend five more years in Ravensbrück! Before her first imprisonment, she'd poured all her energies into the struggle for Communism; after her second, she did all she could to fight against it. And she wrote* Milena, *a marvelous book, unique in the literature of the camps in that it is the story not of her own life but of another's.*)

ACTORS

Who are these agents of concern, these people who care? They could be anyone. In the camps, there were Kapos and *Blockälteste* who cared about the people under them; there were overseers and prison guards who allowed goodness to come before duty. Buber-Neumann tells of a Soviet guard who was supposed to supervise a group of women working outside the camp. He would regularly abandon his watch to go into town to buy them food, leaving them on their own. "It took him over half an hour to get back. During that half-hour, seven prisoners trembled with fear for the life of an ordinary guard" (*Sibérie* 131). Even common criminals, the bane of every camp, were capable of acts of caring; nonetheless, such acts were much more frequently the work of political prisoners.

Obviously, some human relationships, especially those between close family members, are more apt to inspire caring than others. Caring is the maternal attitude par excellence. From Salonika to Auschwitz, from Moscow to Magadan, in the cattle cars that carried them to the concentration camps and the gulags, mothers continued to nurse their babies and did their best to keep them in dry diapers. Filip Müller and Zalmen Gradowski both write that even in the gas chambers mothers stroked the hair of their children to calm them. Other family ties were also likely to elicit caring responses. A twelve-year-old girl sends packages of food to her grandmother in the camps. "Dear Nana," she writes, "I've broken the sugar into tiny pieces, just the way you like it" (Buber-Neumann, *Sibérie* 169). A child of thirteen, on learning that her cousin has been arrested and taken to the railway station, races there with a small package in her hand. "She had dashed into a shop with her few pennies and bought me all that she could afford—cherries," writes the cousin, Rudolf Vrba (54). In Auschwitz a young girl, "terrified of touching dead bodies, is ordered to pick one up; her sister . . . slips her own hands between her sister's and the corpse" (Leitner 68). Men contrive to smuggle food to the women they love who are in the same camp; spouses and lovers forsake privileges in order to stay together. Friends do the same for friends. Inmates of the camp in Mordovia recall with great emotion how one man, Yuli Daniel, cared more about the fate of a comrade in misery, Andrei Sinyavski, than about himself (Marchenko 374). Doctors and nurses, whether male or female, cared about others and perhaps not just out of professional habit but from a sense of deeper vocation as well.

Here another question arises. When I call caring the maternal attitude par excellence, do I mean that it is somehow more "feminine" than "masculine"? And if so, is it a matter of biology or of socialization? And is this division of virtues along gender lines something to be applauded or decried?

Let me begin with this observation: on the whole, women survived the camps better than men did, not just in terms of numbers but in terms of psychological well-being. There must be some explanation for this advantage, and it is tempting to look for that explanation in differences that have to do with gender. It could be that the guards, who for the most part were men, mistreated their male prisoners more severely than they did the women. The confrontational nature of male relations, the desire to display one's superiority and establish one's power over a rival, may account for the greater brutality against male prisoners than against female prisoners, whose unequal status in the eyes of their guards may have been much more of a foregone conclusion. But there also appear to have been significant differences in the behavior of the prisoners themselves: the women were more practical, more likely to help one another than were the men. Germaine Tillion notes that men were more likely to deaden themselves, to become hard and indifferent, to turn on one another. "It seems to me," Tillion writes, "that friendly support was more consistent, more solid, and more widespread in the women's camps" (38; see also 230). Perhaps that is why, after liberation, women tended to readjust to the outside world more easily than men did.

Ginzburg makes a similar observation: "Our poor male companions! The weaker sex. . . . For it was they who keeled over dead where we merely bent with the wind while we stayed the course. They were better than we at using an ax, a pick, or wheelbarrow, but they were greatly inferior in their ability to withstand torture." How does she explain this difference? "Although one might have thought the men were stronger than we were, they seemed somehow more defenseless and we all felt a maternal pity for them. They stood up to pain so badly . . . and they would not know how to mend anything or be able to wash their clothes on the sly as we could" (*Within* 165; *Journey* 344–45). It would seem that with physical strength comes psychological weakness, and vice versa. The women's accounts of life in the camps give a very different impression from the men's. The camp in which Marchenko was imprisoned is striking in its inhumanity, whereas Ratushinskaya's, though not far from his, is marked by an atmosphere of warmth. It is a question not so much of different conditions as of different behaviors: where men often reacted self-destructively, women showed caring and concern for one another. Perhaps the most surprising thing in Ratushinskaya's memoirs is the happiness these women felt just being together; they managed to create a climate of freedom, dignity, and mutual support that they would perhaps not find again, once liberated. "How good it is to be back in the Zone!" Ratushinskaya exclaims when she is discharged from the infirmary (196). To be sure, Marchenko feels sad in bidding farewell to his companions as he leaves the camp, but there is really no comparing the general atmosphere of the two groups.

These differences in behavior merely reflect the roles that society traditionally assigns men and women. At the risk of recalling the obvious, let me briefly go over the following points: the division of sexual roles is biologically based insofar as only women can bear and nurse children; the consequences of those nine or eighteen months in the life of a woman continue, however, throughout her entire lifetime (and they extend to women who do not become mothers). This division of roles finds its way into other domains and is reflected in other oppositions—the practical and personal versus the abstract and impersonal (politics, science, and the arts); body versus mind; involvement in personal relationships versus solitary goal-oriented pursuits. Whether or not she has children, a woman will most likely find herself responsible for child care and for the care of parents and husband as well. Even if, in recent decades, the legal status of women has evolved toward one of greater equality and even if certain traditionally female responsibilities have now been taken over by institutions (day-care centers, lunch programs, nursing homes), tradition remains a force to be reckoned with. Thus it is that a young girl, Fania Fénelon, looks around her at the women asleep in her Auschwitz barracks and says, "I look at them and a protective tenderness unfolds inside me, a tenderness that rises from the darkest past, and I wonder where this feeling could possibly come from, since I am one of the very youngest" (*Sursis* 87).

Two stories illustrate the kind of caring that is hard not to associate with women. The first one comes from the same account by Fénelon. Transferred to Bergen-Belsen, she strikes up a friendship with a doctor named Marie. The two are talking one day when a Polish prisoner comes to Marie for help. She is not sick—she is about to give birth. At first, Fania and Marie panic, but then they collect themselves and have the woman lie down on a table. Silence is imperative, so the woman, "teeth clenched, uttered not a moan. She knew the fate that awaited children at the hands of the SS." Fortunately, the child arrives quickly. There are no scissors: Marie cuts the cord with her teeth. There is no water: Fania rips the lining out of her coat, fashions a crude version of swaddling clothes, and wraps up the baby, still covered with blood. "The woman, who has not yet said a word, puts on her drawers again, lowers her skirts, puts on her shoes, and takes her child in her arms in a wonderful gesture of possession and protection" (*Playing* 251–52). Both mother and child survive.

The second story takes place twenty years later, in Russia, and it is recounted by a man, Anatoly Marchenko. The prisoners are being transferred by train to another camp; there is a car reserved for women, one of whom carries a baby in her arms. Its diapers are already filthy, but when she asks permission to wash them, the guards refuse: it's against the rules. Prisoners are allowed to use the toilets at the appointed hour only and even then not for very long. "When the women started to be let out for their toilet break, the child's mother was the first to go," Marchenko writes. "Somehow she managed to wash the baby's things out in the wash-basin and leave them there. The next woman rinsed them as much as she had time for and again left them there. And the next and the next. By the time all the women had been led out, the things were well washed and the last one brought them back with her. Then they dried them inside the cage" (30).

A caring attitude may not arise "naturally" from the female and maternal traditions, but it is nonetheless cultivated in them, especially in the latter. The figure of the mother took on special importance for the inmates, particularly for the women, who could identify with it. At her mother's death, Ginzburg remembers her acts of silent heroism that she herself seemed to take for granted (*Within* 307). Ginzburg's mother is no different from many others in this respect, but can an act be called heroic if it is silent? Buber-Neumann has a similar image of her own mother; unfortunately, when Buber-Neumann finally returns home after her liberation, her mother hardly recognizes her. She sits on the doorstep and keeps repeating: "Has she really come home? Has Margarete really . . ." (*Ravensbrück* 324).

(My mother used to say nearly the same thing during my last visits to Bulgaria, when, in infinitely less dramatic circumstances, I would make my annual visit from France to see her. When she recognized me, she grew animated and called me by name, caressing my face with her wrinkled hands and kissing me over and over. Her life had passed in acts of caring and kindness, particularly after she became ill at the age of forty and was forced to give up her job. While my father devoted himself body and soul to a variety of projects (organizing institutions, putting up buildings, teaching), she worried about the family: the children, my father, her unmarried and somewhat bohemian sister. During her last years, she lost her mind; forgetting that her sister had died, she would grow anxious after dinner. Are there any leftovers, she would ask, because when Dora comes home she'll be hungry. . . . This devotion was not intentional; she just did not seem able to do otherwise. On the other hand, she never complained about her situation, never gave the impression that she was sacrificing herself; in fact, I believe she was happy about it for she seemed incapable of experiencing pleasure except through others. She did not like caring for herself, only for others; if ever she found herself alone, she grew bored. In addition, she was miserable when someone had to do something for her; she didn't want people to pay any attention to her. She died very quietly, while the family was out of the room; after all, she did not like to disturb anyone. My father, however, has another interpretation: he says that she prayed to God to take her so that she wouldn't be a burden to her husband.)

A number of women writers who have at least partially renounced the traditional female role of caregiver have asked whether women ought not to free themselves from this role altogether and try to emulate the male half of humanity, to concern themselves with humanity, for instance, rather than with individual human beings. I have in mind not Simone de Beauvoir so much as Etty Hillesum, a Dutch Jew who died in Auschwitz but whose journal has fortunately been preserved. A remarkable writer, Hillesum asks herself if she will "always continue to be in search of my one man." She wonders "to what extent that is a handicap, a woman's handicap. Whether it is an ancient tradition from which she must liberate herself, or whether it is so much a part of her very essence that she would be doing violence to herself if she bestowed her love on all mankind instead of on a single man." Hillesum is drawn to the first explanation, although she lived her short life according to the second: "Perhaps the true, the essential emancipation of women still has to come. We are not yet full human beings; we are the 'weaker sex.' . . . We still have to be born as human beings, that is the great task that lies before us" (*Interrupted* 27–28). To renounce caring, the traditional destiny of women —is this the great task? Perhaps then women will become more like men, but both will be that much less human. If there is a great task, isn't it rather to make men understand—all men, that is, not just a few —that, unless they too learn to care, they run the risk of being not men but only male, unrealized in their humanity? For what does it mean to remain human—to sacrifice oneself to abstractions or to care about others?

I don't wish to suggest that the feminine and the maternal warrant unconditional praise. What is admirable as an act—in this case, caring —can cease to be so when it becomes entrenched behavior, a mere automatism. It would be better, I think, for maternal caring to be spread a bit throughout the world rather than restricted to a category of individuals for whom motherhood is a profession. Mothers, too, need people to care about them, and children do not wish to be mothered eternally. And caring can assume forms that run counter to the usual idea of maternal protectiveness: during the war, often the best way to care for children—in Jewish families, for instance—was to part with them, even to abandon them. An entire family could easily be tracked down, whereas a Jewish child, alone, had at least a fair chance of being rescued by a Christian family.

BOUNDARIES

I want to distinguish here between true care for someone else and other feelings or actions that resemble it, if only superficially. To begin with, caring is not the same thing as the *solidarity* felt by members of a group among themselves. Solidarity is a feeling that can manifest itself in all sorts of situations. Say I am a provincial who has moved to Paris; it is out of solidarity with others from my region that I try to help them out when they themselves come to Paris. Or perhaps I am simply a French citizen; it is also out of solidarity—now with my fellow Frenchmen—that I refuse to extend to foreigners the benefits of the public health-care or school systems. Even if one makes an a priori distinction between these two types of solidarity—solidarity as a support system in the face of adversity and solidarity as a means of securing certain advantages—and recognizes only the former, it is not the same thing as caring. Solidarity with the group to which I belong means that I automatically help all its members and that I do not concern myself with the needs of those who do not belong. Understood in this way, as a mutual aid society, solidarity is no more than a quantitative extension of the principle of self-interest; it replaces egotism with what Primo Levi calls "we-ism," the selfishness of the collectivity.

Solidarity with our own implies the exclusion of all others. Its victims thus are foreigners, strangers, those who are different. Even in the camps, newcomers first run up against the hostility of the group that has already formed. The group is not sure it wants the newcomers to share in the benefits of its solidarity, and they are kept outside the circle, lest they jeopardize whatever advantages the group has already won for itself. All groups tend to develop this corporate spirit as a defense against intrusion from without. Philip Hallie tells how the mayor of Chambon-sur-Lignon, a village in the Cevennes that became a wartime haven for the persecuted, declared himself ready to hide and protect Jews, but only those Jews who were truly "one of us." For him, as for certain French Jews, foreign Jews only meant trouble; it was because of them that "good" French Jews risked persecution. The Darbyist sect of Protestant fundamentalists in the same region practiced a different kind of solidarity. Out of admiration for those whom they saw as the "people of the Book," they preferred to save Jews rather than, for example, other Frenchmen. Pétain played constantly on this reflex, as did Hitler: they deported "only" foreign, recently naturalized, or newly assimilated Jews or "only" Jews, but not other French citizens, and so on down the line.

For reasons that are easy to understand, solidarity in the camps meant, first of all, national—or, more precisely, linguistic—solidarity. In a Babel like Auschwitz, how could one feel solidarity with people whose language one did not understand, people with whom one could not communicate? Antelme writes of several very real moral conflicts that arose during the horrendous displacements of prisoners from one camp to another at the end of the war, when rations were gradually reduced to nothing. The Poles shared their food among themselves, refusing to give anything to the French. When the French finally began receiving packages from the Red Cross, they divided them equally—among themselves; when the Russians approached the French and begged for food, they were chased off with clubs and sticks, even though they were allies. Antelme recalls, "The torture the Russians around us are undergoing barely affects us. Our attention is concentrated upon the food." But the group could be more exclusive still: "We have reached the point where it is unthinkable to share food with anyone except a guy from the [same railroad] car" (276–77). And yet, as we saw with Eugenia Ginzburg when she came upon cranberries in the forest, even a few mouthfuls to alleviate one's own hunger allows a change of attitude: people will generally help those whose need is greatest, whether or not they are of the same nationality.

Groups that formed along lines other than those of national origin acted no differently. The Communists, for example, formed tightly knit collectives from which all those who did not share their convictions were of course excluded. Communists, especially German Communists, often held positions of responsibility in the camp hierarchy. These positions enabled them, among other things, to erase the name of a comrade if it appeared on the selection list for the gas chambers.

Yet there was no changing the total number of persons selected. Thus
if one name was removed, another had to replace it. The solidarity of
some can sometimes mean the death of others.

To act out of solidarity with a group is a political, not a moral, act.
Free choice is not involved, and the decisions one makes derive from
particulars, not universals. This does not mean that solidarity is something that can or should be dispensed with: what social welfare system, for example, can generously extend its benefits to any and all
who might wish to claim them? At its best, however, group solidarity
acts as a kind of preparation for, or an apprenticeship in, a generosity
that extends beyond the group. Ginzburg describes the first encounter between two groups of prisoners: their initial reaction of mutual
rejection is followed by one of inclusion. "We were figures from a
nightmare," she recalls. "This could be seen in their faces as they
looked at us with an expression of horror, and in their readiness to
share their last rags with us" (*Journey* 332). Where else might one
learn to care for other people if not with those who constantly surround us?

Caring also differs from solidarity in that those who receive care
cannot automatically count on it; they are, after all, individuals, not
members of a group. Caring cannot include everyone, not everyone in
the world or even everyone in the same camp. The choice is made
according to criteria other than nationality, profession, or political
persuasion; each person who is cared for is deserving in and of him-
or herself. Yet here, too, having a common language is important—
how does one discern the individuality of a person one cannot understand?

There is a second boundary that should also be defined, that between caring and *charity* (or any of its synonyms). Unlike solidarity,
charity makes no distinctions; it excludes no one. The recipient of the
act of charity need only be suffering or be somehow in jeopardy. With
charity, there is no danger of its being turned to the advantage of any
particular group. It is incontestably a moral act. Charity differs from
caring, then, precisely in its being directed toward everyone rather
than toward particular individuals; the typical beneficiary of the charitable act is the nameless beggar lying in the street, not the person
lying on top of me in the cattle car or under me in the infirmary.

Pascal, in fact, expressly recommends that one avoid knowing personally those to whom one would extend charity so as not to risk dimin-
ishing the virtue of the act by becoming attached to the recipient and
acting out of love for the person rather than out of love for God.

John Glenn Grey, who lived through the Second World War,
though not in the camps, describes a similar feeling, which he calls
"protective love." He cites the example in *War and Peace* of
Karatayev's saving Pierre's life: the man would have helped an animal
in exactly the same way. Grey qualifies this love as maternal, but a
mother would not, of course, love just any child in place of her own.
In this kind of love, "the object of one's care is less essential than the
presence of the need to take care and to preserve" (85), which is why
I believe the love Grey describes is more a variant of charity than an
act of caring. Caring cannot be universal, for it implies feeling personal sympathy with the object of one's concern. Ginzburg can never
bring herself to feel this way toward the common criminals imprisoned with her, and so she does not concern herself with them. Under
these circumstances, helping them would have been a form of charity.

The charitable relationship is an asymmetrical one: I do not see
how the beggar can possibly help me; that is why I do not seek to
know him. It is also why the act of charity, or of pity, can humiliate its
recipient; there is no way to reciprocate in kind. Caring for someone,
on the other hand, usually elicits similar concern in return, even
though it may be years in coming, as it is with parents and children.

Finally, caring is not to be confused with *sacrifice*, first because acts
of sacrifice, much like those of charity, inevitably come with a certain
religious coloration, while caring remains exclusively within the
sphere of the human. In addition, sacrifice implies separation from
something one holds dear; it suggests the acceptance of a painful
deprivation that is redeemed by a sense of duty. To care about someone does not mean sacrificing one's time and energy for that person.
It means devoting them to the person and taking joy in doing so; in
the end, one feels richer for one's efforts, not poorer. Like charity,
sacrifice cannot be reciprocated (for me, the word *sacrifice* brings to
mind not ritual sacrifice but mothers sacrificing their professional
lives to care for their children, wives sacrificing their personal lives for
the sake of their husbands' careers, and so on). It is for this reason

that sacrifice often gives rise to frustration, resentment, and demands. If one makes a sacrifice, one wants others to feel it too, to know how much it has cost. Caring is its own reward, for it makes the giver happy.

The supreme sacrifice—that of one's life—even if made for an individual and not for an abstraction, derives nonetheless from the tradition of heroic virtues and not from the logic of caring. Father Kolbe gave his life to save that of another man. But more than that, as I have suggested, it was to proclaim his faith in God; it scarcely mattered to him who in particular it was whose life he saved. The mothers, daughters, fathers and sons who went to their deaths with those they loved acted in a very different spirit. Their attachment to the specific individuals whom they cared about was stronger than their desire to live. In a sense, these people are more selfish: they do not want to die so that the other may live; they would prefer that both survive, so that they can continue to enjoy each other. Since that is impossible, they accept death—with the other, and not in his or her stead. That, writes John Glenn Grey, is the spirit of friendship, which is altogether different from the spirit of sacrifice: "For friends, dying is terribly hard, even for each other; both have so much to lose" (91). Sacrifice glorifies death; caring makes sense only in life.

EFFECTS

The act of caring confers an immediate benefit on its recipient. What is more, the giver can hope to receive benefits in return, should the roles be reversed. According to Richard Glazar, the caring of others explains the good fortune of those who survived: "The truth is . . . they survived because they were carried by *someone,* someone who cared for them as much, or almost as much, as for themselves" (Sereny 186). A person could not survive, Germaine Tillion confirms, "without a few outstretched hands" (38). And Charlotte Delbo writes, "Everyone who returned knows that, without the others, she would not have come back" (*Convoi* 17). "By 'the others,' " she says, "we meant those members of our group who hold you up, or carry you when you can no longer walk, those who help you hold fast when you're at the end of your rope" (*Auschwitz* 193). Anna Pawelczynska shares this view: "There is not one survivor," she writes, "who did not find support and help among fellow prisoners. No one could have survived on his own physical and mental strength" (121). The recipient, moreover, receives a further benefit, that of being recognized as a human being who is capable of becoming not only the instrument of an action but also its end. One doubts one's own worth, one's very reason for being, if it is not confirmed by others. "As soon as you find yourself alone," writes Delbo, "you think: What good does it do? What's it all for? Why not give up . . ." (104). The attention of others provides a reason to go on.

Here are two examples, from among many others, of the lasting effects of caring. Karlo Stajner, who survived seven thousand days in Siberia, describes how one morning, after five years of solitude in the gulags of the far north, he suddenly received a letter from his wife. "This was my first happy day in my years as a prisoner. Now I had the answer to the question: Why go on living? Yes, it was worth going through all those torments to experience even one day like that" (226). (The Russian wife of this Yugoslavian Communist had been nine months pregnant when her husband was arrested; the little girl died shortly after birth.) This first letter was followed by others, and Stajner knew he could stay alive because now he had his wife to think about. When, after eighteen years of separation, she was finally allowed to join him, he kissed her and said, "You haven't changed!" Later he would write, "The following days were the most beautiful in my life" (388). But Danilo Kiš, who knew both of them, did see the change: there was something disquieting about her face, for in the middle of it shone two dead eyes.

Albert Speer writes in his memoirs of a trip he made to the region of Dnepropetrovsk in February 1942, on the eve of his nomination as minister of armament production for the Third Reich. He had been outside in the cold for a long time when some Russian peasants working nearby caught his attention. They seemed very agitated and kept pointing to his face, which, without his realizing it, had become frostbitten. One of the peasants scooped up some snow and began to rub it over Speer's frozen skin; another took out an immaculate handkerchief and carefully dried his face. Twenty-five years later, when

Speer began his memoirs, this scene came back to him; it was the point from which he began trying to rethink his past (something he does not always manage to do), and it became the cornerstone of his conception of good and evil.

The giver of care, however, is also a beneficiary. Apart from any future reward, that person profits simply from the accomplishment of the act. The testimony is unanimous on this point. "Probably this is the best way to retain one's humanity in the camps," Ratushinskaya remarks, "to care more about another's pain than about your own. We were not seeking to perform heroic acts; if anything, these were acts of self-preservation" (238). But why should this be so? There are several possible explanations. Perhaps by caring about others, one experiences a recovery of one's own dignity and self-respect because one is doing something recognized as morally laudable, and that feeling of dignity, in itself, strengthens one's ability to stay alive. Olga Lengyel finds a reason to live when she is asked to set up an infirmary. The well-known paradox holds true: the more she gave of herself, the more she found she had to give. "I knew that I was doing something useful," she writes, "something that was enough to give me the strength [to go on]" (158). Viktor Frankl, who became a psychiatrist after his liberation, explains this indirect benefit in terms of the need of all human beings to find meaning in their lives, to find some sort of goal beyond mere survival. In the face of the daily absurdity of the camps, helping someone or simply paying attention to someone could be a very meaningful act.

It has also been observed that individuals find much more strength within them when looking after someone else than when they are taking care of themselves alone. A prisoner in Robert Antelme's *Human Race* seems to have that idea in mind when he tells his comrades, "In order to hang on, each one of us has got to get out of himself, he's got to feel responsible for everybody" (196). Margarete Buber-Neumann can think of no other explanation for her own survival. "I was always able to find people who needed me," she writes. "Again and again, I made friends. It is only under such conditions that the true meaning of friendship can be learnt" (*Ravensbrück* 40). How does one survive the despair of confinement in a windowless underground cell? Once again, by taking care of others. When two of her friends are thrown into the cell with her, finding ways to ease their suffering helps Buber-Neumann forget her own. What should have been pain becomes happiness instead. "Compared with what went before, the time I spent with Maria Graf and Maria Presserova seemed almost serene and happy" (281). In moments of despair, she clings to the idea that Milena needs her. "I mustn't leave her all alone in the camp! Who will take care of her if her fever starts up again?" (*Milena* 185). The reward lies in the act itself; in caring for another, one continues to care for oneself as well. Here, the one who spends the most is actually the richest.

For the caring person, there are other things besides benefits that come with the act of concern. There are dangers, too, for both giver and receiver can somehow fail the other. If caring for others is part of one's normal way of life, then to be thwarted—as is almost inevitable—provokes painful feelings of guilt. Although millions of people died at Auschwitz, Ella Lingens-Reiner still holds herself responsible for the death of a friend, someone whom she had promised to look after if the woman ever fell ill. "I know that she waited for me and counted on me. And I did not come" (84). For Ginzburg, her greatest torment was not any of the terrible punishments inflicted on her but rather the memory of the spanking she had given her little boy Vasyia for some trifling thing he'd done. "This memory tortured me like fire," she writes, for she had failed—or so she believed—in her caring for him. "The pain that night was so great that it brimmed over into the future and reaches me today when I write of it after twenty years" (*Journey* 118).

The other danger is that this person who represents so much for us will suffer or even die. As lovers well know, the more one allows oneself to love someone, the more vulnerable one becomes. What happens when the loved one is no longer there to receive that love? This, of course, has always been the fate of parents and children. When Louis Micheels, an Auschwitz inmate, learns that a new train-load of Dutch Jews is due to arrive, he realizes that he might see his father and "have to witness his suffering and slow death. I could not imagine anything more horrible," he says. "I would joke like most others about going up the chimney, but when it concerned somebody close, it became unmentionable or unimaginable" (87, 122). Neither

Elie Wiesel nor Germaine Tillion was spared this experience: "There are ills which are unendurable and incompatible with human strength," Tillion writes, "the suffering and death of a loved one" (10).

To live life in the camps according to an ethic of caring is to render oneself especially vulnerable, for in addition to one's own suffering, one takes on that of the people one cares about. Milena speaks from experience when she says, "It's awful to see someone you love crying" (Buber-Neumann, *Milena* 175). One is much more protected if one is fighting for an ideal: the loss of one person can then be relativized; one's hopes for the triumph of the cause remain intact. But can one protect oneself by ceasing to care for those one loves, by ceasing to love them? In choosing to suffer, as Pola Lifszyc did, both for and with another, one adds to the world's misfortunes; yet such actions, through their goodness, make the world as a whole more, not less, acceptable.

The ineradicable human feeling of caring will always be a comfort to those who have parents or children, a wife or a lover, a friend or a comrade. But what about the others, those who know no one and whom no one seems to know, the outsiders, the strangers—that is to say, these same people, you and me perhaps, but in different circumstances? Who will help them? For these people, the caring of those who love them is not enough.

The Life of the Mind

INTELLECTUAL AND
AESTHETIC EXPERIENCES

In his account of life in the camps, Viktor Frankl describes how a group of inmates, having been transferred from Auschwitz to Dachau, made an unexpected discovery. "One evening," Frankl says, "when we were already resting on the floor of our hut, dead tired, soup bowls in hand, a fellow prisoner rushed in and asked us to hurry outside to the assembly grounds and see the wonderful sunset!" (62–63). Nature, it seems, was more beautiful at Dachau than at Auschwitz, and living conditions, all in all, were less unbearable. That difference was enough for a hitherto forgotten pleasure, the admiration and contemplation of nature, to be reborn. Eugenia Ginzburg recalls the day she was finally brought before the tribunal after a long "preventive detention." She was about to hear her sentence, perhaps her death sentence, but instead of anguishing over what might await her, she was filled with wonder at the glimpses she managed to snatch of the outside world. "Outside the windows there were some large, dark-green trees," she writes. "Their leaves were rustling and I was moved by the cool, mysterious sound. I could not remember having heard it before. It was strangely touching—why had I never noticed it?" (*Journey* 170–71).

In reading such passages as these, one senses that the experience they describe, which can certainly be called an aesthetic one, was not only pleasurable for those who lived it but also morally uplifting. Here the mind casts off its immediate and practical preoccupations, turns to the contemplation of beauty, and in doing so becomes beautiful itself. And so, to the ordinary virtues of dignity and caring can be added a third, one that Edelman touches on, but just barely, in his account of the ghetto uprising. I call this virtue "the life of the mind," not to oppose it to physical acts but simply to use a single term to designate two activities—the search for the truth and the search for the beautiful—that in themselves would seem to have nothing to do with moral action. Such activities are not the exclusive province of intellectuals, scholars, artists, and the like. They are accessible to everyone.

In certain extreme situations, particularly in prison, people can read books, and they are willing to pay dearly to obtain them. Charlotte Delbo reports trading a full day's ration of bread for a paperback copy of *The Misanthrope*. Reading has a powerful effect, and it appears that, given writing of adequate quality, that effect is independent of the book's particular content. The important thing is not whatever messages the book may seek to convey but the beauty it incarnates and the freedom of mind and spirit the reader experiences in entering into communication with its creator, and through that person, with the world at large. Gustaw Herling tells the story of Kostylev, a young Communist who accidentally stumbles on Flaubert's *Sentimental Education* and Constant's *Adolphe* in a library. The experience of reading them affects him so powerfully that he neglects his duties as a party member and soon finds himself arrested. He has no regrets, however: "If I have ever known, even for a short time, what freedom is," he says, "it was while I was reading those old French books" (73). Herling goes on to describe his own experience in the Vologda camps and the devastating effect that Dostoevsky's *House of the Dead,* which he discovered there, had on him.

When there are no books to be had, people try to compensate by an effort of memory, in the manner of the characters in Ray Bradbury's *Fahrenheit 451*. Ginzburg, who knew by heart the works of countless writers from Pushkin to Pasternak, never missed a chance to recite from them, much to the enjoyment of those around her. One particular episode stands out: on the train to Siberia, Ginzburg decides to recite some poems to her companions to distract them from their troubles. A guard enters the compartment. He has heard reading, and books are forbidden. Ginzburg assures him she is reciting from memory, but he refuses to believe her. "If you can go on for half an hour without a break, O.K.," he challenges her. "Otherwise, it's irons for you, all the way to Vladivostok!" (*Journey* 294–95). The car falls silent; all the prisoners hold their breath. Ginzburg, their latter-day Scheherazade, smiles and begins to recite *Eugene Onegin*. Half an hour later, someone brings her a cup of water; she drinks it and goes right on. The wager is won, and everyone—the "reader" and her listeners alike—feels that a small victory has been achieved against the evil around them. Ginzburg herself continued to believe in this kind of resistance throughout her incarceration: "I felt instinctively," she wrote, "that as long as I could be stirred to emotion by the sea breeze, by the brilliance of the stars, and by poetry, I would still be alive, however much my legs might tremble and my back bend under the load of burning stones" (343).

In *Survival in Auschwitz,* Primo Levi brings to life another remarkable scene of a poetry recitation. During his imprisonment in the camp, he has been teaching Italian to his friend Jean, the Pikolo, in exchange for French lessons. This intellectual activity, a tiny island of freedom, is soon followed by a more ambitious project: Levi decides to introduce his friend to the music of Dante. He begins reciting canto 26 of *The Inferno,* the scene that tells of Odysseus's voyage. Although hardly a connoisseur of poetry, Pikolo understands the importance of the scene. "He has received the message," Levi says, "he has felt that it has to do with him, that it has to do with all men who toil, and with us in particular" (103). As for Levi, he feels he absolutely must continue reciting; he would give all he has—that is, his day's ration of soup—if only he could recall the few verses he has forgotten so that his friend could hear them. "It is vitally necessary and urgent that he listen," Levi writes, "that he understand . . . before it is too late; tomorrow he or I might be dead, or we might never see each other again" (104). Had it been thus, there would have been one less human consciousness in which Dante might live on, a moment of spiritual transcendence would not have occurred, and the world would have lost one more fragment of its beauty.

Not everyone shared Levi's sentiments. In his reflections on Auschwitz, Jean Améry, who was confined in the same sector of Monowitz and who believes he actually slept in the same barracks as Levi, maintains that being an intellectual or a writer (as he was himself) was a handicap, not an advantage. As an intellectual, you have no practical skills, he says, and what you know is useless. One day, the sight of a flag waving in front of an unfinished building catches his eye and a stanza from a Hölderlin poem runs through his mind: The walls stand speechless and cold / The flags clank in the wind. But the emotional and mental response these words had formerly provoked in him now did not come. "Nothing happened," Améry writes. "The poem no longer transcended reality. All that remained was objective statement: the Kapo roars 'left!', and the soup was watery, and the flags are clanking in the wind. Perhaps the Hölderlin feeling . . . would have surfaced if a comrade had been present whose mood would have been somewhat similar and to whom I could have recited the stanza. The worst was that one did not have this comrade; he was not in the work ranks, and where was he in the entire camp?" According to Améry, he and the other intellectuals at Auschwitz acquired the certainty that "for the greatest part the intellect is a *ludus* and that we are nothing more—or, better said, before we entered the camp we were nothing more—than *homines ludentes*. With that we lost a good deal of arrogance, of metaphysical conceit, but also quite a bit of our naive joy in the intellect, and what we falsely imagined was the sense of life" (*Mind* 7, 20).

But perhaps Améry himself was in large part responsible for that impression. A professional intellectual, he kept trying to establish a high-minded relationship with a peer, someone with whom he could share his delight in the beauties of the mind. Pikolo was certainly not a real intellectual; nor, for that matter, was Levi, who at the time was only a chemistry student who loved literature. Indeed, it is perhaps because Levi considered the life of the mind an ordinary virtue and not something reserved for an elite that he was able to keep faith in it and safeguard its power.

When memory does not permit the reconstruction of books themselves, conversations about them can serve as their stand-ins. In the camp where he was imprisoned, Herling took "lessons" in French literature from Boris N., an old professor; for both men, these lessons became an occasion for passionate discussions about abstract subjects utterly foreign to the life they were forced to lead. Milena Jesenska and Margarete Buber-Neumann arranged secret rendezvous at which they spoke not of escape plans but of Kafka, literature, art. "For the prisoner," writes Buber-Neumann, "the mind is an island, small but safe, in the middle of a sea of misery and desolation" (*Ravensbrück* 84).

While many prisoners found communion with beauty directly—in nature or in art—or in more mediated ways through recitation or performance, far fewer actually wrote. The reasons are obvious: life in the camps was hardly conducive to creativity. And yet it is in the very midst of that life that future writers, often quite consciously, lay the foundations for the works they would later write. Ginzburg and Levi both knew that if they survived they would try to write. As Etty Hillesum, who did not survive, says, "A camp needs a poet, one who experiences life there, even there, as a bard and is able to sing about it" (*Interrupted* 190). The Polish Jewish poet Leon Staf, who lived in the Warsaw ghetto, expresses a similar thought. "Even more than bread we now need poetry," he writes, "in a time when it seems that it is not needed at all" (Suhl 121). Without poetry, the world would be irremediably poorer.

What is true of language and literature is also true, though perhaps to a lesser degree, of the other arts. When Milena Jesenska and Margarete Buber-Neumann find a Brueghel reproduction in a magazine, they immediately tear it out and tack it to the wall; they see this act as "a protest against our condition as prisoners," and rightly so (*Ravensbrück* 84). Milena understands the artist's need for encouragement, and she lies and steals so that Mischka, a gifted young Polish painter, can go on drawing pictures of life in Ravensbrück (*Milena* 162). Music is no exception. Micheels, for instance, cannot forget the pieces by Bach that he heard a guitarist play at Auschwitz: "The contrast between the purity of his music and our misery seemed to imbue every phrase with special depth. The horror of our situation made the beauty of life so much more poignant and precious" (56). Laks and Coudy, musicians themselves, recall how "during the short time the music lasted we became normal human beings once more as we listened with religious awe" (185). And prisoners like Fania Fénelon, who actually performed, felt the same way: "Each piece unfolded easily inside me, smoothly, measure after measure. . . . I forgot everything else. I was happy. . . . The symphony soared, compelling and marvelous. . . . The girls were transfigured" (*Playing* 106–07). What is important is not merely the sense of escape—however brief and illusory—that making music can provide but also the feeling of having brought a little more beauty into the world and of participating, through this beauty, in the universal.

Aesthetic experiences are merely one form that the life of the mind can take. Another, closely related form is the impulse to know the world and understand it. For the prisoners, understanding the world in which they found themselves was clearly a matter of survival; moreover, it was a prerequisite for any sort of political struggle against the camps. But understanding the world can also be part of a larger project, that of explaining it. Here, one seeks out the truth not simply because it can help one survive or because it can help others fight a hateful system but because unearthing the truth is an end in itself. Ginzburg, who understood her efforts at remembrance in terms of the first two purposes, describes the third in this way: "Truth does not need to be justified by expediency. It is simply the *truth*. Expediency should take its cue from truth, and not the other way around" (*Within* 421). The camp inmates were made to know the far limits of human experience; it became their duty to humanity to report, in all honesty, what they saw and what they felt, for even in the most horrible experience there is some possibility for mankind's enrichment; only total oblivion calls for total despair. Shifting from the perspective of the individual to that of humanity as a whole, one can see that no life is lived in vain if it leaves behind some trace of itself, some story that, when added to the countless other stories by which we know who we are, contributes, even if in the smallest way, to making the world a more harmonious and more perfect place. This is the paradox; stories of evil can create good.

Hence the dying enjoin the survivors: Remember everything and tell it, not just to fight against the camps but so that, having left something behind, our lives will have had some meaning. At the top of his manuscript, Zalmen Gradowski writes, "Dear discoverer of these writings! I have a request of you: this is the real reason I write, that my doomed life may attain some meaning, that my hellish days and hopeless tomorrows may find a purpose in the future" (Roskies 548). In speaking about oneself, one helps establish the truth about the world. From each family at least one member must survive, not so that he or she can perpetuate the biological line but so that the entire family will not disappear without a trace. One has to stay alive not for the sake of life itself but as a bearer of memory, as a possibility for narrative. "We were terribly afraid that . . . people would never notice a thing," Marek Edelman says, "that nobody in the world would notice a thing: us, the struggle, the dead, . . . that this wall was so huge that nothing, no message about us, would ever make it out" (Krall and Edelman 7).

To observe, to remember, and to pass on to others what one has seen is already to take a stand against inhumanity. "Understanding one's situation is exhilarating in itself," Germaine Tillion writes, "perhaps because awareness of a burden is one way of overcoming it, perhaps also because awareness and comprehension are the more profound vocations of the human species, and one of the goals of humanity's place on the evolutionary scale" (164). To know, and to let others know, is one way of remaining human and, for that reason, is an act with a moral dimension. It is not that the individual becomes a better person by pursuing the life of the mind but simply that a more intelligible world is a more perfect world; to contribute to that end is to work toward the good of humanity.

THE LIFE OF THE MIND
AND THE MORAL LIFE

That there is inherent moral virtue in either the production or the reception of aesthetic pleasure or in the intellectual effort to understand—in other words, in the life of the mind—is not entirely self-evident. People are far more inclined to see the life of the mind and the moral life as independent of or even opposed to each other. Borowski presents what seems to him an existential dilemma: "Is it better for a man locked inside the ghetto to sacrifice his life in order to make counterfeit dollars to buy armaments and make grenades from tin cans, or is it better for him to escape from the ghetto to the 'Aryan' side, to save his life and thus be able to read Pindar's *Epinicae*?" (*This Way* 172). The character in Borowski's book who formulates these alternatives chooses the second path—art and mind over morals and politics. And yet the accounts of concentration camp survivors say something quite different, essentially that the two are not mutually exclusive. Poetry readings and Bach concerts at Auschwitz were not only aesthetic activities but moral ones as well, for in making the world better than it had been before, they also improved and enriched the lives of those who took part in them.

When Etty Hillesum decided to accept that it was her vocation to be a writer, she did not choose a disinterested aesthetic over a concern for others. Instead, as she herself aptly puts it, "Life has confided so many stories to me, I shall have to retell them to people who cannot read the book of life itself" (*Interrupted* 192). Primo Levi was fully aware that Dante's message "has to do with all men who toil." Readers and listeners are not directly "helped" by literature, nor do they have to be. Books are not Band-Aids. Yet to be touched by the beauty of art is to be in some way elevated and enriched. The accounts born of the experience of life in the camps, Hillesum's and Levi's, Ginzburg's and Delbo's, and even Borowski's, have value as moral acts, not just because they bear witness or because they advance political struggle but because they help unveil before us, their readers, the truth of the world. The search for truth nourishes the moral life.

Still, one might counter with any number of examples demonstrating that it is possible to cultivate the mind without such activity being in any way virtuous. Albert Speer could not help finding aesthetic pleasure in watching the bombardment of his own city. "From the flak tower," he writes, "the air raids on Berlin were an unforgettable sight, and I had constantly to remind myself of the cruel reality in order not to be completely entranced by the scene" (288). Where was the morality in his contemplation of that sight? Or, for that matter, in the act that allowed him to realize his architectural dreams? All Speer wanted was to create beauty, or, in practical terms, to design and construct buildings to his own taste. But the market for architects was limited and the competition severe; he received only one commission his first year, to renovate a floor of a building that belonged to his father. It was just at that moment that the prime minister asked Speer to become his official architect. "Not yet thirty," Speer remembers, "I saw before me the most exciting prospects an architect can dream of" (32). Speer's desire was perfectly understandable, perhaps even legitimate. "I was on the way, I thought at the time, to creating a body of work that would place me among the most famous architects of history," he wrote, and for the next five years, he devoted himself completely to this task (127).

His backer in this endeavor was, nevertheless, a man named Hitler, and while Speer dreamed his dreams of a classical renaissance, his country was devouring its European neighbors one after another. (But ah, Speer sighs, wasn't it thus that Faust sold his soul to Mephistopheles?) At Treblinka, Stangl, cinched into a custom-made riding jacket, enjoyed parading about on a white horse among his future victims: should we, too, take delight in his sense of beauty?

(In 1944, during the first few months after the Communists took power in Bulgaria, they massacred tens, perhaps hundreds, of thousands of people. There is no official count. Those killed included former fascists, policemen who had been complicit in the suppression of the resistance, but also those, particularly in the countryside, whom the new government wanted to get rid of for one reason or another: local dignitaries or members of the intelligentsia such as schoolteachers, attorneys, and reporters—in other words, anyone who might recognize an authority independent of the one designated by the new powers. The victims vanished without a trial; they were rounded up and taken to the forests, beaten to death with axes or gun barrels, and summarily buried. During those months, however, my father must not have been altogether unhappy, for here at last was a government that appeared to understand his passion—the modernization of Bulgaria's libraries. And so with great enthusiasm, he threw himself into the construction of the new National Library. Today, he still remembers certain of his friends telling him: "Your head is in the clouds! You don't see what's going on all around you here on earth! You think of nothing but your libraries. But maybe it's better for you that way. . . .")

Imprisoned in Auschwitz, Louis Micheels is transported by listening to music. But he is not alone in this regard. Maria Mandel, Auschwitz's *Lagerführerin,* has a particular weakness for Madame Butterfly's aria in the opera by Puccini. She enters the musicians' barracks at all hours of the day or night and demands that someone sing it for her. Each time she hears it she is filled with wonder. Josef Kramer, the commandant at Birkenau, who shares Mandel's penchant for music, encourages the activities of the camp's women's orchestra. His favorite piece is Schumann's "Reverie," which he listens to with rapt attention. "He abandons himself to his tender feelings," Fania Fénelon writes, "and down his impeccably shaven cheeks, allows tears, precious as pearls, to run" (*Playing* 92). Apart from Mandel and Kramer, surely the most fervent musical devotee was Dr. Mengele himself. "Could people who love music to this extent, people who can cry when they hear it, be capable, at the same time, of committing so many atrocities on the rest of humanity?" asks Szymon Laks, who performed in the men's orchestra at Auschwitz (Laks 70). Alas, they can be. And so if Fénelon found transport in making music, so did many others. In the State Security offices in Berlin, a special room was stocked with musical instruments. Adolf Eichmann regularly practiced the violin there, accompanied on the piano by his SS comrade Bostramér. They played chamber music of the romantic period.

Because they harbored no illusions as to the role of music in the camps, the members of the women's orchestra at Auschwitz found it hard to give themselves over to the pleasures their playing could bring. Music was used to hasten the steps of the prisoners; it provided distraction for the guards and eased their consciences. To make music is to feel free and to bring joy to others; but in the shadow of the crematoriums, does this still hold true? "At Birkenau," Fénelon says, "music was both the best and the worst of things. The best because it filled in time and brought us oblivion, like a drug; we emerged from it deadened, exhausted. The worst because our public consisted of the assassins and the victims: and in the hands of the assassins, it was almost as though we too were made into executioners" (*Playing* 125). This ambiguity, in which "the best of things" is not really very good at all, is familiar to anyone who has lived under a totalitarian regime. Those who wield power flatter their country's artists and treat them generously (relatively speaking), for as long as they do not cross the line and become dissidents, their creations, beautiful though they may be, pose no real threat. But it is not necessary to restrict the discussion to totalitarian countries. Such notions as the "beauty" of crime, murder as art, the dandy who wants his life to be governed by aesthetic rather than ethical rules have been solidly ensconced in Europe since the nineteenth century. "The connection between aestheticism and crime is a well-known fact," Erich Kahler says. "The subtlest sensitivity to artistic values sometimes makes a person particularly insensitive to ethical values" (77).

What is true of the artist is also true of the scientist. Like all creators, scientists are happy to have the means to bring their projects to fruition, and thrill to the command to outdo themselves. Germany's great scientists gave their blessings to Hitler's regime, which was especially generous to them. Heisenberg was encouraged to pursue his research in atomic fission, Wernher von Braun his work with long-range missiles. Indeed, what other government would have placed so many millions of marks at their disposal? The intellect is given free rein and there's no room left for ethics. But isn't science always estranged from morality, obeying only the drive to know and understand? Who cannot cite examples proving that intelligence does not automatically produce goodness? It is a cliché, of course, and has been at least since Rousseau, that the blossoming of arts and letters does not necessarily contribute to the improvement of social conduct; that even great intelligence does not always entail high moral standards. Recent arguments in defense of culture, all of them more or less conscious avatars of Enlightenment thought, seem based on a total disregard of the caveat that cultural growth need not have a moral corollary. Intellectual pursuits may lead to material abundance, but they do not prevent our moral frailty.

As powerful as such arguments are, the edifying effects of the life of the mind cannot be ignored. What is necessary, therefore, is not so much to choose between two opposing theses as to determine just where either thesis applies and how they bear on each other.

Characteristic of the acts that arise out of the ordinary virtues is that they are intended to benefit particular human beings. But who these intended beneficiaries are varies according to the virtue. Acts of dignity are addressed to the subject of the action himself, or rather to that subject's consciousness. My action must be worthy of my self-respect, give me dignity in my own eyes; I am thus both actor and judge, even if the criteria by which I judge myself are no more than an internalized reflection of the opinions of others. With acts of caring, the beneficiary is someone other than myself, a person or a group of people whom I know individually. Acts that stem from the life of the mind are also directed toward others, but the identity of those others is irrelevant; moreover, they are often far too numerous ever to know personally. As Etty Hillesum observes, writers write not for their daughters or their fathers but for some of their compatriots or contemporaries or for people thirty years in the future. The writer, painter, or musician may not be conscious of addressing an audience but a creation is always intended for someone. The audience, even if a multitude, must be thought of as individual human beings and not be diffused into some abstraction like "humanity" or "mankind." In this sense, the ordinary virtues, unlike acts of heroism, are *personal* virtues. By the same token, acts that belong to the life of the mind are moral if their aim is the welfare of those whom they are intended to reach; they cease to be moral if they bring about destruction or death. To develop new weapons may require great intellectual capacities, but that does not mean it is a moral act.

The passive side of the life of the mind—contemplation of beauty, for instance, or understanding the world, activities that do not necessarily lead to creative projects—fits into this framework with somewhat more difficulty. And yet we have seen how often such activities do touch the lives of others. The prisoner at Dachau who chanced upon a beautiful sunset was not satisfied to contemplate it alone; he wanted his fellow inmates to share his joy. Milena Jesenska was not happy recalling her favorite pieces of literature just for herself; she needed to experience them with her friend. As a prisoner, Viktor Frankl wanted more than simply to advance his understanding of the world of the camps; he wanted others to know what he knew. This inclination to share intellectual or spiritual experiences suggests, I think, that even when they occur as solitary experiences, they are to be situated within the framework of communication because they put us in touch with everyone who could have been in our place.

This interpretation of the ordinary virtues may explain why they fall so naturally into three groups rather than, say, two or five. I started out with no preconceived schema; I simply collected and grouped together, as I read, those acts that seemed to illustrate one ordinary virtue or another. In hindsight, however, I see that the number of virtues and the relationships among them follow from the nature of their beneficiaries or, if one prefers such language, from the structure of intersubjectivity. In the case of dignity, the "I" addresses itself to the same "I"; in that of caring, the "I" addresses itself to one or several individual "you"s—in other words, to particular human beings with whom there has been established a relationship of reciprocity, a possibility of a reversal of roles (the fundamental form of human interchange). And finally, in the case of acts that belong to the life of the mind, the "I" addresses itself to more or less numerous "they"s who remain anonymous and are no longer part of a present and ongoing dialogue. In this sense, there can be only three virtues, just as there are three grammatical persons in the conjugation of a verb. This fact suggests a twofold relationship between ethics and communication: the latter provides the former with both the content of its ideal (the ultimate goal of communication being universality) as well as a framework for its manifestations.

A HIERARCHY OF VIRTUES

How do the ordinary virtues bear on one another? What sort of hierarchy do they form? That question has no simple answer, as it all depends on one's point of view. From the subject's point of view, dignity is the primary virtue. From the human community's point of view, the most important virtue is caring. But from a world historical perspective, it is the life of the mind that counts most, because the effects of its products are the most lasting: centuries after their deaths, we are still grateful to Plato and Shakespeare for having left the world more beautiful and more intelligible than they found it. Artistic and intellectual activity is undertaken on everyone's behalf, whereas caring may have only a few beneficiaries and dignity only one, the self. That there should be several different hierarchies is no accident: the self cannot possibly have the same interests as the community, nor the community those of the world at large. But one could also say that caring is by its very definition coincident with the moral stance that holds other people to be ends in themselves, whereas for the life of the mind this engagement with others is optional, and when dignity is at stake, the subject's welfare can be an altogether extraneous issue. That is why in the latter two cases, moral limits are so easily overstepped.

Actual experience, however, often conflates what analysis separates. My consciousness is an internalization of the discourse of others; the "I" is formed by the "they." The concern I feel for those close to me confirms my sense of dignity, and the life of the mind often addresses itself to a "you," a life companion, for example, before seeking its audience in a more amorphous "they." It is impossible to cultivate one virtue at the expense of the others, and when they conflict with one another, no formula can tell us which to choose.

For although the virtues may mesh with or be transformed into one another, conflicts between them do indeed arise. Consider the virtue of caring. If one takes care of others, it is at least partly to satisfy one's standards of what is good, or, one might also say, to live up to one's sense of duty; caring about others can produce inner satisfaction. Caring and dignity can thus exist in harmony with each other. Yet as Kant knew, these two virtues can also clash, for dignity is, above all, freedom, while caring involves a restriction of freedom. As soon as I accept that my actions must have others besides myself as an end, I am no longer entirely free. Bettelheim defines the terms of this inevitable antagonism as "autonomy" and "integration"; although opposing impulses, they are equally indispensable to the individual's well-being.

A mundane example is provided by a Dutch farmer who hid several Jews during the war. He describes the conflict that arose outside the door to his bathroom. Six refugees used it, and so it was necessary to make a schedule, with a certain number of minutes allotted for each person, and to insist on punctuality. Sometimes things went well, but often people would exceed the limit, each by some small amount; the delays would then add up until the sixth person's turn might begin twenty minutes late. There was no "natural" reason for these delays, but it was the only time during the day when the refugees could break the rules, exercise their freedom, and so regain a bit of their dignity. Of course, those who had to stand and wait outside the bathroom door saw in those same acts a lack of care and consideration (Stein 236).

This particular conflict might have been resolved had those involved been able to exercise even a little freedom in their other interactions. In extreme circumstances, however, such freedom is usually not possible. But similar conflicts occur in far less dramatic situations. Who has not known people who spend their lives worrying about others—mothers, for example, who never stop being wives and daughters—all the while building up resentment because they feel that they've neglected themselves and thereby lost their dignity and self-respect? One might, in this regard, formulate a rule of precedence: caring is a morally superior act only insofar as it does not encroach upon the dignity of the one who cares.

Conflict can also arise between acts of caring and the life of the mind. In the eyes of Alma Rose, the conductor of the women's orchestra at Auschwitz, musical perfection took precedence over her musicians' welfare and ultimately became an end in itself, so that she forgot whose interests the music was serving. Here one can no longer speak of virtue, ordinary or otherwise. Well before the war, as Rose recalls, "stories of arrests and deportations seemed things in another world. They didn't affect me, or even interest me. Only music counted" (Fénelon, *Playing* 112). And later, toward the end of her life, she says again, "Dying is unimportant; what is important, truly important, is to play music" (204). Her arrival in Auschwitz allowed her to devote herself to music, and the shortcomings of her musicians were simply obstacles to be overcome. Her goals were musical, not humanitarian. Rose shouted and slapped and rationalized. "Here or elsewhere," she said, "whatever one does should be done well, if only out of self-respect" (121). Once again, we see how artistic and intellectual activity can give rise to feelings of dignity—pride in the knowledge of a job well done—while ignoring the interests of the individuals involved. (When she died, Alma Rose was paid a moving tribute by the SS; they blanketed her coffin in white flowers and, with bowed heads, wept over the remains of their Jewish prisoner.)

The theme of the self-centered artist also predates the concentration camp, of course. Do the poet's beautiful verses justify the suffering of those closest to him? The answer depends, first of all, on which perspective one adopts—that of world history or that of the human community. Bettelheim cites Beethoven's nephew, whose life was ruined by his brilliant uncle: "While lasting works of art may be created," Bettelheim remarks, "those persons closest to the artist may be destroyed in the process" (*Heart* 25). From a moral standpoint, the two perspectives are simply not the same, which is why I disagree with Viktor Frankl, who, in explaining the need to find meaning in our lives, fails to distinguish between two different types of goals. "Man does not [behave morally] in order to satisfy a moral drive and to have a good conscience; he does so for the sake of a cause to which he commits himself or for a person whom he loves" (158). Now, there is a great difference between these two objectives; one is simply not as humane as the other. Here, then, is another rule: the life of the mind can be admirable, but it does not justify the creative individual's making instruments of those around him; nor does it justify the loss of dignity these people suffer by being made to play that role. "If Shakespeare returned to earth tomorrow," George Orwell writes, "and if it were found that his favourite recreation was raping little girls in railway carriages, we should not tell him to go ahead with it on the grounds that he might write another *King Lear*" (161).

In the camps, the life of an artist or a scholar was worth just as much (or, rather, just as little) as that of the most inconsequential prisoner. One life was as good as another. During the Warsaw ghetto uprising, many people wanted special efforts made to ensure the safety of the poet Yitzhak Katznelson. "We desperately wanted him to survive," Tzivia Lubetkin remembers, "so that he would be an eyewitness and tell what truly happened" (Borwicz 59). One can certainly understand this desire, part of the war of memory being waged alongside the military struggle, but Katznelson—who, as it happened, did not die in the uprising—"absolutely refused to hide or be hidden." That he should survive in someone else's place, that being a poet made him more valuable than other people, was something he would not accept. Primo Levi, for his part, was shocked when a visitor suggested that Levi had survived Auschwitz because God had wanted him to tell the story of the camps. "Such an opinion seemed monstrous to me," Levi says. "I might be alive in the place of another, at the expense of another; I might have usurped, that is, in fact, killed" (*Drowned* 82). The suggestion is but a step away from the much-contested practices of Rudolf Kastner, the wartime leader of the Hungarian Jewish community, who agreed to sacrifice "ordinary" Jews in order to save a few "important" ones, people who, as it turned out, were either wealthy or members of Kastner's own family. If money does not make one person more deserving of living than another, neither does a commitment to the life of the mind, even though history may remember the names of poets and scholars and not those of the people who brought them tea in their bedrooms or sewed on their buttons.

ORDINARY AND HEROIC VIRTUES

Let us now return to the broader confrontation between ordinary and heroic virtues. First, to summarize: traditional heroic virtues (strength, courage, loyalty, etc.) may be indispensable during grave crises, in times of life-or-death struggle, uprising, or war; there are such things as just wars, and heroes are needed to win them. But even in these extreme situations, heroism is easily perverted when one forgets that heroic acts must be directed toward people rather than performed simply for the sake of heroism. The hero who gives his life to save his city or his country is held in different regard from the hero who does what he does for the sheer beauty of the gesture. Outside these extreme situations, however, classical heroism no longer has such justification, at least not in the modern democratic state. But while it is true that the virtues associated with this sort of heroism are in decline, they are transforming into elements of what I have called modern heroism—the obsession with winning, the need to succeed at all costs. However valuable these qualities may be for political, economic, or scientific success, their moral value is nil.

The ordinary virtues—dignity, caring, the life of the mind—are appropriate to times of peace. Yet as the accounts of life in the camps suggest, they also have their place in times of war or crisis whenever the objective is not merely to win but to remain human as well. When wars end, the heroes return home; if they are not to sink into a life of madness, crime, or drugs, they need to feel that they have not made a mockery of everything they respected before they went off to battle. "War and politics are not waged with good feelings," heads of state are fond of saying in their more "pragmatic" modes. Yet to forget all human feeling is to be assured of losing, if not the battle, then certainly the war. It is for this reason that I find it hard to agree with Améry, who, while acknowledging the value of those who extend a helping hand to their weaker comrades, nonetheless considers the rebel a far superior being. "The rebel," Améry says, "is the hero absolute" (*Humanism* 26). Perhaps he is, but are heroic values necessarily superior to all others?

It is also for this reason that I would insist that the various ordinary virtues are not all of equal moral value. Caring implies, by definition, taking other individuals into account. And while acts of dignity and the products of the life of the mind are always directed toward individuals—myself or my audience—these individuals can be simply a pretext, a nod to convention. Dignity then becomes taking pride in a job well done, even if the job is to exterminate millions of people, as Höss's was. Similarly, when the life of the mind addresses itself only to "humanity" or some other such abstraction, it succumbs all the more easily—as we saw in the realm of intellectual and artistic research—to the sheer logic of success, heroism's modern avatar.

My positing of an opposition between heroic and ordinary virtues is scarcely original. A modern version of it can be found in Sartre's "Existentialism Is a Humanism." In this well-known essay Sartre tells of a young man who comes to him for advice during the occupation. The young man is vacillating: Should he remain with his mother, who has already lost her eldest son in the war and whose husband is now a collaborator? Or should he try to join up with the Free French Forces and fight the Germans? Sartre's essay seeks to demonstrate two things: first, that essence does not precede existence, that human qualities do not exist prior to the acts that reflect them; and, second, that it is impossible to choose between the two alternatives in the name of some moral principle. All one can do is to try to avoid falling either into error (through faulty reasoning or a lack of information) or into bad faith (a lack of sincerity). All solutions are good, Sartre says, as long as one exercises one's autonomy and chooses for oneself rather than submits to the demands of tradition or falls back on physical determinism or other external imperative. "You are free, therefore choose, that is to say invent!" Sartre tells the young man. "No rules of general morality can show you what you ought to do. . . . Whenever a man chooses his purpose and his commitment in all clarity and sincerity, whatever that purpose may be, it is impossible for him to prefer another. . . . The one thing that counts is to know whether the invention is made in the name of freedom" (297, 298, 306, 308).

What is novel in Sartre's essay is not the particular dilemma he describes but rather his assertion that it is the attitude of the subject who chooses, not the content of the choices, that makes one choice preferable to another. As for the dilemma itself, it appears as far back as the *Iliad*, at the end of book 6, where it is not a young student but Hector, the Trojan hero, who must choose. Hector is leaving for battle when his wife, Andromache, stops him and begs him to stay with her and their infant son, Astyanax. Hector loves his wife and child; on another occasion (in book 15) he will say that to die in their defense would be to choose a glorious death. He does not, however, confuse means with ends: the classical hero defends the weak not by remaining at their sides but by going off to fight. Hector does not waver: "I have learned to be valiant / and to fight always among the foremost ranks of the Trojans, / winning for my own self great glory, and for my father" (6.444–46). For Hector, the sexual division of virtues is clear. "Go therefore back to our house," he tells Andromache, "and take up your own work, / the loom and the distaff, and see to it that your handmaidens / ply their work also; but the men must see to the fighting" (6.490–93). The choice here is defined by an external code (which the Sartrean hero rejects). Hector is not free; he simply conforms to his ideal.

Yet this ideal does not rule the ancient world unchallenged, as even Homer himself seems to suggest in perhaps the most curious detail in what is already an extraordinary scene. As Hector leans forward to kiss Astyanax, the infant, terrified by his father's armor, shrinks back screaming. To regain his son's love, Hector must remove his helmet.

Book 2 of the *Aeneid* replicates this scene but reverses the outcome. During the sack of Troy, when Aeneas wishes to join the battle, his wife, Creusa, tries to stop him, holding out their son, Ascanius, to him as a way of persuading him to stay. At first, Aeneas leans toward the model of the ancient hero, but after Jupiter sends him a sign or two of divine displeasure, Aeneas finally makes exactly the opposite choice from Hector's: he lifts his father onto his shoulders, takes his son by the hand, and, followed by his wife, escapes into the night. Aeneas and Hector may be brothers-in-law, but Virgil belongs to a different age from Homer's; the *Aeneid* sings the glories of a founder of cities, not those of a consummate warrior. Yet here again, it is society (or fate) that decides for the individual, whose own will, for all intents and purposes, is not involved.

In the modern world, the two value systems—that of the heroic virtues and that of the ordinary virtues—exist side by side, and convincing arguments can be made for both solutions. Still, does it follow that, as Sartre puts it, "there are no means of judging" (308) and that the best we can do is to insist that the choice be free rather than imposed from without? The two possibilities offered the Sartrean hero are equally worthy, but is it enough to invoke the principle of free choice if we are speaking of Stangl, the commandant of Treblinka, wavering between his devotion to his wife and his patriotic duty (which meant keeping the camp running smoothly)? Although Sartre does not admit it, clearly we cannot entirely disregard the nature of the choice or concern ourselves exclusively with the attitude of the subject who chooses. If authenticity means simply being true to oneself, then it is not a virtue, even if, as Sartre rightfully reminds us, within the modern perspective an act cannot be moral unless it is freely chosen. But even in the case of the hesitant young man who came to Sartre for counsel, to say that his alternatives are of equal worth is not quite accurate and requires that one disregard all the contextual elements that might influence the decision one way or the other. For that reason, I continue to believe that it is right and not arbitrary to reject Okulicki's decision to fight and to embrace Anielewicz's, even if both men opted for revolt and in so doing took the model of classical heroism as their point of reference.

KINDNESS AND GOOD

Sartre suggests another way of looking at these alternatives, this time as a choice not between heroic and ordinary virtues but between "two kinds of morality," one of them concrete and directed toward individuals, the other abstract and directed toward a wider collectivity (296). Although Sartre's example is not entirely felicitous—one's homeland being always a question of particulars, and the decision to act on its behalf deriving not from any kind of universal morality—it does offer an illuminating distinction between what one might call the morality of sympathy and that of principles (what others have called a "horizontal" and a "vertical" morality). A principle is an abstraction that every relevant particular case serves to illustrate. Sympathy, on the other hand, is a sentiment one feels as a direct result of someone else's experience; it can take the form of compassion, in which one seeks to alleviate another's pain, or that of vicarious joy, prompted by the sight of another's good fortune.

The examples of conflict between the morality of sympathy and that of principles which I find in the accounts of survivors do not accord the two equal standing. Ella Lingens-Reiner tells of a young girl who, while convalescing in the hospital barracks, takes the food of a dying woman. The "theft" is discovered, and the *Älteste* of the barracks, a zealous Communist, punishes the "thief" by assigning her to an especially exhausting job. The young girl dies. "The *Lagerälteste* had acted from a conscious moral principle," says Lingens-Reiner. "She wanted to uphold the law of decency, but in her rigid, meager, cramped determination, she could not find the way to simple human tolerance and kindness" (92). Virtually the same situation presented itself at Elgen, a collective farm at Kolyma in the Soviet gulag. Zimmerman, the farm's director, being an "honest" woman, is prepared to mete out lethal punishments to anyone who steals so much as a potato. She "killed many people without any thought for herself, acting, from her point of view, on the most idealistic of principles" (Ginzburg, *Within* 75). Buber-Neumann became the object of this sort of obduracy at Ravensbrück. Her crime was not theft, but even so she had violated the moral code of the Communist cell (by claiming that similar concentration camps existed in the USSR); the ostracism that followed nearly cost her her life when later she was stricken with blood poisoning (*Ravensbrück*, 190–91).

The literature describing the mores and dilemmas of the Puritans has taught us about such contradictions between noble principles and the ignoble acts they supposedly inspire. Morality can be a cold and unyielding monster. In the name of the common good, certain individuals are killed; when defending abstract principles, one can forget the people one is supposed to be helping and protecting. But it is on the basis of the extreme experiences of the recent past that Vasily Grossman has worked out a sort of theory, which he puts in the mouth of old Ikonnikov, a minor character in the novel *Life and Fate*. Ikonnikov holds that there are two moral ideals, "kindness" and "good." Men have always sought to act in the name of the good, he explains, but every religion and philosophical doctrine, each race and each class, has defined the good in its own way. The more narrowly the term is defined, the more necessary it becomes to try to impose that definition everywhere. As a result, "the very concept of good became a scourge, a greater evil than evil itself" (405). And this is as true of Christianity's ideal, "an idea of good [that is] fine and humane," as it is of the ideal of Communism (406). He who *desires* good does evil: "Whenever we see the dawn [of an external good], the blood of old people and children is always shed" (406). Goethe's Mephistopheles describes himself as "Part of that force which would / Do ever evil, and does ever good" (*Faust* 1.1335–36); Grossman, however, seems to fear those with the opposite intention, who, in desiring only good, ultimately do evil.

Fortunately, says Grossman, aside from good and evil, there exists "everyday human kindness. The kindness of an old woman carrying a piece of bread to a prisoner, the kindness of a soldier allowing a wounded enemy to drink from his water-flask, the kindness towards age, the kindness of a peasant hiding an old Jew in his hayloft" (407–8). It is the kindness of one individual toward another, kindness without ideology, without thought or speeches or justifications, a kindness that does not ask that its beneficiary deserve it. This kindness is "what is most truly human in a human being," and it will endure as long as the human race exists. But it must never be made a rallying cry: "Kindness is powerful only while it is powerless. If Man tries to give it power, it dims, fades away, loses itself, vanishes" (409).

Several remarkable letters written by Vasily Grossman and only recently published (under the title "Memoria") underscore the connection in his mind between the theme of kindness and the image of his mother, who was killed in 1941, in the first wave of Hitler's massacres of Soviet Jews. In 1961, Grossman wrote her the following letter: "My Precious One, Twenty years have passed since your death. I love you and think of you each day of my life; my grief has stayed with me all these years. . . . I am you, dear mother. As long as I live, so shall you live. And when I die, you will live on in this book [*Life and Fate*], which I have dedicated to you and whose destiny is so like your own. . . . During the ten years of writing it, I thought of you almost constantly. This work is an expression of my love, of my devotion to my fellowmen; that is why I offer it to you. For me, you are all that is human, and your terrifying fate is the fate of all humankind in inhuman times. All my life I've believed that everything in me that is beautiful, honest, and good, everything in me that is love, comes from you. But everything in me that is bad—do not forgive me for it—is not you. And yet you still love me, mama, you love me even with all the bad (*Dawgava* 11)."

The morality of principles, for Grossman, is hardly distinguishable from evil itself; the only commendable morality is the morality of sympathy. It contrasts with the morality of principles in two ways: in negative terms, it relies on no particular concept or doctrine; in positive terms, it yields the kind of act that is performed by one individual for the sake of another. As I argued earlier, acts of ordinary virtue are, by definition, directed toward specific individuals (they are "personal" acts). But without a human subject who takes it on him- or herself to carry out such acts, we cannot talk of kindness—or, to use my terminology, virtue—at all. Virtues are not only personal; they are also in this sense subjective. Justice and virtue are therefore not the same. A set of principles and laws embodied in an institution, justice can benefit particular individuals, no less than acts of dignity or caring or those of the life of the mind can; but justice does not imply any particular virtue on the part of the person who practices it, for whom therefore the just action is no cause for self-congratulation. Moreover, we require not that our judges be especially virtuous or moral, only that they comply with the rules of justice. The domain of morality begins where the individual who states the abstract rule goes on to apply it to him- or herself. Justice is objective; it is independent of the person who formulates it or represents it. The difference between justice and virtue is not unlike the difference between intelligence and wisdom— the latter can result only from the subject's lived experience.

It is by the presence or absence of individual human beings as beneficiaries of certain acts (personalization) that we have been able to distinguish ordinary virtues from heroic virtues, which tend to serve abstractions—humanity, country, or the ideal of heroism itself. The obligation to identify a subject as agent or source of these moral acts (their subjectivity) now allows us to make another distinction, this time between morality, or a moral life, and moralism. Moralism consists of practicing justice without virtue, of simply invoking moral principles without feeling that they apply to oneself, of presuming one's own goodness simply on the basis of having declared adherence to principles of good. To say that one is in favor of morality is not a moral act; most of the time, it merely signifies conformity or a desire to live at peace with one's conscience. Subscribing to noble principles does not make one noble, as the moralists of antiquity well knew. It is this very distinction, I believe, to which Marcus Aurelius refers in his famous precept: "No longer talk at all about the kind of man that a good man ought to be, but *be such!*" (10.16).

The requirement that the individual perform moral actions (and not be content merely to aver their righteousness) applies not only to ordinary virtues but to all forms of morality. In the name of morality one can legitimately make demands only on oneself; to make moral demands of others to the exclusion of oneself is to imagine that one has risen above it all and achieved a perfectly objective god-like vantage point. Although a moral ideal is by definition universal, moral action cannot be generalized. Justice is not morality; there is nothing moral in allotting myself as big a slice of the pie as everyone else's. Kant expresses this asymmetry when, in referring to those human ends that are also duties as "one's own perfection and our neighbor's happiness" (201), he reminds us that we cannot reverse these terms: there is nothing moral in seeking either my own happiness or my neighbor's perfection; in fact, the latter is exactly what is meant by "moralism."

Seeking my own perfection and securing the happiness of others are not two separate actions but rather opposite aspects that the same action presents to its subject and its beneficiary respectively; it is by seeking my neighbor's happiness that I contribute to my perfection. Therefore, if I want examples of good, I must find them outside myself. For examples of evil, however, I must first look inward. The mote in my own eye ought to bother me more than the beam in my brother's. Conversely, the person who holds himself up as an example to others is in fact acting immorally, no matter how commendable his conduct may otherwise be. Hannah Arendt refers to this characteristic of moral action when she summarizes the Christian ethic in these terms: "Goodness can exist only when it is not perceived, not even by its author" (*Condition* 74). Another philosopher, Philip Hallie, who has examined the difference between "vertical" and "horizontal" morality in the context of extreme situations, has remarked, "Aside from the distinction between good and evil, between helping and hurting, the fundamental distinction in that ethic is between giving *things* and giving *oneself*"; the former can be considered moral only insofar as the things one gives are a part of oneself (72).

(Maurice Blanchot, an author I once admired, entitled one of his recent publications "Les intellectuels en question." He has many judicious things to say in this piece, and yet I find it disturbing. For example, he devotes several pages—full of keen observations—to Paul Valéry's involvement, early in the century, in both the anti-Semitic campaign and the anti-Dreyfus party and then offers this severe judgment: "I do not find [in this examination] anything that can excuse his adding his name to the very worst of those who called out for the death of the Jews and the annihilation of their defenders" [13]. What bothers me in reading those words is the knowledge that between 1936 and 1938 Blanchot himself espoused the positions of the nationalist and anti-Semitic Action française and signed his name to articles published in the periodical Combat excoriating the Jews and linking them repeatedly to the Bolsheviks. Later, Blanchot underwent a radi-

cal conversion, becoming both pro-Communist and philo-Semitic. As far as I know, however, he has never found the moral courage within himself to write even one line about his blindness of years past. That one line would have been a true moral act and would have had a more powerful influence on us, his readers, than all those lengthy pages he devotes to the errors of others. Indeed, his puzzlement over Valéry might have lessened considerably had he reflected on his own case. But Blanchot never offers us that line, neither in this text nor in any other (not even in his recent writings about Heidegger's involvement with the Nazis), even as he reminds us of his obligation to bear witness. "As the years pass," he writes, "and witnesses become ever rarer, I cannot remain silent" [20]. Yet the single "personal confession" [28] he offers concerns his hatred of the Nazis, scarcely a compromising admission today, all things considered. What are words worth if they are not echoed by actions? While Blanchot's article is wanting neither in historical details nor in accurate judgments, it has no moral value. Because it does not implicate the author, it does not permit the reader to do so either: the wicked ones are always the others. As Blanchot himself says, but of Valéry, "a painful memory, a painful puzzle" [12].)

The same is true of judgments about the past. To denounce slavery constitutes a moral act only at those times when such denunciation is not simply a matter of course and thus involves some personal risk. There is nothing moral in speaking out against slavery today; all it proves is that I'm in step with my society's ideology or else don't want to find myself on the wrong side of the barricades. Something very similar can be said about condemnations of racism, although that would not have been the case in 1936 in Germany. Today the crimes of Stalin and Hitler are a matter of historical record; to pronounce on their guilt yields me no particular moral advantage. On the other hand, if I discover that either I myself or people with whom I identify have participated in acts like those I have condemned, then the conditions do exist for me to take a moral position. It may be true that German culture was responsible for the disaster of Germany, that Russian culture was responsible for the disaster of the Soviet Union;

yet to say so adds nothing to my personal virtue unless I happen to be German or Russian.

If I reproach others for failing to be heroes or martyrs, then I am speaking from the standpoint not of virtue but of justice, and justice of a highly questionable sort; if I level the reproach against myself, things are different. Take the debate about the uniqueness of the Holocaust. Whether or not it is unique, the moral position for those aligned with the victims consists in not reaping any advantage from its exceptional character; for those aligned with the executioners, the truly moral position is not to seek advantage from the possibility that there might be similarities between it and other events. As Charles Maier suggests, Jews should emphasize the ordinariness of the Holocaust, Germans its uniqueness. Essentially the same point was once made to Vasily Grossman by an Armenian. Touched to learn that a Jew had written about the Armenians, this old man from Yerevan "wished there had also been . . . a son of the martyred Armenian people who had written about the Jews" (*Dobro vam!* 270). Grossman, moreover, was not the first Jewish writer to turn his attention to the history of the Armenian genocide; it was the subject of Franz Werfel's extraordinary 1933 novel, *The Forty Days of Musa Dagh.*

Conversely, certain just behaviors would be that much more just if carried out without reference to their being moral. The judge who, in dispensing justice, gives more thought to his personal edification than to the application of the law, risks being a very bad judge. The politician who addresses each problem by seeking not the solution most consonant with the public good but the one that advances him one step further on the path to sainthood is likely to be a bad politician. Similarly, voters ought not to love their leaders with the same love and concern they have for their parents or their children. Where justice is at stake, one must put aside all consideration of the personal moral benefits that one's actions might bring. This does not mean that morality and politics or morality and justice cannot draw on the same principles or have the same ultimate goals; it simply means that they should be clearly distinguishable from each other in practical application.

This second basic requirement of a moral life—that I myself be the one to carry out the actions I recommend—implies a never-ending questioning of the self. This process should not be reduced to its most famous, and perhaps most arguable, examples, which are, in the Christian tradition, repentance (followed by absolution from sin) or the self-inflicted punishment of the ascetic saints; in the Communist tradition, the practice of compulsory and humiliating self-criticism, of which the Moscow trials represented the apogee; and, in the realm of individual neurosis, inexpiable guilt feelings. Not exempting oneself from the moral principles to which one subscribes implies neither the ritualization of acts of contrition nor the exaggeration of one's personal faults.

This is how I understand Grossman's characterization of kindness as the absence of doctrine: an action is moral not in itself but only in relation to its author, a specific time, and a particular place. Of course, it is not at all impossible to conceptualize, or generalize about, acts of kindness (we speak, for instance, about the need to concentrate on individuals, not abstractions, about the need to make demands on ourselves and not on others). The concept can help us grasp the nature of these acts, but it does not guarantee that we will perform them. Unless we restrict the meaning of "good" to that of "political good," the abstract definition of good and the exercise of kindness are not opposed to each other, or at least no more than a rule of grammar is opposed to actual linguistic practice. The possibility of encountering each of them separately does not mean that they are mutually exclusive. It is for this reason that the morality of sympathy and that of principles are not opposites either, even though one can find people practicing one but not the other. Like theory and praxis, they are complements. To care about others, then, is to carry out the categorical imperative.

NEITHER MONSTERS NOR BEASTS

Ordinary People

We usually associate the extremity that is the concentration camp not with acts of virtue but rather with the outbreak of evil unprecedented in magnitude. I have tried to go beyond this conventional picture, but there is no escaping the fact that, in the literature of the concentration camp, evil is the main character. As a project, interpreting evil appeals less to me than does understanding goodness, yet I feel I cannot avoid this task, inasmuch as the evil we are concerned with here is not only extreme but also, it would seem, particularly resistant to explanation. Or perhaps I should say, the traditional explanations that come so readily to mind when we face evil in its usual guises are of little help to us here.

First of all, we cannot understand the evils of the concentration camps by interpreting them in terms of abnormality unless we define abnormality—tautologically—as the behavior in question: nothing about the personalities or actions of the authors of evil, apart from this behavior, allows us to classify them as pathological beings—in other words, as monsters, whatever our definition of the terms *pathological* and *normal*. It is for this reason no doubt that studies of concentration camps by psychoanalysts or psychiatrists are somewhat disappointing, even when their authors write from firsthand experience; almost without exception, these studies use the language of pathology when discussing either the inmates or the guards (or both). Clearly such characterizations are inadequate. This is not an a priori judgment on my part but the nearly unanimous opinion of the survivors themselves.

Camp survivors seem to agree on the following point: only a small minority of guards, on the order of five or ten percent, could legitimately be called sadists (and thus abnormal). This type of individual, moreover, was not appreciated by those in the higher echelons. Writing of his experiences as a prisoner in Auschwitz, Benedikt Kautsky says, "Nothing would be more mistaken than to see the SS as a sadistic horde driven to abuse and torture thousands of human beings by instinct, passion, or some thirst for pleasure. Those who acted in this way were a small minority" (Langbein 274). Himmler supposedly even gave instructions to remove from duty any SS man who appeared to take pleasure in hurting others (Fénelon, *Playing* 182). Similarly at Buchenwald, Bruno Bettelheim writes, "only a small minority were actually perverted, willing to kill and injure when so ordered" (*Heart* 224). Germaine Tillion recalls that the staff of the medical experimentation unit at Ravensbrück showed themselves to be "not a very inspiring lot but, on the whole, not too different from what might be found in any hospital" (77). Prisoners in the Soviet gulags voiced much the same impressions: "There are not many dedicated sadists among the jailers, after all; the majority of them are none too bright but cunning functionaries" (Ratushinskaya 149). Ginzburg seconds that opinion in her description of the men who sent her to Kolyma: they were "merely functionaries," she writes, "earning their pay" (*Journey* 171).

Who were these five or ten percent? The exceptions? For the most part, they were individuals scarred by physical defect, grave psychological handicap, or simply vicious fate. As Tillion remarks of the Ravensbrück SS, "Their ranks included a large number of physical misfits whose bodies seemed thrown together and who could have had personal grudges to take out on the female sex in general" (61). At Auschwitz the most brutal guards were not the *Reichsdeutscher* but the *Volksdeutscher*, Germans born outside Germany, who felt they needed to prove themselves true Germans. Scholars have pored over the personal histories of the Nazi leaders, hoping no doubt to discover the causes of the evil they created and so banish its specter:

wow!

Sadism: sexual pleasure obtained from inflicting cruelty upon another; extreme cruelty.

Reinhard Heydrich, for instance, deputy chief of the Gestapo, who initially presided over the "final solution," may have been part Jewish, and Hitler, too; they had to compensate, the story goes. Goebbels walked with a limp; Himmler and Hitler had bizarre sex lives. Apart from the fact that there is nothing particularly pathological or exceptional about such traits, they apply to only a few individuals, whereas the evil that needs to be explained was the affair of millions. As Primo Levi says, "Monsters exist, but they are too few in number to be truly dangerous. More dangerous are the common men" (Afterword 214).

If the concept of monstrousness is of limited utility in helping us understand evil, positing some reversion to bestial or primitive instincts takes us no further. We all know the popular expressions: in every human breast there lurks a wild beast, ready to strike out the moment circumstances permit, or each of us harbors within him- or herself a primitive being, a savage awaiting the chance to shatter the thin veneer of civilization and satisfy the most primal urges. As far as the camps themselves are concerned, we have already noted that many people, seeing in them a collapse of the social order, believe they represent the reversion to a Hobbesian state of nature, to the "war of all against all." Yet one need only look at the facts themselves to see how far off the mark these explanations truly are. In the first place, torture and extermination have not even the remotest equivalent in the animal kingdom. Nor was there any breakdown of the social contract in the camps: the guards who tortured and killed were obeying the laws of their country and the orders of their superiors. As Dwight MacDonald remarked shortly after the war, what the crimes of the Nazis teach us is that those who enforce the law are more dangerous than those who break it. If only the guards had given themselves over to their instincts! Unfortunately, they followed the rules.

The last of the more familiar explanations, ultimately no more useful than the first two, holds that concentration camps are a direct outgrowth of ideological fanaticism. There were indeed fanatical Communists among the guards of the gulags, just as there were fanatical Nazis among the concentration camp guards, but proportionally the fanatics were no more prevalent than the sadists. The predominant type was a different sort altogether: a conformist, willing to serve whoever wielded power and more concerned with his own welfare than with the triumph of doctrine. Up and down the ladder of power, one finds only "pragmatists" and cynics. For such men, especially after they seize power, ideology (although not irrelevant) is a pretext rather than a motive. Those who knew Mengele used to say of him that he was a cynic, not an ideologue. Albert Speer spoke similarly of Hitler, that he was a pragmatist, not a fanatic. No doubt this was true of Beria as well. Vasily Grossman remarks that "The new state did not require holy apostles, fanatic, inspired builders, faithful, devout disciples. The new state did not even require servants—just clerks" (*Forever Flowing* 193). It has often been pointed out that in the single most intense moment of anti-Semitic fanaticism in Germany—*Kristallnacht* of 1938—about one hundred people lost their lives. If the extermination of the Jews had proceeded at that pace, the Nazis would have needed 140 years to kill as many as they managed to in five.

TOTALITARIAN CRIMES

Traditional explanations, then, shed little light on the crimes of totalitarianism, on the extremity of the camps; these crimes were new, right down to the principle on which they were based, and thus require new explanatory concepts. Hannah Arendt's use of the phrase "the banality of evil" in reference to Eichmann represents one attempt in that direction. Judging from the number of misunderstandings that this coinage has provoked, it was perhaps less than felicitous. Nevertheless, the idea remains an important one.

Sitting among the spectators at the Eichmann trial in Jerusalem and faced with Adolph Eichmann the individual, Arendt had to acknowledge that despite the prosecutor's efforts to demonize him, this man who was responsible for one of the most devastating evils in the history of humanity stood before the court a profoundly mediocre, indeed common, human being. "The trouble with Eichmann," Arendt writes, "was precisely that so many were like him, and that the many were neither perverted nor sadistic, that they were, and still are, terribly and terrifyingly normal" (*Eichmann* 276). It is in this—and only in this—sense that the evil that Eichmann represents is "banal" and not "radical" or inhuman. (Note that, for Arendt, "radical" and "extreme" are not the same.) To call this evil banal is not to trivialize it: precisely what made this evil so dangerous was that it was so easy, that no exceptional human qualities were required for it to come into being. The wind had only to blow in the right direction, and the evil spread like wildfire. The paradox of this concept, according to which an evil can be extreme without being radically different from its less virulent forms, is doubtless responsible for the misunderstandings surrounding it; it must be said, however, that the facts are themselves paradoxical, the evil in question being at once ordinary and exceptional.

Still, the notion of the banality of evil is less an explanation than a way of putting aside the usual formulas and indicating a direction for further inquiry. Arthur Seyss-Inquart, the Nazi governor of Austria and then Holland and one of those convicted at Nuremberg, long ago said in response to Höss's testimony about the exterminations at Auschwitz that "there is a limit to the number of people you can kill out of hatred or a lust for slaughter"—so much for fanaticism and sadism—"but there is no limit to the number you can kill in the cold, systematic manner of the military 'categorical imperative' " (Gilbert, *Psychology* 256). In order to explain an evil of this magnitude, we must thus look not to the character of the individual but to that of the society that imposes such categorical imperatives. The explanation will be political and social, not psychological or individual.

What attributes of a society make possible the commission of such crimes? For me, the answer is a point of departure, not an end point: the societal trait that allows such crimes to be carried out is totalitarianism, the only attribute that Nazi Germany shares with the Soviet Union, Bulgaria, and China. The Germans, the Russians, and all the others who committed these unspeakable crimes are human beings no different from any others; what sets them apart is the political regime under which they lived. This is not to argue that national differences are altogether irrelevant. We do not have to accept Nazi notions of inferior races and culpable peoples to ask why totalitarianism took hold in Germany, for example, but not France, in China but not India, and to seek causal factors in such things as one country's tradition of militarism, another's history of brutal repression, or even the "slave mentality" of yet another. My aim, however, is not to analyze cultural and national traditions, and I subscribe to Germaine Tillion's conclusion that "no 'people' is immune to [this] kind of collective moral disaster" (188). In this opinion, she concurs with Buchenwald survivor David Rousset, who warned just after the war that "it would be duplicity, and criminal duplicity, to pretend that it is impossible for other nations to try a similar experiment because it would be contrary to their nature" (112).

Tillion's conclusion is all the more invaluable because upon her liberation from Ravensbrück she could not make so impartial a statement. In the first version of her book, she was prepared to accept a historical explanation for the disaster and to rely on such notions as the German and Polish "national characters." Later, she revised her opinion: "I hasten to say that today, I am ashamed of this judgment," she wrote in 1972, "for I am convinced that in a similar situation, any other national group would have committed similar abuses" (28). For the French, at least, blaming the German national character by comparing it to their own is all the more dubious a proposition for their having been among the most zealous collaborators in the implementation of the final solution. The totalitarian machine absorbed the "lessons" of Russian czarism, Prussian militarism, and Chinese despotism, but it also made of them something quite new, and it is this entity that acted on the minds of individuals. Primo Levi shares this conclusion. "Certainly," he writes, "the greatest responsibility lies with the system, the very structure of the totalitarian state" (*Drowned* 44).

(What interests me here, however, is not totalitarianism as such but rather its influence on individual moral behavior) In this context, some characteristics of totalitarianism are of more importance than others. The first of these characteristics has to do with the place totalitarianism assigns to the enemy. All extremist doctrines invoke the principle (found, sadly, in the Gospels) that "he who is not with me is against me." Not all of them, however, take up its corollary, that "all who are against me shall perish." Nor do all extremisms have at their disposal the means of the totalitarian state to carry out the threat implicit in this principle. What characterizes totalitarianism more specifically is that the enemy is an internal one. (Nazi Germany and the Soviet Union pursued aggressive foreign policies, it is true, but in that respect they behaved like any other imperialist powers.)It is the notion of an internal enemy—or the extension of the principle of warfare to relations between groups within the country itself—that sets these two apart from the rest. In a speech he made to the commandants of the concentration camps at the beginning of the war, Theodor Eicke, the great inspiration behind the camps and one of their most aggressive promoters, echoed an idea that Lenin had already formulated in the wake of the October Revolution. "The obligation to destroy an internal enemy of the State," Eicke said, "is in no way different from the obligation to kill your adversary on the battlefield" (Höss 101).

The generalization of the idea of war leads inevitably to the conclusion that internal enemies should be killed. Totalitarian doctrines always divide humanity into two groups of unequal worth (which are not coincident with the categories of "our country" and "other countries," for here we are not dealing with simple nationalism) and maintain that the inferior beings must be punished, even annihilated. Totalitarian doctrines, then, are never universalist in character; under them, all men do not have the same rights. In Nazi doctrine, that fact is obvious: the "inferior races"—Jews, Gypsies, and others—are all subhumans, parasites. But it is just as true of Soviet discourse (to say nothing of Soviet methods), which throughout the purges of the 1930s was identical to that of the Nazis; slogans such as "Dogs must die like dogs" or "Crush the vermin" were the order of the day. According to Stalinist doctrine, moreover, the internal struggle was supposed to intensify as the day of true Communism approached. A class enemy in one case, a race enemy in the other; under both regimes, however, this much is the same: the enemy is necessarily an extreme enemy, against whom a war of extermination is justified.

The second characteristic of totalitarian systems, like the first, is also bound up with the repudiation of universality: the state becomes the custodian of society's ultimate aims. The supreme values that are supposed to govern the individual's conduct are no longer accessible to him; the individual can no longer think of himself as one of humanity's many representatives and consult his conscience to determine which goals to pursue and according to which criteria to judge the actions of others. Imposing itself as an intermediary between the individual and his values, the state replaces humanity as the standard by which to distinguish good from evil and thus determines the direction in which society will evolve. Through this usurpation of society's and the individual's ultimate aims, the totalitarian state becomes indistinguishable from those aims, both from its own perspective and in the eyes of its subjects.

A third characteristic of totalitarian systems is one to which the adjective specifically refers: the state aspires to control the totality of an individual's social existence. The party (Communist or National Socialist) is not content to seize political power in the narrow sense (as a classical dictatorship would) by eliminating the opposition and taking over the government. Rather, it extends its control over the entire public sphere of each person's life and encroaches substantially on his private life as well. It controls what work the individual does, where he lives, what he owns, his children's education and leisure, even his family life and his love affairs. In this way the state secures its subjects' submission; in a totalitarian system, there is no refuge, no escaping the state's control. During periods of hard-line totalitarianism (in Eastern Europe and the Soviet Union under Stalin, in Germany under Hitler during the Second World War), obedience is obtained by direct threat of physical violence and death; in more "relaxed" times, the totalitarian state is content to deport its subjects, deny them work, prevent them from traveling abroad or owning property, keep their children out of the university, and so on.

Each of these characteristics of the totalitarian system is at the root of certain moral behaviors specific to the totalitarian subject. Inasmuch as the totalitarian regime requires an absolute enemy, an embodiment of evil, hostile acts against that enemy become not only permissible but also commendable. This is no more than the extension of the principle of war: the soldier is honored for his determination in confronting the enemy, that is, for his capacity to kill; what is forbidden during peacetime becomes laudable in times of war. One must be strong, stronger than the enemy, above all. Inevitably those who under totalitarianism heed this injunction enjoy—in both senses of the word—power over their enemy.

The fact that the state appropriates all societal goals, making itself sole arbiter of which ends are to be pursued, has a twofold effect. The subjects of the totalitarian regime can take comfort in being relieved of personal responsibility for their decisions. At the same time, the totalitarian power demands that its subjects restrict themselves in thought and deed to instrumentality and treat every action as a means to something else rather than as an end in itself. In the realm of material production, the fulfillment of that demand does not yield particularly brilliant results, as expanding bureaucracies and the loss of personal initiative present formidable obstacles. In the domain of moral conduct, however, the demand is far more productive. The question is often asked how "ordinary people," "decent husbands and fathers," could have committed so many atrocities. Where was their conscience in all this? The answer is that by usurping social goals and restricting people to instrumentalist thinking, the totalitarian power manages to have its subjects accomplish whatever tasks they are assigned without its having to disturb the individual's moral structure at all. Guards who committed atrocities never stopped distinguishing between good and evil. Their moral faculty had not withered away. They simply believed that the "atrocity" was in fact a good thing and thus not an atrocity at all—because the state, custodian of the standards of good and evil, told them so. The guards were not deprived of a moral sensibility but provided with a new one.

Individuals caught up in so total a web ultimately become docile, submitting to orders passively. The fact is that totalitarian subjects believe there is a way out for them: by deciding to submit "only" in their outward behavior, in their public words and gestures, they console themselves with the thought that they remain masters of their consciences, faithful to themselves in their private lives. In reality, this sort of social schizophrenia is no solution at all and tends to work against those who try to make it one. Whatever pains the totalitarian regime may take to indoctrinate its subjects, it is quite satisfied with "merely" public docility, because it needs no more than that to remain firmly in power. At the same time, its subjects live in the comforting illusion that "in their innermost selves" they remain honorable and pure. Social schizophrenia thus becomes a weapon in the hands of those in power; it lulls to sleep the conscience of the totalitarian subject, reassures him, and lets him underestimate the seriousness of his public deeds. Master of his heart of hearts, the subject no longer pays much attention to what he does in the world.

(I must admit that during the years I lived under a totalitarian regime the idea of resisting never crossed my mind. In the first place, to my comrades and me such a venture seemed clearly slated for disaster. The disproportion between the vast power of a police state and the sprinkling of isolated individuals like us was simply too great. To revolt would have been proof of either a profound naïveté or a conspicuous taste for masochism. The conditions that would later make possible the actions of the dissidents—the regime's dependence on public opinion in the West, for example—did not yet exist. Yet there was an even stronger reason for our passivity. Totalitarian regimes give the illusion that they control your life "only" in the public sphere, that they leave you in charge of your private life. And thus, unfettered—or so we thought—we tasted the joys of friendship and love, of the mind and the senses; our passionate discussions of all manner of elevated subject, often lasting well into the night, gave us the illusion of freedom. Doubtless we were still too young to understand that the boundary between private and public was neither fixed nor impermeable and that, by believing that we had escaped totalitarian control over at least one part of our lives, we were giving the state free rein to regulate our social existence, which is to say, our lives as a whole. In looking after our survival and ensuring our relative well-being, we were consolidating the power of the regime itself.)

The submissiveness of totalitarian subjects has another, still more tragic consequence for any subject unfortunate enough to be considered one of the internal enemy. The totalitarian state obtains the submission of all its subjects, including its victims, by combining total control of sources of information and means of coercion (the police) with the threat of physical violence and death. The fact that the victims are so numerous counts for little; because they cannot organize, each victim stands alone and thus powerless before an infinitely superior force. As everyone knows, during and after World War II certain Jewish writers reproached entire Jewish populations for having allowed themselves to be led "like sheep to the slaughter," for having failed to take up arms and fight back. (This argument was made by men as different from each other as Bruno Bettelheim and Raul Hilberg, Jean Améry and Vasily Grossman; but it was first employed by resistance leaders, as a way of spurring people to action.) Other writers later contested this charge by stressing those acts of Jewish resistance that did take place here and there. The debate, however, is a spurious one. (There is only one answer to the question of why the Jews did not revolt more vigorously: such revolt is impossible in a totalitarian regime. Why did Soviet prisoners of war in Germany not revolt? Why did five million Ukrainian peasants passively submit to starvation by Stalin in the early 1930s? Why are a billion Chinese not in revolt right now? Obviously one cannot, in these cases, speak of Jewish tradition or the ghetto mentality.

Totalitarian crimes are crimes of a new species altogether and we must recognize their specificity, but doing so does not oblige us to revise our notions about "human nature." There is nothing either extrahuman or subhuman about these crimes, and yet something historically unprecedented has clearly occurred. Their cause resides neither in individuals nor in nations but in the political regime under which they are committed. Once the totalitarian system is in place, the vast majority of the population—people like you and me—are at risk of becoming accomplices in its crimes; that is all it takes. Indeed, that it should be such a simple matter for people to fall into behaviors they understand are evil is one of the lessons of these tragic events, as Germaine Tillion points out, calling our attention to "the tragic easiness with which 'decent people' could become the most callous executioners without seeming to notice what was happening to them" (189). To say that the cause of totalitarian crimes resides not in the individual but in the political regime does not mean the individual bears no responsibility for its crimes, a point to which I shall return.

(Until 1944, Bulgaria belonged to the pro-German camp and had a government that was said to be fascist. Its pro-Germanism and its fascism must not have been rock solid, since Bulgaria was one of the very few European countries that did not surrender "its" Jews. It was possible to demonstrate publicly against the wearing of the yellow Star of David, in the National Assembly deputies could protest the roundups of Jews, and the Orthodox clergy could announce their intention to lie across the tracks that the transport trains would take with their human cargo. The fact is that Bulgarians fought this fas-

cism, and in that struggle the Communists were in the lead. They were joined by numerous sympathizers, including my father, at the time a modest librarian and man of letters, but someone who already held pro-Communist opinions. Could he have imagined then—at a time when his response, in no way an extreme one, was simply to support the antifascist struggle—that he would be helping to establish another totalitarian regime, one with a network of camps ten times the size of that of its predecessor, one that would hang, shoot, or strangle to death all representatives of the opposition that it had imprisoned, one that would tolerate neither public demonstrations by opponents nor the expression of personal opinions? How could he have deduced extremity from the ordinary?)

UNITY OR UNIQUENESS

The inclusion of the Communist and National Socialist regimes in the same category, that of totalitarianism, has long been a matter of contentious debate and remains a problematic issue to this day. These two regimes obviously have their similarities as well as their differences, and everything depends on which similarities or differences are deemed most important. Much has been made of the seemingly unbridgeable ideological abyss separating the two systems, yet as soon as one begins to look not at abstract theoretical pronouncements but at the ideologies that can be directly deduced from actions, the gap narrows. Just as the Third Reich was not without its share of socialist ideas, so too was Stalin not without his Nietzschean inspirations. Indeed, the extent to which the two dictators emulated each other is striking. Before the war, Hitler both admired Stalin and imitated him on many points. He modeled the Gestapo after the NKVD; the Communist massacre at Katyn prefigures, down to its details, the butcheries of the *Einsatzkommandos*, the mobile death squads that Hitler would operate behind the Russian front. As for Stalin, he would later issue orders that no mercy be shown any soldiers reluctant to fight to the death, and in this he was directly inspired by analogous orders given by Hitler. Toward the end of his life, Stalin was even tempted to apply Hitler's "final solution" to the Jews of Russia. The entente between the two heads of state, culminating in the infamous Hitler-Stalin pact of 1939–41, was a moment of truth, not a lapse of judgment.

With respect to the camps, whether one stresses differences or similarities again depends on one's perspective. It can be argued, for example, that the Soviet Union had no precise equivalent of the Nazi death camp: even if Auschwitz and Kolyma produced comparable numbers of victims, the Soviets never industrialized the killing process. (A closer parallel is perhaps Cambodia.) There were thus proportionally fewer fatalities in the Soviet camps; moreover, medical care was less inadequate. In the Soviet Union, guards and prisoners not only came from the same country but almost always spoke the same language, and the prisoners took some comfort in this. On the other hand, German political prisoners in the Nazi camps had the advantage of knowing they had always been the enemies of the Nazis, whereas in the Soviet Union, it was Communists who imprisoned other Communists, a circumstance that prompted the collapse of the many victims' mental universe. If Soviet guards showed more compassion than their Nazi counterparts, they could also be more capricious. Greater misery reigned in the gulags, but the kind of order applied in the German camps was a lethal one.

This analysis has been taken up many times before; the object of my inquiry, however, is not the regimes themselves but the experiences of individuals. From the inmate's point of view, the Communist and Nazi camps were often identical, and so one can appreciate the quandary of someone like Buber-Neumann, who experienced both: "I ask myself, deep down, which is really worse," she writes, "the lice-infested corncob-walled cabins in Birma [in Kazakhstan] or the nightmare-order of Ravensbrück" (*Ravensbrück* 53). Or, as she says in her testimony at the David Rousset trial in 1950, "It is hard to decide which is the least humane—to gas people in five minutes or to strangle them slowly, over the course of three months, by hunger" (Rousset et al. 183). These similarities of the Nazi and the Communist camps are further confirmed—comically, one could say, were it not for the gravity of the subject—in the arguments offered by the representatives of the French Communist party who testified against Rousset; they accused Rousset, who had been deported to the German camps and later spoke out to denounce the Soviet gulags, of forgery, suggesting that he had used descriptions of the German camps to portray the Soviet ones and had merely substituted names and dates. I find this admission all the more chilling for its being unintended.

There are other similarities as well. The concentration camp and the gulag played similar roles in their respective societies and were the result of mutual emulation and real points of contact between the two social systems. Once again, Hitler took his lead from Stalin; according to Rudolf Höss, "The secret police (RSHA) sent the camp commandants detailed reports on the Russian concentration camps, based on testimony from escaped prisoners. Particular emphasis was given to the fact that the Russians annihilated whole populations through forced labor" (Höss 224). But Stalin profited from Hitler's experience, too; he even reopened the gates to Buchenwald, Sachsenhausen, and other camps in Germany as soon as the last of their inmates had been freed and began filling them once again, this time with enemies of his regime, not only Nazis but other non-Communists as well, some of whom were former inmates! The number of postwar occupants of these camps is estimated at 120,000; the number of deaths by execution, exhaustion, disease, and hunger there, at 45,000.

These former detainees of German nationality who were liberated by the Russians and immediately reimprisoned by their liberators were not the only prisoners to experience both regimes. Russian prisoners of war, upon their release from their German captors, were systematically sent to camps in Siberia as punishment for having surrendered to the enemy instead of dying in battle. After the signing of the Hitler-Stalin pact, on the other hand, the Soviets turned over to Hitler German and Austrian Communists who were languishing in Soviet camps. Margarete Buber-Neumann was among them and describes a highly symbolic scene at Brest-Litovsk in 1940: "The NKVD officer and the SS officer raised their hands to their hats and saluted each other" (*Sibérie* 213). This continuity simply highlights a deeper kinship; it is not surprising, then, that after the war former Soviet prisoners compared their condition with that of the victims of Nazism. The Hitler-Stalin pact brought out into the open the collusion between the two regimes and so stands as a kind of culmination point in the history of twentieth-century totalitarianism; for its victims, the pact represents the moment of their greatest despair. Describing his impressions of the period, Gustaw Herling writes, "I think with horror and shame of a Europe divided into two parts by the line of the Bug [River], on one side of which millions of Soviet slaves prayed for liberation by the armies of Hitler, and on the other millions of victims of German concentration camps awaited deliverance by the Red Army as their last hope" (175–76).

And so to return to the question of which should take precedence, the uniqueness of the Holocaust or its similarity to that other great moral disaster of our time, the answer is: it depends on the task at hand. The historian or the political scientist must examine—and even dwell on—those aspects of the Nazi camps and Soviet gulags that make these institutions unique and distinct from each other. But if the moral behavior of the individual is our subject, then unity must take precedence over uniqueness.

ORDINARY VICES

Having suffered the persecutions and humiliations they did, it was important for the victims to be able to say, We too are human beings like you. Both Primo Levi's *Survival in Auschwitz (If This Is a Man)* and Robert Antelme's *The Human Race* are pleas for the recognition of the victims' humanity, for it is in this common humanity that the victims' hope resides. "It's because we're men like them," Antelme writes, "that the SS will finally prove powerless before us. . . . The executioner . . . can kill a man, but he can't change him into something else" (219–20). Today, however, when everyone recognizes the humanity of the victims, it is not enough to be able to say, "We are human like them." We must also grapple with the more problematic comparison, between ourselves and the executioners, and be prepared to say, "They are human beings like us." Those who took an active part in the perpetration of evil were ordinary people, and so are we: they are like us, and we are like them.

A statement like this may not mean much at all in the mouth of someone who was not directly affected by the events in question, but for those who experienced them in the flesh, it is not an easy thing to admit. One former Auschwitz inmate recounts how he and his friends constantly asked one another whether "the German was a human being like everyone else. Each time, the response was a categorical 'No, the German is not a man. The German is a *Boche,* a monster, and what's more, a monster conscious of his monstrosity'" (Laks and Coudy 157). Thus it is with even greater admiration that I read Etty Hillesum's journal entry for Thursday, February 19, 1942, in which she relates a discussion she has with a friend while waiting at an Amsterdam tram stop. "What is it in human beings that makes them want to destroy others?" her friend asks. And Hillesum replies, "Human beings, you say, but remember that you're one yourself. . . . All the appalling things that happen are no mysterious threats from afar, but arise from fellow beings very close to us" (*Interrupted* 70–71, 72).

Others took a number of years to make the same discovery. In the 1946 edition of *If This Is a Man,* Levi defends the humanity of the inmate, but not until forty years later can he write, in *The Drowned and the Saved:* "They were made of the same cloth as we, they were average human beings, averagely intelligent, averagely wicked: save the exceptions, they were not monsters, they had our faces" (202). Solzhenitsyn recalls the years when he was an officer of the Red Army and was leading his company across a ravaged Prussia; he remembers the criminal acts he found himself capable of committing. We know now that this self-knowledge is the requisite starting point for moral action; as Solzhenitsyn says, "There is nothing that so aids and assists the awakening of omniscience within us as insistent thoughts about one's own transgressions, errors, mistakes." Thirty years later, after his imprisonment and deportation, he comes to the following conclusion: "Gradually it was disclosed to me," he writes, "that the line separating good and evil passes not through states, nor between classes, nor between political parties either—but right through every human heart—and through all human hearts" (615–16). If the others had been in our place, they would have behaved like us; had we been in theirs, we could have become like them.

In general, we find this truth a very hard one to accept. It is infinitely easier for each of us to believe that the evil lies outside of us, that we have nothing in common with the monsters who perpetrated it. (We respond in much the same way to those particularly monstrous crimes that every now and then seem to capture the attention of the media.) If we prefer to forget Kolyma and Auschwitz, it is because we fear discovering that the evil of the camps is not alien to the human race; this same fear makes us prefer the (rare) story in which good triumphs. Psychoanalysts like Alexander Mitscherlich and Bruno Bettelheim, who have studied the concentration camp experience, are right to insist on this point: these evils are not as foreign to us as we might wish, which is precisely why we refuse to admit the fact and instead gravitate so readily to explanations rooted in the notion of monstrousness.

Let there be no mistake about what this assertion does or does not mean. In no case should we (or could we) infer from it that there is no difference between the guilty and the innocent, between the executioners and the victims. In her writings on the banality of evil, Arendt repeatedly warns us not to interpret this phrase to mean that there is a little Eichmann in each of us and therefore that we are all the same. To do so would be to ignore the distinction, basic to the notion of justice, between the capacity to act and the action itself; it would be to turn a blind eye to degrees of difference of one and the same trait. Primo Levi stresses this point: the fact that the executioners were human like us in no way allows us to conclude—as Liliana Cavani seems to have done in her film *The Night Porter*—that "we are all victims or murderers" (*Drowned* 48). If we draw that conclusion, we obliterate with a single stroke of the pen the guilt of some and the suffering of others and renounce all justice in the name of some caricatured notion of the unconscious. To be sure, perpetrators and victims are not different by nature, but the law punishes only acts that have been committed and nothing else. In this respect, justice differs not only from compassion, whose object is the entire human being, but also and to a greater degree from anthropology, which concerns itself with human dispositions rather than any particular action. Anthropology seeks to understand; the law makes it possible to judge.

Here, we are obviously treading a narrow path with pitfalls on either side; misunderstandings are easy under these circumstances. Much is at stake, however, for we must reject not only Manichaean conceptions of evil but too rigid an application of the principle of the excluded middle. We must try to grasp the whole situation, to articulate two propositions which only *seem* to contradict each other: first, that the crimes are inhuman but the criminals are not and, second, that some ordinary people committed some extraordinary acts.

Philip Hallie studied in detail one of the rare examples of goodness during those dark years, that of André Trocmé and his neighbors, who rescued Jews in the southern French region of the Cévennes. Hallie writes that "there is an unbridgeable difference between those who can torture and destroy children and those who can only save them" (225). Instinctively, one wants him to be right; there is, one hopes, a wide abyss between "them" and "us." Indeed, I take as honest a look at myself as I can, and I believe I can say in all good faith that I could never throw living children into a furnace. Yet this way of putting it seems to me to obscure the issue in two ways: first, by taking only the two extremes of what is really a continuum and, second, by eliminating any consideration of the particular circumstances surrounding the act and of such processes as habituation and inurement. Accounts that attest to the power of these processes speak in near unanimity. Rudolf Vrba—an Auschwitz escapee, a member of the resistance, and a thoroughly admirable human being—describes how it sometimes felt to witness a beating: "I grew used to the sight of these punishments that first day. I began almost to welcome them indeed, for when Koenig and Graff were busy (with the beatings), I could steal, which meant I could survive" (130). Margarete Buber-Neumann makes a similar admission, recalling a visit to the camp infirmary in 1944: "Making my way down corridors filled with the death rattles of dying women, I was obsessed with a single thought— never to see this sight again, never again to hear these cries" (*Ravensbrück* 42). Bettelheim is correct, I feel, when he concludes, "A few screams evoke in us deep anxiety and a desire to help. Hours of screaming without end lead us only to wish that the screamer would shut up" (*Survival* 260).

Let us return to the essentials. Etty Hillesum, one of Eichmann's victims, would never, in any circumstance, have acted as he did, but she is able to understand Eichmann and those like him by looking at herself. Mendel, the Jewish protagonist in Primo Levi's *If Not Now, When?*, is a victim of persecutions, yet when he looks within himself, he says, "Maybe each of us is Cain to some Abel, and slays him in the field without knowing it" (83). And it is in speaking of himself and his fellow prisoners that Levi concludes: "We . . . had the potential to construct an infinite enormity of pain. . . . It is enough not to see, not to listen, not to act" (*Drowned* 86). For evil to come into being, the actions of a few are not sufficient; it is also necessary that the vast majority stand aside, indifferent; of such behavior, as we know well, we are all of us capable.

What have Kolyma and Auschwitz taught us about human nature that we did not know before? Is man fundamentally evil? Is he, as Hobbes would have us believe, a wolf toward his fellowman? Or is he by nature good, as Rousseau insisted? For my part, I do not think we can derive from these experiences any new lessons about the nature of man, neither optimistic theories of progress nor apocalyptic theories of decline. Totalitarianism is incontestably worse than democracy, that much is (now) clear; as for people, they are by nature neither good nor evil, or else they are both at once: selfishness and altruism are equally innate. "Does human nature undergo a true change in the cauldron of totalitarian violence? Does [man] lose his innate yearning for freedom?" Grossman asks (pondering in this instance the alternative of freedom or submission, not that of good or evil). He answers in the negative. "Condemned to slavery," he writes, "man is made a slave by fate, and not by nature" (*Life and Fate* 216). Evil is not accidental; it is always there at hand, ready to manifest itself. All it needs to emerge is for us to do nothing. Nor is good an illusion; it persists, even in the most desperate circumstances. There is no more reason to resign ourselves to cynicism than there is to indulge in naive dreams.

Having familiarized ourselves with what I've called "ordinary virtues," those moral acts that each of us can perform without having to be either a hero or a saint, we now need to envision an opposite array of "ordinary vices," behavioral traits that are equally common to all and that do not necessarily make us exceptional beings—monsters or beasts. Brought to light by the extremity of the totalitarian camps, these traits are very much in evidence in more peaceful circumstances as well. I begin by considering a few that I find particularly striking: the fragmentation of behavior, or the disconnection of conduct from conscience; the depersonalization of beings caught in the chains of instrumentalist thinking; and the enjoyment of power. I have chosen these concepts—perhaps they are really no more than themes for reflection—because they involve only a moderate degree of abstraction. More general than the observable acts to which they refer, they nonetheless do not derive from any unitary psychological, anthropological, or political theory that would reduce all actions to a single cause. Once again, what interests me are the banal sources of exceptional actions, the ordinary attitudes that could make "monsters" of us, too, were we to have to work in a concentration camp.

Fragmentation

S urvivors of Auschwitz as much as latter-day observers repeatedly point to one trait that was common to all the camp guards, even the cruelest ones. That trait is behavioral inconsistency. In the same place, often in the course of the same day or even hour, a person could help one prisoner and, without batting an eyelash, send another to his death. It is not that good and evil had reached some kind of equilibrium—evil had the upper hand, by far—but rather that there was no guard who was wicked through and through. Instead, all the guards seemed subject to constant shifts in attitude and temperament, so much so in fact that there is no better word to describe their behavior than "schizophrenic," even though none of these people, as far as we know, had any specific mental illness. What we have here is the "social schizophrenia" specific to totalitarian regimes. As Primo Levi observes, "Compassion and brutality can coexist in the same individual and in the same moment, despite all logic" (*Drowned* 56).

Let us take as a first example of discontinuity an excerpt from the private diary of Dr. Johann Paul Kremer, a member of the Auschwitz medical corps in 1942. On September 5, Kremer writes, "This noon was present at a special action in the women's camp—the most horrible of all horrors. *Hschf.* [Adjutant] Thilo, military surgeon, is right when he said today to me we were located in 'anus mundi.' In the evening at about 8 p.m. another special action with a draft from Holland." The following day, September 6, Kremer writes: "Today an excellent Sunday dinner: tomato soup, one half of chicken with potatoes and red cabbage (20 grammes of fat), dessert and magnificent vanilla-cream" (214–15). Is it really the same person who one day watches the "most horrible of all horrors," describing it with what would become a famous expression, *anus mundi,* and then, scarcely twenty-four hours later, thinks only of recording what he had for dinner? The juxtaposition is actually even more brutal: when he made his entry of September 6, Kremer surely could not have avoided rereading the previous day's entry just above it. He reread the one, then added the other: a horrific execution, a fine dinner.

One finds similar discontinuities in other characters of sinister reputation. The torturer Wilhelm Boger sometimes helped the Jews who worked under him. Johann Schwarzhuber, who as *Lagerführer* of Birkenau was directly responsible for the death of thousands, one day intervened to save the lives of sixty-eight boys from Terezin who had been marked for the gas chamber. Dr. Frank took special care of the Jews around him but never missed his turn on the incoming railway platform where the selections—that euphemism for on-the-spot death sentences—took place. Even Mengele was capable of giving individual patients the best of care, in between selections. These shifts in mood were not really random occurrences; seemingly chaotic, they nonetheless obeyed certain rules. An inmate whom a guard knew personally, for instance, had greater chances of eliciting his compassion. The inconsistencies in behavior occasionally had an ideological component; some overseers, for example, were accommodating to Russian and Polish prisoners but merciless to Jews. The situation was much the same in all the camps, and even on the outside; in fact, according to Speer, Hitler himself could slip in an instant from intolerance to charity.

Depending on one's point of view, this coexistence of good and evil within the same person can be cause for hope or reason to despair. Even the basest individual has his or her good points; conversely, the presence of good in no way guarantees against the emergence of evil. The most awful thing about informers, Grossman writes, "is the good that is in them; the saddest thing of all is that they are replete with virtues, that they do good deeds. . . . That is what is really awful: the

fact that there is so much good in them, in their human essence"
(*Forever Flowing* 82–83).

To this first form of fragmentation, which manifests itself as an
alternation between benevolence and malice, we can add a second,
more systematic form, a consequence of the fact that two of the "ordinary virtues," caring for others and the life of the mind, do not necessarily coexist. We have already seen the passion so many of the Nazi
guards had for music; yet the same Josef Kramer who wept when he
heard Schumann and who had been a bookseller before becoming
commandant of Birkenau was also capable of crushing a prisoner's
skull with his truncheon because the woman wasn't moving along
quickly enough; at Struthof, his previous assignment, he would push
naked female prisoners into the gas chambers with his own hands and
then watch their death throes from a specially constructed window. "I
had no particular feeling in carrying out these operations," he testified
at his trial (Tillion 209). Why did music make him weep, but not the
deaths of other human beings? The same Maria Mandel who would
hasten from her duties as head guard of Birkenau to hear Alma Rose's
orchestra perform "her" aria from *Madama Butterfly* also personally
ordered, and took part in, beatings—when she wasn't urging doctors
to perform more selections. The deeds of Dr. Mengele, a music lover
who was forever whistling strains from Wagner, are of course notorious. Pery Broad, another guard, played Bach and also tortured prisoners in their barracks. Eichmann played Schumann and organized the
deportation of the Jews. The point is not that music had ceased to be
good; but because of personal fragmentation, this aesthetic activity
did not affect behaviors in any significant way. The small good that is
music was largely outweighed by the vast evil of the circumstances in
which it was produced.

In the Soviet camps, under Stalin, the guards had more literary
inclinations, but a love of Pushkin was no more salutary in its moral
effect than was a fondness for Bach. The massive printings of both
Russian and foreign classics, an act that inspired the admiration of
Western intellectuals and facilitated their approval of Communism, in
no way reduced the population of the gulags; as in Nazi Germany, the
number of prisoners climbed into the millions. Germany, too, was
hardly a country lacking in culture. "In German cities," Borowski

writes, "the store windows are filled with books and religious objects, but the smoke from the crematoria still hovers above the forests" (*This Way* 168). Indeed, people with university educations could be every bit as cruel as the illiterate, so long as the life of the mind was cut off from the rest of life. One can only smile at the naïveté of the Nuremberg prosecutors who found an aggravating circumstance in the fact that the *Einsatzkommandos* were not "uneducated locals incapable of appreciating life's higher values" but persons with advanced degrees—eight attorneys, one university professor, a dentist, and so on. As if a sense of morals were something one learns at universities!

PRIVATE AND PUBLIC

Another form of discontinuity, the split between the private and public, seems to have played the paramount role in totalitarian crimes. Expanding the notion of the enemy to include not only enemy soldiers but also the regime's internal opposition, its adversaries at home, totalitarianism generalizes the state of war and with it the schism characteristic of the warrior psyche. As John Glenn Grey notes, "Men who in private life are scrupulous about conventional justice and right are able to destroy the lives and happiness of others in war without compunction" (172). This separation of public and private could be found in nearly all the guards: they behaved with the utmost brutality toward the inmates while continuing to lead private lives filled with love and concern.

Borowski tells the story of kapo Arno Boehm, who "administered twenty-five lashes of the whip for each minute a prisoner was late or for each word uttered after the evening bell and who also wrote brief but moving letters to his elderly parents in Frankfurt, letters filled with love and longing" (*Monde* 149). When Josef Kramer stood trial, his wife came to testify in his behalf. "Our children were everything to my husband," she said (Langbein 307). *Lagerführer* Schwarzhuber, too, showed great fatherly concern, fastening a name tag around the neck of his six-year-old child so that the little boy would not be thrown into a gas chamber by mistake as he wandered about the grounds of Birkenau. Even the sinister Höss sounds human when, in his last letters, he writes about his children.

As for Maria Mandel, she was not content, as Kramer was, simply to protect Alma Rose's women's orchestra and encourage its activities; she also had a weakness for children—not her own, for she had none, but those of others. One day she discovered two Jewish children whose mother was trying to hide them. She called them into her office, leaving the mother trembling on the doorstep. "Five minutes later they reappeared, each clutching a packet of cake and chocolate. . . . She was capable of a normal, motherly woman's reaction, and of turning herself into a wild beast" (Lingens-Reiner 146). Fania Fénelon recounts an incident that ended less well. Mandel rescued a Polish child from the gas chamber, took him home with her, and showered him with gifts and caresses; for the first time, the inmates saw her laugh. Several days later, however, she strode into the barracks, looking especially grim, and demanded to hear *Madama Butterfly*. The inmates later learned that she'd been ordered not only to give up the child but to deliver him to the gas chamber herself. Fénelon reflects that, most of the time, "her brain, like all German brains, was compartmentalized, made of watertight compartments, like a submarine. One might fill with water, while the others remained dry and untouched" (*Playing* 226). This time the compartment to which she had consigned her private life threatened to spill over into the one belonging to her "professional life"; she had therefore to reestablish the seal between them. Maybe so, but are German brains the only ones to be so constructed? And are all Germans really cast from the same mold?

Personal documents at our disposal—letters, interviews, memoirs —concerning a few individuals who practiced this separation between public and private afford us a close-hand look at how the process worked. One particular case, that of Eduard Wirths, the head doctor at Auschwitz, has been analyzed in detail by Robert Jay Lifton. Wirths, it seems, subscribed to Nazi doctrine and was thus a professed anti-Semite, but before his appointment to Auschwitz, while still a country doctor, he had continued treating Jewish patients, something many of his colleagues refused to do. He performed "medical" experiments on Auschwitz inmates but was known for his personal scruples;

in a world of rampant corruption, he stands out in his refusal to obtain any provisions beyond those to which his ration-book tickets entitled him. In Wirths's mind, his love for his family seemed to make up for the drawbacks of his professional life: "Nothing is impossible, as long as I have you, my beloved," he wrote to his wife. The faster the selections succeeded one another, the more he filled his letters with questions about the children's first teeth and with commentaries on the photographs she had sent him. In his letters one sees a growing relationship between the two sides of his life, as if he were working at Auschwitz only out of love for his children: "It must be done for our children, my angel," he writes, "for our children." Wirths's daughter recalls a loving father; her desire to understand the past takes the form of the following question: "How is it possible for a good man to do bad things?" (Lifton 396, 411).

Gitta Sereny interviewed Franz Stangl, the commandant of Sobibor and Treblinka, while he was in prison. Stangl was a zealous policeman, much more a careerist than a fanatical ideologue, who came to the concentration camps after working in the euthanasia "institutes." He, too, was a man who adored his wife. During their early separations, he wrote to her every day; later, he transferred this attachment to his children. In his lengthy conversations with Sereny, he himself explains his life at the time in terms of a fragmentation that recalls Fénelon's image of the submarine. "The only way I could live," Stangl says, "was by compartmentalizing my thinking." Burning corpses is not a pleasant pastime; he therefore latched on to the idea that he himself wasn't lighting the fires but only supervising construction projects or arranging the transfer to Berlin of the gold found on the victims. "There were hundreds of ways to take one's mind off it [the liquidations]. I used them all. . . . I made myself concentrate on work, work, and again work" (Sereny 164, 200).

Stangl sought to convince his family and himself that his work was more compartmentalized than it really was, that one could be involved with the arrival of the trains but not with the fate of their passengers, with the construction of buildings but not with what went on inside them. "I see it," he told his wife, "but I don't *do* anything to anybody" (136). Eventually Frau Stangl learned the truth. She was shocked. (For the next several days, she refused to have sex with him!)

In the end, however, she resigned herself; after all, he was a very good husband. Much later, when Stangl was in prison, his middle daughter, Renate, told Sereny, "He was my father. He understood me. He stuck to me through thick and thin, and he saved me when I thought my life was in ruins. 'Remember, remember always,' he once said to me, 'if you need help, I'll go to the ends of the earth for you.' . . . I, too, would go to the ends of the earth for him. . . . I love him. I'll always love him" (350). How strange that Stangl's words, as reported by his daughter, are so like those lived but unspoken by Pola Lifszyc, who truly did go to the ends of the earth for her mother. For Pola Lifszyc, the ends of the earth was a place called Treblinka, and Stangl was its master. He presided over the executions of Pola and her mother. If circumstances had so ordered, would he have jumped aboard the cattle car to be with his daughter, to suffer the same fate as she? Who can say?

Some people tend to question the authenticity of such familial devotion. Others brush it aside in the belief that it has nothing to do with the crimes of which men like Wirths or Stangl were accused. Being a good husband and father, they argue, justifies nothing and explains nothing. I, for my part, am convinced that such testimonials are true and that they are indispensable to our understanding of the personalities of the guards. My impression is that these individuals needed to fragment their lives in this way so that no spontaneous feelings of pity might hinder them in their "work" and also so that their admirable private lives might serve as a counterweight, at least in their own minds, for the things that may have troubled them about their professional activities.

That an individual might be virtuous in private life does not mean that his or her public activities or the doctrines he or she professes will necessarily benefit from that virtue. Vasily Grossman makes this point about Lenin, founder of the Soviet gulag system. In a way, Stalin is a handier adversary: his personal brutality is consistent with his policy of extermination; Lenin's personality, on the other hand, is much more seductive. "In his personal and private relations," Grossman writes, "Lenin invariably showed sensitivity, delicacy, gentleness, courtesy. . . . Lenin in whom the thirst for power burned and who was capable of everything and anything in his struggle to seize it, was extremely modest personally, and he did not seek for himself the power he won" (*Forever* 202–4). Exemplary traits like these make it tempting to excuse the system because of the individual: can a man so honest, someone who doesn't care about getting rich (Wirths, living solely off his ration book), who is so attentive in his personal relationships (Stangl with his family)—can such a sincere idealist really bring about so much evil?

The answer is, obviously, yes. It was this same Lenin who also developed the concept of the internal enemy, organized massive repression, fulminated against pity and sympathy. "The man in the arena of world affairs," Grossman writes, "turns out to be the exact opposite of the man in his personal life. Plus and minus, minus and plus" (204). Lenin's internal fragmentation was every bit as complete as Stangl's. And since Lenin was a successful politician whose public personality touched infinitely more people than his private behavior did, the former has to count for more than the latter in our overall assessment of him. His intellect, his modest tastes, his ascetic lifestyle neither influenced nor justified his political acts, but they may perhaps have helped him convince himself—as his admirers tried to convince themselves much later—of the rightness of his ideas.

Another form of disconnection between convictions and actions is exemplified by the Pharisee whose conduct belies the lofty principles he claims to espouse. This division, in which moralism replaces true moral action and stands in its way, can be found in many intellectuals who preach generosity and tolerance but who, we sometimes later learn, are irascible and self-serving in their personal lives. Whereas in the camps, people professing vicious doctrines might act with virtue, here the opposite is true: the doctrine professed is virtuous, but the person who professes it is not. We are to do as he says, not as he does. In his eyes at least, the visible surface is supposed to compensate for the imperfections of the hidden core: I beat my wife at home, but outside I strike blows against American imperialism. This particular pattern of fragmentation, of course, was not altogether unknown in the camps: Henry Bulawko remembers how Moshe, the leader of his work unit, always kept a club within easy reach. "He was a pious man," Bulawko says. "He said his prayers three times a day—and every day, he beat us" (Langbein 171). The *Einsatzkommando* operating in the region of Simferopol, inside Russia, was ordered to kill three thousand Jews and Gypsies before Christmas. The order was carried out with exceptional speed so that the troops could attend the celebration of Christ's birth; Otto Ohlendorf, the group's leader, delivered an emotional sermon to his men that Christmas Eve.

Basically, for those with cause for self-reproach, it matters little if it is the public or the private sphere where the harm was done. What counts is that there are two spheres and that one of them—the one they take to define their essential being—can, from their point of view above all, make up for the other. In *Eichmann in Jerusalem,* Hannah Arendt comments on the attempts of various Nazi officials to use this notion of a divided self to defend themselves. "The sinister Dr. Otto Bradfisch," she writes, "former member of one of the *Einsatzgruppen,* who presided over the killing of at least fifteen thousand people, told a German court that he had always been 'inwardly opposed' to what he was doing," while a former *Gauleiter* argued that "only his 'official soul' had carried out the crimes for which he was hanged in 1946, his 'private soul' had always been against them" (127). There is no question of accepting these arguments as the excuses they were intended to be, yet the fact that they are offered as such permits us to understand how ordinary people can become murderers and how people living under totalitarian regimes can submit, as they inevitably do, to the external order and still preserve a little of their self-respect.

CAUSES AND EFFECTS

Because far more attention has been paid to the Nazi camps than to the Communist gulags, there has been a tendency to explain the fragmentation in the guards' behavior in terms of a German national character or of German history. The Germans, by these accounts, are a people who value only intimacy and the inner self and are indifferent to public acts and behavior. It has been this way, the story goes, at least since Luther, who, as the founder of Protestantism, proclaimed the separation of religious and secular life and sought to concern himself only with the former. Faith alone counted; actions did not. As

we've seen, Fania Fénelon thought all Germans had compartmentalized brains; Alma Rose, a German, reproached her for having the
opposite defect: "You French are so irresponsible," she said, "you
seem to forget that there's a time for everything; you confuse work
and play, you mix everything up!" (*Playing* 116).

Despite their penchant for "mixing everything up," we know today
that during the war the French proved themselves quite able to separate their sense of family responsibility from their indifference to the
Jewish children who were being deported to Auschwitz. We also know
that the German character does not explain the atrocities committed
in the Communist camps and that, whatever the supposed defects of
this national character, concentration camps existed in Germany only
under its two totalitarian regimes, the National Socialist and the Communist.

The fact that the concentration camp, unlike the penal colony, is a
uniquely twentieth-century institution might prompt us to inquire
whether fundamental traits like fragmentation are not somehow
linked to other aspects of modern society. It is tempting to make a
connection between this fragmented mentality and the ever-growing
specialization that has invaded not only the world of work but also
that of interpersonal relations. Of course, division of labor has existed
since neolithic times and was stigmatized well before Karl Marx;
nonetheless, the growing complexity of workplace tasks during this
century has increased the need for labor specialization enormously.
Who can pretend not only to have mastered the techniques particular
to his or her line of work but also to grasp all the implications or
consequences of it? Might not the division of individual lives into
watertight compartments be an understandable response to the progressive compartmentalization of the world at large?

(*This attitude, I've noticed with some surprise, has its supporters these
days. The disclosure of Heidegger's Nazi involvement has prompted
some of his disciples and admirers to seek excuses for him, the most
convenient of which is to say that the philosopher who was a genius
and the man who was a Nazi need have nothing in common. One
apologist, on the other hand, sees unity where others have found rup-
ture and goes so far as to say that Heidegger's mistake was precisely*

his desire to establish continuity between his philosophy and his life. Hitler made the same mistake. One must always act the good citizen; as long as one doesn't seek to put them into practice, one can profess whatever views one likes. As if the world were not sufficiently compartmentalized already and we had to struggle to put up still more walls!)

The splintering apart of the world—with its corollary of professionalism and the psychological fragmentation that results—is especially characteristic of totalitarian countries; what was originally a feature of industrial production becomes a model for the functioning of society as a whole. First separation: the party or state takes charge of all social goals, and thus of the definition of good and evil. The subjects are to concern themselves only with the means—in other words, everyone with his or her own area of expertise. As Albert Speer remarks, "The ordinary party member was being taught that grand policy was much too complex for him to judge it. Consequently, one felt one was being represented, never called upon to take personal responsibility" (33). Second separation: each profession sets itself apart from the others. Once again, in Speer's words, "Worse still was the restriction of responsibility to one's own field. That was explicitly demanded. Everyone kept to his own group—of architects, physicians, jurists, technicians, soldiers, or farmers. . . . The longer Hitler's system lasted, the more people's minds moved within such isolated chambers" (33).

Separation suited Speer just fine on days when he found his Nazi commitment flagging: "I felt myself to be Hitler's architect. Political events did not concern me. . . . I felt that there was no need for me to take any political positions at all. Nazi education, furthermore, aimed at separatist thinking; I was expected to confine myself to the job of building." Later, when Speer became minister of armaments, he maintained this point of view, even though his work had changed. "The task I have to fulfill is an unpolitical one," he said in 1944 (112). Finally, in February 1945, he began to see that he had to take some interest in matters beyond his own specialty. "Something must be done, you know," he told Grand Admiral Karl Dönitz, in the course of a meeting. To which Dönitz tersely replied, "I am here only to represent the navy. The rest is none of my business. The Führer must know what he is doing" (426). It was up to the Führer to decide on objectives, and for everyone else to mind his or her own area of expertise. This is the totalitarian subject's standard way of thinking.

The most thoroughgoing product of this system, however, is not Speer or Dönitz but Adolf Eichmann. In reading the transcript of his questioning by Captain Avner Less, one is struck by the fact that, even in 1961, Eichmann's attention is focused not on the horrendous acts of which he stands accused but on the possibility that his accusers may be running roughshod over the neat delineation of responsibilities among the various divisions of the Third Reich. To his mind, the separations were watertight and remained so. His department was responsible only for organizing transfers of peoples, for finding trains and selecting stations, a limited and specific task as far as he is concerned. "The only matters we dealt with in IV B 4 [Eichmann's department] were purely technical" (*Eichmann* 136). Any thoughts about ultimate ends were brushed aside; the question was purely one of means, and even then, only those means relevant to one segment of the process. "As for who was going to the gas chambers and who wasn't, or if it was time to begin or not, or if we were supposed to stop or speed up, . . . I had nothing to do with any of that" (112). Each time that Less offers up a hideous fact for his consideration, Eichmann fails to react to the basic issue, taking up only the question of which department had responsibilities in a given domain. The sterilizations? No, that wasn't us. It was another department. Whoever says it was us is completely unreliable. The extermination of the racially mixed? Same thing. On a completely different floor, a colossal mess! The only thing that concerned him at the time, Eichmann says, was "avoiding conflicts with other departments about assignments and responsibilities" (221).

Both in the course of his interrogation and during the trial itself, the prosecution sought to establish that Eichmann had personally participated in this or that particular killing. He defended himself fiercely: "I had nothing to do with the execution of the Jews!" he argued. "I never killed a single one. . . . I never killed anyone and I never gave the order to kill anyone" (339–40). Höss made similar protestations. "I never mistreated an inmate," he claimed, "and I never killed a single one with my own hands" (Höss 251). Stangl, too, when he speaks of his work at the euthanasia "institute," insists that he was never "involved . . . in the operational sense" (Sereny 57); he also claims never to have killed anyone at Sobibor. This response, repeated again and again by so many of the accused, excuses nothing; it does, however, explain a great deal. There is little sense in wanting to prove that Eichmann, Höss, and Stangl tortured and killed like any common killer, with their own hands as it were, when in fact they participated in the murder of millions. But they each did so by concerning themselves with only one small link in a vast chain and by seeing their task as a purely technical problem.

Compartmentalization and the bureaucratic specialization to which it gives rise are at the root of this absence of feelings of responsibility one finds in those who carried out the "final solution," as well as in every other agent of the totalitarian state. At one end of the chain there are people like Reinhardt Heydrich: his sleep is never disturbed by the millions of deaths that took place on his orders. He never sees a single suffering face; all he does is manipulate large and odorless numbers. Then comes the policeman, a Frenchman, let's say. His carefully circumscribed job is to ferret out Jewish children and take them to a camp where they are turned over to German personnel. This policeman does not kill anyone; he merely carries out a routine order to arrest and expedite. Now Eichmann enters the picture, his purely technical job consisting of making sure that a certain train leaves Drancy on the fifteenth and arrives at Auschwitz on the twenty-second. Just where is the crime in that? And then we have Höss, who gives the orders to empty the trains and lead the children toward the gas chambers. And finally, the last link: a group of inmates, a special commando that pushes the victims into the gas chambers and releases the lethal gas. The members of this commando are the only people who kill with their own hands—although they quite obviously are victims themselves, not executioners.

No element in this chain (which is actually much longer) feels responsible for what has been accomplished; the compartmentalization of the work has suspended considerations of conscience. Only at either end of the chain is the situation slightly different. Someone has to make the initial decision, of course, but that takes only one person, a Hitler or a Stalin, and the fate of millions veers into the macabre.

That person, moreover, never deals with the actual corpses. And at the other end of the chain, there must be someone to deliver the final blow, someone who will know no peace of mind until the day he dies (a day that, at all events, is not far off) but who nevertheless is not really guilty of anything. Those who made all this possible—Speer, Eichmann, Höss, and all the countless other intermediaries, the police, the bureaucrats, the railway employees, the manufacturers of the deadly gas, the suppliers of barbed wire, the builders of the high-performance crematoriums—can always shift their responsibility onto the next link in the chain. We can tell them that they were wrong, that even in a totalitarian state the individual remains responsible for his or her actions or failure to act; still, we have before us an entirely new kind of responsibility that cannot be considered the same as that of the ordinary criminal. The nonrecognition of this responsibility by the perpetrators of totalitarian crime and their consequent dismissal of the moral problem make it easier for such crimes to be committed.

It would be hypocritical, however, to see the effects of compartmentalized labor as peculiar to the totalitarian state when in fact all of us are well acquainted with them, regardless of where we live. Today we can shake an accusatory finger at the workers in the German factories that produced Zyklon B, but, as George M. Kren and Leon Rappoport ask, "Would workers in the chemical plants that produced napalm accept responsibility for burned babies?" (141). And why mention only the most spectacular methods of extermination? Are other weapons any different? Can anyone who manufactures explosives or cannons or missiles possibly imagine that they will never be used to kill people? And how can one know if they'll be used against "innocent" civilians or "guilty" soldiers—guilty, that is, of belonging to the enemy nation?

(I open today's newspaper; on page 12 there is an article about Bourges, a city I happen to know a bit. "The economic engine behind Bourges's growth is the military," the article says. "The factories of this industrial complex, all dedicated to the manufacture of ground weaponry (heavy cannon), employ some 2,000 highly skilled workers and . . . keep an extensive network of subcontractors busy as well. The bottom line? Bourges is proud of its low unemployment rate of 7 *percent"* (Le Monde, *29–30 April 1990). Here, then, is something elected office holders of every stripe, Communists, democrats, and nationalists, can agree on: Let us make even more weapons, they shout in a single voice. But who will buy these arms? Against whom will they be used? That's not the politicians' problem. Bourges is proud. . . . Why think about burned babies?*)

The effects of internal fragmentation are no less widespread. Soldiers in the field who are bent on killing can be wonderful family men at home; inside them are two noncommunicating compartments, one for war, another for peace. This dissociation is not solely an effect of war; it has often been pointed out that the same American soldiers who landed in Europe and were so horrified by the anti-Semitism of the Nazis practiced racial segregation at home. And the French, who claimed their inspiration in the principles of the Revolution, liberty and equality, imposed regimes on their colonies that allowed the subject populations neither.

In a totalitarian system, social schizophrenia—the division of life into impermeable compartments—is a defense mechanism for anyone with some moral principles left to preserve. I may act passively and ignobly in this or that fragment of my life, but in the others, the ones I deem essential, I remain a respectable person. Without this division, I could not function normally. Like the fever that accompanies an illness, fragmentation itself is not the evil but my defense against it. Yet fragmentation makes evil possible, even easy, and it is for this reason that fragmentation is an "ordinary vice." Robert Jay Lifton, who in his book on Nazi doctors devotes a great deal of attention to this subject, refers to it as a "doubling" of the self (even though there are often more than two compartments). He describes the countless means by which the compromised individual manages to maintain a positive self-image: by agreeing to do one thing but not another, by isolating the private from the public, by trying to make up for public vice with private virtue.

The Nazi doctors were not alone in manifesting this kind of behavior; one finds it among all professionals who fail to apply the same ethical standards in their work as they do at other times and who, as specialists, accept the unacceptable by reassuring themselves that in their "other" life, their "real" life, they behave with dignity and honor. The physicist who helps make nuclear weapons convinces himself that what he's doing isn't bad, because he also happens to be a good citizen and model husband. He believes in unity where it does not exist, where instead there is a fragmentation he fails to recognize. When we choose to ignore the horrors of the totalitarian world as we do today, when we imagine that the monsters responsible for those horrors are not like us at all, we are again trying to defend ourselves by fracturing the world into hermetically sealed compartments. All, or almost all, of us prefer comfort to truth.

A certain measure of fragmentation is indispensable to the individual's psychological survival. We all know the limits of our actions and that we cannot rearrange the world to conform to our desires. We make certain matters our priority and neglect others. I may feel implicated in the world's misfortunes, but I do little about them. I don't even help all the street beggars I encounter between my house and the entrance to the metro; they are not a priority for me. How, then, to recognize the boundary beyond which fragmentation becomes censurable, even criminal? One way is to consider the context; in the fight against poverty, for example, giving alms is not the most effective weapon. Another way is to take into account the degree of evil I refuse to see; torture and death do not belong to the same category of evils as—to take examples from daily life—the problems caused by the pervasiveness of advertising or by the general decline in the quality of culture.

Inside the camps, the inmates saw the harm that fragmentation could do and promised themselves that if ever they were freed they would shun it in their own lives. "What a purposeful, humane life we would create for ourselves," Eugenia Ginzburg remembers, "matching our deeds to our ideas" (*Within* 68–69). Milena Jesenska wanted much the same thing: "She was deeply repelled by the discrepancy between words and actions" (Buber-Neumann, *Milena* 172). Dr. Frankl, during his imprisonment, heard the call to *"live* my thoughts instead of merely putting them on paper" (183). These decisions, all of which begin with a condemnation of fragmentation, raise, however, a problem we've already encountered in relation to dignity, which is that consistency between idea and action or between the private and the public is not necessarily good. The consistent Nazi is not better than the one who occasionally strays from his path and does something commendable. Dr. Frankl's decision pleases me only because I agree with his ideas. Alone in his prison cell, Hitler might have one day made the same decision, but that hardly delights me. A little more fragmentation, some additional moments of good will like those Speer remembers wouldn't have been a bad thing. Here, too, our judgment ultimately depends on the content of the acts carried out and of the ideas expressed. Fragmentation is an ordinary vice that can greatly facilitate the advent of evil but also temper its effects to some small degree; in and of itself, however, fragmentation is not an evil.

Depersonalization

THE DEHUMANIZATION OF THE VICTIMS

Totalitarian ideology sees the individual as an instrument, as a means by which to realize a political or even a cosmic project. Hitler spoke determinedly of "the nothingness and insignificance of the individual human being and of his continued existence in the visible immortality of the nation" (Rauschning 222–23), while Himmler demanded of each member of the SS "the total sacrifice of his personality to the accomplishment of his duty to the nation and to the fatherland" (Höss 95)—all the more reason, I suppose, for the SS to be willing to sacrifice the lives of others to the great cause. One can find equivalent statements in the writings of Lenin and Stalin, the word *Communism* replacing *nation*. Totalitarian doctrines can thus properly be called antihumanist. Humanistic philosophy, as I take that term to mean, considers the individual an ultimate end. This is the practical moral imperative of that other German, Immanuel Kant: "Act so that humanity, both in your own person and that of others, be used as an end in itself, and never as a mere means" (*Metaphysics* 42) The philosophy of humanism recognizes that at times individuals must inevitably be treated as a means; it insists, however, that they not be considered solely that.

Here is one of those rare points on which totalitarian practice conforms with the theory: the human being is in fact taken to be a means; he is therefore no longer a genuine "person" (who by definition, at least in the Kantian sense, is an end in himself). Bettelheim maintains that "the goal of the system was depersonalization" (*Heart* 39). In fact, it was not. Depersonalization was more a means of transforming individuals into the components of a project that transcended them. What is true, however, is that depersonalization is ubiquitous under totalitarianism, and nowhere did it triumph more completely than in the camps. Far more than any sadistic or primitive instincts, it is depersonalization, of the other and of oneself, that is responsible for totalitarian evil.

In its normal operations, the totalitarian system reduces individuals to their functions, but at least these functions tend to be multiple. The camp, once again, is a mirror of the world around it, magnifying what it reflects. Only one function is recognized there, and that is work; moreover, because the camps have access to an endless supply of labor, it becomes unnecessary for those in charge to worry about the upkeep of this instrument and thus about the preservation of human lives. In the totalitarian world beyond the concentration camp walls, individuals, even if not valued as persons, are still treated as human beings, because it is when treated as such that they best fulfill their task. Inside the camp, however, they are no longer truly considered part of the human race. Even before she was sent to her camp, Eugenia Ginzburg was told by one of the examining magistrates, "Enemies are not people. We're allowed to do what we like with them. People indeed!" (*Journey* 63). To be classified as an enemy is enough to be excluded from humanity. Once Ginzburg arrived at her Siberian destination, she found this attitude to be common currency. As she says in her description of the director of the penal *sovkhoze* at Elgen, "He derived no satisfaction from our sufferings. He was simply oblivious to them because in the most sincere way imaginable, he did not regard us as human. Wastage among the convict work force was to him no more than a routine malfunction" (*Within* 71). Conversely, the way to get better treatment from the guards was to establish a personal relationship with one of them, in other words, to have oneself recognized as an individual. Knowing how to speak the same language as the guards proved indispensable for that reason: deprived of speech, the individual loses a large part of his or her humanity.

Turning people into nonpersons, into animate but not human be-

ings, is not always easy, whatever one's ideological principles. Faced
with a concrete individual, guards can find it hard to overcome their
own resistance to this process. And so various techniques of depersonalization are put into action, aimed at helping the guard forget the
prisoner's humanity. Here are a few of these techniques.

There is, to begin with, the transformation imposed on the victims.
Before being killed, they are stripped naked. Human beings tend not
to congregate naked, they do not move about from place to place
naked; to deprive them of their clothing is to make them like animals.
Guards have testified that it became impossible for them to identify
with their victims once those people became a mass of nude bodies:
clothes are a mark of humanity. The same effect was achieved by
forcing the camp inmates to live in their own filth or by subjecting
them to a starvation diet that turned them into scavengers, ready to
swallow just about anything they found. "They were no longer men,"
Höss said of the Russian prisoners of war. "They'd turned into beasts
who thought only about eating" (160). Of course, Höss neglected to
add that he was the person responsible for this change. All these
means had the same end, which was not lost on the guards. "Why,"
Gitta Sereny asked Stangl, "if they were going to kill them anyway,
what was the point of all the humiliation, why the cruelty?" Stangl
replied, "To condition those who actually had to carry out the policies.
To make it possible for them to do what they did" (Sereny 101). It was
thus a two-stage operation: one first induced "animal-like" behavior;
one could then, with a clear conscience, treat these people like animals or worse.

There are other techniques, less brutal but no less effective. Each
inmate is stripped of his name, that cardinal sign of human individuality, and given a number. When speaking of their prisoners, the guards
avoid using words like *people* or *individuals* or *men*, referring to them
instead as "pieces" or "items" or employing other impersonal turns of
phrase. More than thirty years after the fact, Sereny finds Stangl still
using language of this sort: "They were well ahead with the work up
there," he says, referring to a mass execution and the disposal of the
corpses (170). Two grave diggers from Vilno recall that "the Germans
even forbade us to use the words 'corpse' or 'victim.' The dead were
blocks of wood, shit, with absolutely no importance" (Lanzmann 13).

A secret memorandum, dated June 5, 1942, concerning modifications to be made to the trucks that would serve as mobile gas chambers at Chelmno is particularly chilling. The human beings marked for death are always referred to as "the cargo" or "the items," or they are not called anything at all, as in "ninety-seven thousand have been dealt with" (Kogon et al. iii–iv).

Large numbers in themselves produce the same effect: killing two people is in a sense harder than killing two thousand. "I rarely saw them as individuals," Stangl declares. "It was always just a huge mass" (Sereny 201). All of us tend to react this way. When deaths are announced in the thousands, the sheer number depersonalizes the victims and as a result desensitizes us to their fate. One death is a cause for sorrow; a million deaths is a news item. And the incorporation of individuals into a more abstract category works the same way: it is easier to dispense inhumane treatment to "enemies of the people" or to "kulaks" than to Ivan or Masha; to Jews or Poles than to Mordechai or Tadeusz. Reducing the individual to a category is inevitable when one wants to study human beings; when one is interacting with them, however, the practice is dangerous. A category can never stand before me in the flesh; only a person can.

It was for just this reason that all possible measures were taken in the concentration camps to ensure that face-to-face encounters did not occur, to prevent the executioner from meeting his victims' gaze. Only an individual can look at us (and when I look at a stranger, I try to make sure he doesn't notice me doing so); by avoiding his gaze, we can all the more easily ignore him as a person. In recognizing the other, even the most hardened individual risks moments of weakness. "One day," Eichmann remembers, "Höss told me that Himmler had come and looked over everything very carefully . . . and that apparently he had lost his nerve" (117). Eichmann himself made much of his own inability to look death in the face, to see the figures and the graphs transformed into twisted human corpses. He visited Chelmno, where victims were gassed in trucks: "I didn't stay to watch the whole maneuver. I couldn't stand the screams; I was far too anxious. . . . I fled. I jumped into the car and for a long time I couldn't open my mouth" (111). He attended a mass execution in Minsk: "I saw a woman throw her arms out behind her," he says. "My knees turned to water. . . . I had to leave" (115). He went to Auschwitz: "I preferred not to watch the way they asphyxiated people. . . . They burned the corpses on a gigantic iron grill. . . . I couldn't stand it; I was overcome with nausea" (152). And then to Treblinka: "I stood off to one side; I would have liked not to see anything at all" (153). He ordered a group of Hungarian Jews on a forced march to Vienna: "I didn't see them myself; on principle, I refused to watch these oppressive sights unless formally ordered to do so" (326).

The gas chamber was invented to avoid this kind of "human" reaction, to which even Himmler and Eichmann were not immune, and to keep the members of the *Einsatzkommandos,* who shot prisoners by the thousands, from losing their minds. Once the machine had replaced the man, the executioner could avoid all contact with the victim. This is the way Himmler justified the gas chambers to Höss; there were too many people to kill simply by shooting them, he said, and "if we take the women and children into account, this method would be too painful for the SS" (Höss 263). On the technical level, the same is true of all modern warfare: wherever actual contact is eliminated, efficiency (the rate of fatalities among the enemy) rises. Psychologically, it is easier to kill ten thousand people by dropping a bomb from a plane than to shoot a single child at point-blank range. Furthermore, we tend to criminalize the second more than the first. "The person who launches a bomb by pushing a button," Erich Kahler writes, "or the general or statesman who directs the slaughter from afar, faces only targets and numbers, and must, by necessity, lose the ability to value and distinguish human beings" (70). Robert Jay Lifton has found a significant correlation between altitude and attitude: during the Vietnam War, pilots who flew bombers at high altitudes had clear consciences, while those who fired from helicopters experienced remorse and anguish (494–95). The risk in getting to know an enemy soldier is that he may cease to be an enemy.

Yet the gaze of the other cannot always be avoided; therefore depersonalization ultimately depends on the torturer's having a schema that allows him to maintain an acceptable self-image in his interactions with his victims. This schema was transmitted through ideological indoctrination, which in Germany took the form of a "cult of toughness," the systematic denigration of all feelings of sympathy or pity. This cult preceded Nazism; it is part of what Alice Miller calls "the black pedagogy" (a tradition that, among other things, expected fathers to beat their sons in order to make men of them). It found its way into Prussian military training as well, in the form of the *Drill,* which imposed exhausting exercises and forced marches with heavy packs, all in the name of a doctrine that held that each additional suffering improved the sufferer and was therefore reason for pride rather than complaint. Nazism appropriated these traditions and systematized them. The "tough" training received by the SS men guaranteed that no spontaneous feeling of pity would taint the treatment to which they would later subject their prisoners. A circular from Hitler's chancellery concerning deportations says, "It is the nature of things that these, in some respects, very difficult problems can be solved in the interests of the permanent security of our people only with *ruthless toughness—rücksichtsloser Härte*" (Arendt, *Eichmann* 161). Thus, the SS tended to recruit candidates who seemed the most hard-hearted, and those who aspired to the SS counted on a little of its ruthlessness to rub off on them; they felt that simply by belonging to the SS, they would be perceived as tougher and more virile. Those who belonged to the Cheka, the predecessor of the KGB, felt similarly. Needless to say, this kind of toughness did not imply physical endurance or personal courage (during wartime, prison camp guards were derided by "real" soldiers for being goldbrickers); it merely meant insensitivity to the suffering of others.

Hitler himself spoke contemptuously of pity, that onerous holdover of Christian ethics. "It's just bad luck that we don't have the right religion," Speer recalls him saying. "Why didn't we have the religion of the Japanese, who regard sacrifice for the Fatherland as the highest good? The Mohammedan religion too would have been much more compatible to us than Christianity. Why did it have to be Christianity, with its weakness and flabbiness?" (96). Other religions were preferable to Christianity precisely because they did not place as much value on compassion, on sympathy for the weak. Hitler, moreover, carefully avoided personal attachments; the only one Speer knew him to have was to his dog; indeed, before committing suicide, Hitler killed the dog, thus conferring on his pet the highest possible distinction. The fact that this cult of toughness is both a caricature of masculinity and the antithesis of the ordinary virtues may explain the systematic deprecation of women in Nazi discourse. Thus, during the Nuremberg trials, Göring scorns the humanitarian values as "womanly" (Gilbert, *Nuremberg* 216) and holds heroism to be a strictly masculine affair; the role of women here, if any, is to admire the heroes and reward them with feminine favors for their great deeds (a role in keeping with tradition). Hitler himself was neither attracted to the world of ordinary everyday life nor particularly concerned with the valorization of feminine virtues. "A highly intelligent man should take a primitive and stupid woman. . . . I could never marry. Think of the problems if I had children!" (Speer 92).

Eicke, who was responsible for the actual setting up of the camps, was steadfast in his contempt for those who failed to live up to his harsh ideal: "To perform an act of charity toward an 'enemy of the state' would be a weakness that he would instantly turn to his advantage. Pity for these men would be unworthy of an SS man; in our ranks there is no room for 'softies'; they are better off entering a monastery. We need men who are tough and committed." (Eicke imagined monks to be as fanatical as Nazis but more prone to pity.) "An SS man," he says on another occasion, "must be capable of annihilating even his closest family if they rebel against the state or the ideas of Adolf Hitler" (Höss 71, 100). In the Soviet Union, it is the Young Pioneer Pavlik Morozov who incarnated toughness. Having denounced his parents, he was killed in retaliation by "enemies of the state" and was accorded the status of martyr, a posthumous example for all Soviet children. The lesson is simple: if one's parents do not agree with the ideas of the leader, they are to be denounced. And in yet another speech, Eicke recommends that the SS men rid themselves of "those old bourgeois notions that Hitler's revolution has rendered obsolete. They are symptoms of a weakness and a sentimentality unworthy of an SS führer" (101–2). We know that most of the SS took that counsel to heart and allowed no unseemly pity to hinder the systematic depersonalization of the prisoners. After all, a regime cannot cultivate both pity and torture at the same time. If these men felt any pity at all, it was for themselves, for having to be so tough with the inmates. Sometimes, like Eichmann, they might become "anxious," although their "anxieties" never seemed to keep them from fulfilling their duty.

The cult of toughness—or of virility, as it is also sometimes called—is obviously not the exclusive province of the camp guards, although they did take the ideal to its extreme. We, too, know how to depersonalize those close to us. Our methods are infinitely less spectacular, however; sometimes an offhand word or a thoughtless glance suffices.

THE SUBMISSION OF THE GUARDS

The inmates were not the only ones to undergo the process of depersonalization. In the totalitarian system, and especially in the camps, the guards tended toward this same condition, although they reached it by a different route. The goal of the system was to transform everyone into a cog in a vast machine and thus to deprive them of their will. The guards attest to this transformation in claiming that they were only following orders, that it was their duty to obey. They fail to realize that submission of this sort implies their own depersonalization: they have ceased to see themselves as an end and have agreed to be merely a means.

When the system collapses, the former guards typically fall back on the principle of obedience as their excuse. "We were only following orders," they exclaim, assuming that this formula is sufficient to lift the burden of responsibility from their shoulders. Their accusers, of course, try to prove that this defense is a sham, that the guards acted on their own initiative, in which case their fault would indeed be all the greater. Certain exceptions notwithstanding, it is clear that the demand for blind obedience, the need to have each person see himself as a mere cog in a machine, is highly characteristic of the totalitarian system. Even if the words "I was only following orders" do not always do justice to the actual facts, they correctly evoke the mind of the totalitarian subject. Rather than reject such statements, we must preserve them as a precious admission of a certain truth. The argument that the guards were only doing what they were told they must do may lessen their responsibility in the eyes of the law, but it also reveals the enormity of their moral transformation. Someone who only follows orders is no longer a person. The originality of totalitarian crime resides precisely in this possibility.

Submission is presented first as an obligation. Eicke says of the true SS man that he "must consider every order sacred and execute it without hesitation, however painful it may appear to be" (Höss 95). Echoing the SS motto "Führer, Command and We Shall Obey," Eicke's letterhead bears the following inscription: "One thing counts: the order given" (100–101, 196). These were not mere words. Obedience, however, is not simply accepted; it is sought out and actively assumed. To submit to laws and commands is to fulfill one's duty; one therefore has reason to be proud and can even feel especially virtuous. To comply with the demands of the state, that is, with the supreme demands, allows one a clear conscience. That is why Eichmann could claim that he acted according to moral principles, that he simply did his duty. As Hannah Arendt points out, however, that claim becomes possible only after one has supplanted Kant's categorical imperative—that one must act as if the maxim from which one acts were to become through one's will a universal law of nature—with Hans Frank's reformulation. "Act in such a way," says Frank, the Nazi governor-general of Poland, "that if the Führer knew of your action he would approve of it" (Frank 15–16). Here, the form (to do one's duty) remains, but the content has changed. In place of universal maxims we have the will of a single individual. *"Führerworte haben Gesetzkraft,"* the leader's words have the force of law; this is Eichmann's principle and that of every other obedient citizen as well.

The principle of submission is not confined to behaviors; it concerns beliefs as well. This is to be expected in the camps, where the absence of any autonomy was a given. Elsewhere in the totalitarian state, however, subservience of mind comes as more of a surprise because it concerns the beliefs of an entire population. (Note, however, that outside the camps the distinction between guard and inmate is no longer as clear; each and everyone is both guard and inmate at the same time, if only to a small degree, submitting to the system and imposing it on others.) Surprising or not, in the 1930s, when accusations rained down upon the heads of ordinary Soviet citizens, neighbors discovered that people they thought had led irreproachable lives were in fact perfidious enemies. Did they really believe such things? *"Pravda* said so," Eugenia Ginzburg recounts, "and it must therefore be true" (*Journey* 5). The fact of being arrested is proof of guilt; indeed, the accused is punished before it has been established that any crime has been committed. Better yet, the punishment obviates the need for the crime. In some cases, spouses stop trusting each other; when one is accused, the other believes the testimony of the accuser rather than the evidence of his or her own senses. Ginzburg tells the sad story of an elderly Communist who refused to defend her husband after he had been declared an enemy of the party and who, despite her own sufferings, wrote Stalin a letter "full of love and devotion" (19); later the woman committed suicide. Ginzburg's own husband reacted in a similar way: he did not want the calamities that befell his wife to compromise his confidence in the party.

In the literature devoted to the Nazi camps, this blind submission to law and order is often held up as yet another "typically German" or "Prussian" characteristic. That it is also present in other totalitarian countries is enough to undercut such a notion, but habits of obedience are not confined to these countries, either. When Jorge Semprun, the son of Spanish refugees who settled in France, was liberated from Buchenwald, he immediately returned home. On his very first day back in France, he heard from the mouth of an administrator of a repatriation camp a phrase the Buchenwald guards had not bothered to say to him but certainly must have said to themselves many times: "If I had to have personal opinions, *monsieur,* there would be no end to it," the man said. "I confine myself to carrying out the orders of the Administration" (Semprun 110). The chilling results of Stanley Milgram's famous experiment on submission to authority are well known: a representative sample of free, educated, intelligent American citizens (and not "docile Germans") agree to inflict torture on one of their own once they have been convinced that in doing so they are acceding to the demands of science and to their professors' orders. Not a "typically German" phenomenon at all, submission turns out to be a general human response—given the right conditions.

Of all these conditions, one of the most powerful is the transformation of life in its totality into a state of war (an extension of the notion of "the enemy"). In wartime, you are supposed to stop making decisions on your own and to carry out, blindly and promptly, your superiors' orders, even when they violate your peacetime principles. War is an occasion for legal, even moral, murder. Insofar as the Prussian mind was impregnated with the military ideal, the Nazis could indeed claim to be drawing on a national tradition (of course, they kept only those parts of it that suited their purposes). The army is traditionally the guardian of this wartime mentality in times of peace as well. "When you're in the army, you don't argue," Fritz Klein, an Auschwitz doctor who took part in the selections, offered in his own defense (Langbein 337). But one cannot equate a concentration camp with a battlefield or an "internal enemy" with an "external enemy"; the "war" that the Jews were alleged to have declared against the Nazi state was a convenient fiction invented by Hitler. In addition, even in wartime, all prior principles are not annulled. If they were, we would all run the risk of ceasing to be human.

Docile acquiescence and abdiction of will and judgment can be found well beyond the confines of the camps and the totalitarian states; they are everyday behaviors. What extreme situations do is simply illustrate the most painful consequences of them. Once again, the truth of the individual and that of humanity find themselves on the same side, opposed to that of the collectivity; the laws of the country, the will of the leader, the orders of the state will always be contested by the thinking individual who is inspired by what has been called, at different times, natural law, universal morality, or human rights. The notion of "crimes against humanity" rests on these principles: actions that are entirely within the bounds of existing laws come to be considered crimes, not because they break those laws but because they violate the unwritten maxims underlying the very notions of right and of humanity. Seeking to justify his actions as commandant of Auschwitz, Höss claimed to have followed a principle still in force in democratic England: "My country, right or wrong!" (197). Far from justifying Höss, however, the principle was itself compromised by the revelation of the acts to which it can lead. Auschwitz becomes possible when national interest is held above that of humanity. Obedience to the law may be necessary in order for the state to function smoothly, but that does not make it a source of virtue. If the law is iniquitous, it must be denounced and disobeyed. That it is more possible to do so under certain regimes than under others points to a practical way of distinguishing the better among them from the far less good.

THREE PORTRAITS

In our effort to understand the nature of evil, it is the Nazi variant of totalitarianism that offers the richest material; on the Communist side, we have nothing like the documents produced by certain officials of the National Socialist regime who were more or less forced to explain themselves. And so it is with particular interest that I turn to three of these documents—Höss's autobiography, the proceedings of Eichmann's pretrial questioning, and Speer's memoirs.

Let us begin with Rudolf Höss. He describes his childhood as an apprenticeship in obedience—less to the law itself than to the successive figures incarnating it, first his father, then his superiors, then his commanding officer. Höss confuses good with power, or with the person holding it: "In our eyes, the Führer was always right," he declares, "as was his first deputy, the Reichsführer [Himmler]" (197). Their orders are carried out with no reflection whatsoever; disobedience is inconceivable. "I don't think such an idea even came close to entering the mind of a single one of the thousands of SS officers," Höss says (196). The commandant of Auschwitz, then, works at his own depersonalization, becoming in his own eyes a cog in the Nazi machine. The day comes when he receives the order concerning the "final solution" to the Jewish question; without a moment's hesitation he sets about executing it. Höss acts out of duty, not for the pleasure of killing, as is illustrated by an episode that occurred during the final evacuation of the camps. Soldiers coming upon convoys of inmates amused themselves by firing on them at random. Every so often someone would hit his target. Catching one of his men in the act, Höss takes the soldier to task. "I shouted at him," he says. "I was furious. I asked him why he'd killed that poor creature when he wasn't even in his charge. He answered me with an insolent laugh and told me it was none of my business. I pulled out my revolver and shot him" (237). This is the same Rudolf Höss who sent millions to their deaths, but then Höss had been officially charged with that responsibility, unlike the soldier, who acted on his own initiative. The story may not be true, but it is still a good illustration of how Höss saw himself and understood his actions.

Höss is as depersonalized as he is obedient. He never mentions a single friend; he says he loves his wife but never describes a single act that might confirm it. At Auschwitz he has a mistress, one of the inmates; when he wants to end the relationship, he isn't satisfied simply to leave her—he takes steps to have her killed. On his orders, the inmates are reduced to their pure function, that of work. Those too weak to produce a high enough yield are eliminated at once. "They were dying after a very short time, without having been the slightest use to the rearmament industry. . . . These men were a burden on the camps; good for absolutely nothing, they took space and food away from those who could work" (219). They were going to die soon anyway (from exhaustion), so why not send them directly to the gas chambers? Unproductive, a burden on the camps, these men are never considered an end; at best, they can serve as a means. And if they cannot do that, then they must die.

Höss's depersonalization of others, especially the victims, lets him strike a rather odd pose, that of a natural scientist. In his confession (which he makes after he already knows he has been sentenced to death) he coyly confides in his readers and shares with them his impartial observations on the behavior of the human species and the Jewish race. During his tour of duty at Sachsenhausen, he tells us, he accumulated many "varied and picturesque impressions" (129). Even more so at Auschwitz, that vast laboratory, where he "gathered indelible impressions and ample food for thought" (209). Why did members of the Jewish race go to their deaths so easily? A thorny question that Höss, the professor, will try to clarify for us: "From my observations, I can state categorically . . . ," he says (175). "The life and death of the Jews posed, in fact, a fair number of problems that I was incapable of solving" (209).

(Each time I read Höss's book, I am deeply disturbed. It doesn't matter that it holds no surprises for me anymore. As soon as I start

NOTE
THE WRITINGS
+ NOTES IN
THIS BOOK
ARE <u>NOT</u>
MINE

Dan CHUSING.

reading or copying down passages like those above, a kind of nausea washes over me. None of the other books I've discussed triggers this strong a feeling. So why Höss? Doubtless because of several factors combined: the enormity of his crime, the absence of sincere regret on his part, and the many ways he elicits my identification with him and manages to make me share his way of seeing things. The first-person-singular point of view is also important, as is the absence of any other voice alongside his own, like Gitta Sereny's with Stangl's, Less's with Eichmann's, or even that of the older Speer juxtaposed with that of the young man. Finally, there is the complicity Höss creates by inviting his reader to take advantage of his singular experiences to observe human beings as if they were laboratory animals at a particularly interesting phase of their lives, the hours just before death. When I read Höss's book, I consent to share with him the role of the voyeur who looks on as others die, and it makes me feel unclean.)

For Höss, abstract categories become detached from the reality they are supposed to elucidate, and from then on, only the categories matter. Höss is thoroughly enchanted by the idea expressed in the motto *Arbeit macht frei* ("Work will make you free"), and the whole macabre experiment of Auschwitz taking place before his eyes, even though it is the antithesis of freedom, cannot dampen his enthusiasm. Höss can easily see the problem in general terms (and in other individuals) but never in himself, despite his being a prime example. How else to explain so astonishing a statement as this one: "I am convinced," he writes, "that the situation of many prisoners could have improved if the representatives of the administration had been more humane and less bureaucratic" (48).

Höss reached this degree of depersonalization by systematically cultivating his toughness and by suppressing any compassion or, as he calls it, "softness." He himself interprets this ability as part of his love of the soldier's occupation, for him a calling. His first kill at the front felt to him like a rite of passage: "My first death! I have crossed the threshold into the magic circle" (27). Until his dying day, Höss believed that war alone reveals the truth about life. Having endured harsh treatment himself—at home, in the army, in prison—and stirred by Eicke's speeches, Höss treats others with equal severity. At the first executions and torture sessions he attends, he experiences an "inner emotion" but allows nothing to show. "I did not want to destroy my feelings of compassion for human suffering. I've always felt them, but usually I paid no attention because I was not allowed to be 'soft.' In order not to be accused of weakness, I wanted to have the reputation of being 'tough'" (92–93). In this value system, to be strong means to be hard, or pitiless. Here, the perfection of the totalitarian machine is unmistakable: the more Höss can console himself with that other self—the one still filled with sympathy—the more effective he is in his work. His confession ends with the words "I too had a heart. . . ." (257).

Having succeeded in depersonalizing his victims, Höss regards his work at Auschwitz as a technocrat might his own: all that interests Höss is how his factory is performing. He never wonders about the final product. Not that he has any doubts about Hitler's objectives; in fact, he is so committed to Nazi doctrine that, despite his best efforts, the book he writes can't help exuding anti-Semitism. Yet he continues to insist on certain distinctions. For example: "I want to emphasize the fact that I personally have never felt hatred toward the Jews" (174). As Arthur Seyss-Inquart points out, the "work of death" is particularly successful when it is done without hatred. Höss sees to it that his factory functions smoothly, that there are no hitches, that the various raw materials (poison, human beings, combustibles) arrive in synchrony. In this sense, he represents a prime example of instrumental thinking. It is not the only way of thinking Höss knows, but it is one at which he excels.

Adolf Eichmann, the person directly in charge of the "final solution," was the same type of man. He describes himself as "a pawn on a chessboard" (*Eichmann* 291), a tiny cog with no will or initiative of his own, in other words, a nonsubject. To hear him tell it, he never did anything more than obey, than carry out orders. "Throughout my entire life, I'd been used to obeying . . . from earliest infancy right up to May 8, 1945 . . . an obedience that had become unconditional" (422). In Jerusalem, in his final statement before the court, he observes, "My guilt lies in my obedience, in my respect for discipline, for my military obligations in wartime, for my oath of loyalty"—all attributes we normally esteem. "During these times," Eichmann continues, "obedience was required of all subordinates, as it will be again in the future. Obedience belongs among the virtues." For him, to disobey was both inadmissible and impossible.

Eichmann thus prides himself on what is most troubling about him, his own depersonalization. Not only does he obey orders, but he never *wants* to do otherwise. Personal initiative frightens him; he always tries to make sure he is "covered." If there is one thing that truly shocks him, it is the idea, proposed to him by his interrogator, that he could have disobeyed orders. Never in his life, he says, has anything as low as this—a capacity for disobedience—been imputed to him. Given the magnitude of the crimes for which he was on trial, the comment is a telling one indeed. Eichmann's idea of duty and virtue is grounded in obedience, and yet he never completely stops seeing himself as a person, since he considers himself (though not his victims) to be deserving of pity. If, toward the end of the war, he expressed a desire to put a halt to his labors, it was only to stop "wearing myself out with all this deportation business" (314).

The depersonalization of others in Eichmann's mind is thus more radical than what we saw with Höss. Even during his questioning twenty years later, his language still echoes with it. Repeatedly the act of deportation and execution is referred to with an abstract euphemism, as is the object of that act, the Jews. As for its author, most of the time he is an implicit subject or else absent altogether. His statements deal not with the act itself but with the circumstances surrounding it, which seem to absorb his full attention. Here, for example, is his description of the Wannsee Conference of January 1942, at which it was decided in concrete terms just how the greatest mass murder in German history would be carried out. "Everything went well," Eichmann says. "Everybody was friendly, very polite, very kind, and very courteous. . . . The aides de camp served you cognac, and the business was concluded" (119). Whoever could have guessed what lay behind the vague word "business"? Here are minutes from another meeting, in August 1942, the purpose of which was to discuss ways to speed up the "evacuation": "Difficulties in loading the cars because of the longer October nights" (272). What is being loaded into those cars is not even identified, nor is the destination of the train or the reason for the journey; all attention focuses on a "technical" problem, how to overcome the difficulties caused by darkness.

Another masterpiece of depersonalization reads: "In the context of the solution to the Jewish question in Europe, Hungary too should somehow be relieved" (56). The exact translation of this sentence is: "We also have to deport the Hungarian Jews to kill them." The "we" has simply dropped out (but who is to do the "relieving"?); the Jews are now no more than the "Jewish question" (human beings are supplanted by an abstraction, one that, moreover, takes the form of a problem, and as instrumental thinking would have it, where there's a problem, there's a solution); and the actions themselves are designated by euphemisms of the most general sort ("relieve," "solution").

Eichmann himself sees his work as purely technical, and he never tires of saying so. Counting heads of cattle or Jews is the same thing, a matter of "doing one's job." The important thing is that it be done well. The expression "professional secret" corresponds in Eichmann's parlance to the silence shrouding the mass exterminations; he seems never to understand, however, that his "profession" is precisely that of a mass murderer. At the time of these acts and during his trial as well, Eichmann focuses his attention exclusively on the methods of execution, never on what is at stake in the action itself. If someone brings up a deportation of ten thousand Jews a day (from Hungary), he reacts neither to the meaning nor to the scope of the action, only to the technical "problem." No, he says, we didn't have enough police for operations of that magnitude; there must be a mistake somewhere.

Basically Eichmann's character traits—obedience, abstraction, instrumental thinking—are nothing out of the ordinary. In him, however, they are exceptionally well developed. His capacity for abstraction, for instance, leaves no room at all for human beings; in this regard, Höss was actually the more human of the two. And yet, in his final statement to the court, Eichmann can still declare, "I am not the monster people want me to be" (Wieviorka 187). He knows he is not quite your average man, that he deviated a bit from the norm, but he interprets this positively: I was an idealist, he says, and if I am suffering now, it is because of my idealism. By his definition the idealist is someone who prefers ideas to human beings; in this sense, an idealist is indeed what he was. By contrast, an inmate like Eugenia Ginzburg became the exact opposite of an idealist as a result of her experiences in the camps, whose lessons she summarizes as follows: "How relative are all human systems and ideologies and how absolute the tortures which human beings inflict on one another" (*Journey* 113).

With Albert Speer, we seem to change registers: here we have not some boorish policeman like Höss or Eichmann but a talented architect, a man of education, refinement, and taste, and after his release from prison, a successful writer. Yet his personality, like theirs, reveals many of the familiar characteristics. He, too, wished to be a cog in the machine, to live the "professional life," neglecting, for example, all semblance of family life, all self-reflection. He, too, internalized the notions of law and obedience and declined to exercise his own judgment as to the soundness of the orders he received. He was, by his own account, the type of individual who received an order and never questioned it. In 1947, he concludes that his self-depersonalization was actually part of a larger historical process: "The automatism of [technical] progress," he argues, "will depersonalize man further and withdraw more and more of his responsibility" (524).

Speer's most salient characteristic seems to be the central role he accords to instrumental thinking. He recalls how, even as a very young man, he enjoyed finding himself in challenging situations, the kind that presented a problem and demanded a solution. Indeed, he owes his early celebrity in Nazi circles to his efficiency: working under impossible deadlines, he managed nonetheless to bring to completion various construction projects. Much later in his career, in April 1944, Speer reads in a British newspaper a portrait of himself that pleases him at the time and pleases him still as he writes his memoirs. The article describes him as the very incarnation of the technocrat, "a type which is becoming increasingly important in all belligerent countries: the pure technician, the classless bright young man without background, with no other original aim than to make his way in the world and no other means than his technical and managerial ability. . . . This is their age; the Hitlers and Himmlers we may get rid of, but the Speers, whatever happens to this particular special man, will long be with us" (344–45).

Eichmann's "problem" was the deportation of the Jews; his "solution" was the organization of roundups, the loading of railroad cars, the coordination of train routes. Speer's "problem," from his first day as the Third Reich's minister of armaments, was to produce the most and highest-quality weapons possible. Eichmann never asked himself whether or not the Jews should be gassed; that was not his "problem." Speer never asked himself whether or not the war was just; his problem was "merely" the production of weaponry, not its use. To reach this goal, all means were good: the deportation of foreign workers to Germany, the use of prisoners of war or concentration camp inmates as forced labor. If Speer wanted the lives of certain inmates spared or their food rations increased, it was not out of concern for their well-being but to ensure the greatest possible output from his factories. In his conflicts with the SS, he writes, "apart from all humanitarian considerations, the rational arguments were on our side" (371); he thus reduces common sense to instrumental reasoning. Humanitarian considerations never entered the picture. "The desperate race with time," Speer writes, "my obsessional fixation on production and output statistics, blurred all considerations and feelings of humanity" (375). The "pragmatists," among whom Speer counted himself, were ultimately responsible for at least as many deaths as the "fanatics" were.

Although at the time he writes his memoirs, Speer has already decided to condemn this attitude, he can't help lapsing back into it as he complains about all the obstacles that incompetent bureaucrats, fanatical SS officers, and even waffling leaders (Hitler himself!) placed in his path, in the path of military production. If not for those obstacles, he could have raised productivity levels even higher and Germany could have fought better, might even have won the war. "All my good arguments were . . . blown to the winds," he writes (221). Or on another occasion: "Once again my efforts to organize an effective war economy had been ruined by Hitler's vacillation" (222). And yet if this war, as Speer himself says, was a crime, why the regrets for not having won it? Hitler's vacillation is very attractive, by comparison. In the camps, inmates who were conscientious workers, who staked their dignity on the job well done, could not stop themselves from working efficiently and thus from helping to strengthen the state that had condemned them. Twenty years after the war and despite his overall assessment of it, Speer still cannot free himself from the habit of instrumental thinking; if there is a job to be done, one must do it as best one can, even if it furthers the reign of terror.

Obviously, under these conditions other human beings never constitute an end. If Speer gives any thought to others, it is only insofar as they might serve as a means. And when he adds to this the usual separation between private and public, the work of eliminating humanitarian considerations is complete. "I realize that the sight of suffering people influenced only my emotions, but not my conduct. On the plane of feelings only sentimentality emerged; in the realm of decisions, on the other hand, I continued to be ruled by the principles of utility" (375). At the very end of the war Speer begins to feel responsible, not for the loss of life suffered by the Germans or their enemies but for the destruction of German industrial capacity. He rebels against Hitler and for the first time disobeys his orders—to save machinery and buildings.

The conclusions Speer draws from his life have to do specifically with the power that instrumental thought exerts over mankind; they are about the forgetting of ends. I was, he says, "the top representative of a technocracy which had without compunction used all its know-how in an assault on humanity. . . . By my abilities and my energies I had prolonged that war by many months. . . . Although I never actually agreed with Hitler . . . I had nevertheless designed the buildings and produced the weapons which served his ends" (520, 523). Although Speer has a tendency to minimize his involvement with Nazism, on the whole his explanation seems accurate to me. It also sheds light on lives other than his own.

Speer, Eichmann, Höss: so many links in a single chain. Their personalities are different, as are their social milieux, but their moral behaviors are so many variations on the same basic theme. The accounts they offer of their actions are intended to exonerate and justify them, if only partially. They tend to embellish where they can, emphasizing what they deem least compromising in their pasts. For this very reason, however, these stories are particularly revealing: the authors tell the truth precisely when they believe they have successfully dissimulated it. By portraying themselves as more obedient and more lacking in initiative and conviction than they must have been, they show us that even in their own eyes obedience and depersonalization were enough to transform them into effective means for attaining criminal ends. Höss is particularly hardened, Eichmann exceptionally "abstract," Speer more efficient than anyone else. All three, however, stopped thinking of themselves as subjects, as the authors of their actions, and they stopped thinking of others as their actions' rightful ends. All three were willing to let other human beings be reduced to slavery or be killed, as long as the objectives that they themselves had been assigned were served. Höss, Eichmann, and Speer practiced an "idealism" that was the direct opposite of a concern for others; for them, ideas came before people. The British journalist who painted the portrait of Speer was correct: no matter what their personal destinies, the type of man they personify still has a glorious future before him; instrumental thinking and the depersonalization that goes with it cast their shadow far beyond the concentration camp.

The Enjoyment of Power

Depersonalization cuts both ways, as we have seen. It can affect oneself as well as the other: by seeing the other person as simply an element in a project that transcends him, one forgets his humanity, and by submitting, oneself, to the requirements of the system, one becomes simply another part of the machine. Whether animal or piece of machinery, one ceases to be part of the human condition. There is a particular type of instrumentalism and depersonalization, however, that merits special consideration, the type in which I remain the end of my action while only the other becomes a means, not a means to accomplish some more or less abstract project—the victory of Communism, for example, or cleansing the earth of its inferior races—but a means to realize the satisfaction of a particular individual, me. This kind of satisfaction is fed by one thing only: my cognizance that the other has submitted to me. The power I enjoy over him is direct, unmediated by rationalizing concepts such as law, duty, or the word of the leader. The phenomenon I am describing is that of the *libido dominandi*.

The sense of power can assume a number of different forms. It does not always mean power over others. As a young child (and sometimes later as well), I find pleasure in the power I have over my own body. This satisfaction, though it lacks a moral dimension, nonetheless goes hand in glove with dignity since, like dignity, it arises from an

accord among the various segments of my being. In altogether different circumstances, I can take pleasure in my power over nature; this
enjoyment is the feeling that comes from being able to control the
waters of a river or construct a building that touches the sky. It is an
aspect, an extension of the life of the mind. The power that concerns
us here, however, is of still another sort and has to do strictly with
intersubjective relations—the power of one person over another and
the enjoyment that person derives simply from exercising this power.

The important thing here is that the other person be dependent on
me, not that he have this or that particular experience: it doesn't
matter if his experience is one of joy or suffering, so long as I am
responsible for it. But while I may indeed enjoy bringing happiness to
others, their displeasure offers me more certain proof of my power. A
person's joy is more likely to be at least partly the result of his own
will, whereas his misery is not generally something he has wished for;
instead, it comes from the power I exert over him. Except in truly
exceptional cases, he cannot choose his own physical torture. And
finally, suffering can culminate in the absolute of death (whereas happiness knows no absolute limit). To cause the death of another is to
have irrefutable proof of my power over him.

The enjoyment of power has clear affinities with sadism, although
the two should not be confused. To begin with, even though the
suffering of the other is the most compelling proof of my power, it is
not the only one; his happiness is also proof, if to a lesser degree. In
addition, unlike sadistic pleasure, my enjoyment does not come from
the other's pain itself but rather from knowing that I have power over
him (the sadist, on the other hand, need not be the author of the
other's pain from which he himself derives his pleasure). Finally,
while there is general agreement as to the sexual origin of sadism, the
enjoyment of power is not simply a conversion of a sexual experience.
Freud, in his discussions of the *Bemächtigungstrieb*, or the drive to
dominate, which he sees most clearly at work in the cruelty of children, stresses its nonsexual character; only when it is joined with
sexuality does it veer toward sadism. At the origin of this drive is
simply the drive itself; nothing is gained by translating it into a different vocabulary. The individual aspires to total supremacy because in
achieving it he affirms his selfhood; and the most radical way of

achieving it is to negate the other by making him suffer, or, in the most extreme of cases, by causing his death. With Georges Bataille's interpretation of sadism in mind, Jean Améry reflects on the torture sessions to which he was subjected and writes, "In the world of torture man exists only by ruining the other person who stands before him." Améry describes the "bureaucrats of torture" going about their business: "The name of it was power, dominion over spirit and flesh, orgy of unchecked self-expansion. . . . Amazed, the tortured person experienced that in this world there can be the other as absolute sovereign, and sovereignty revealed itself as the power to inflict suffering and to destroy" (*Mind* 35, 36, 39).

It is this enjoyment of power, and not sadism as it is usually understood, that one finds abundantly present in the camps: enjoyment in the fact that the other is at your mercy, a fact you can prove to yourself by making him suffer or, less frequently, by affording him some pleasure. Yet the confessions of the guards rarely mention enjoyment, doubtless because these confessions tend in one way or another to be apologias and because the enjoyment of power is easily confused with sadism, which generally gets bad press. By contrast, in the inmates' accounts the issue comes up time and again. Fania Fénelon describes the visit of an inspector to her barracks, a Frau Drexler, who ordered all the beds remade and confiscated everyone's meager possessions. "Astonishing to enjoy lording it over such a feeble lot," Fénelon writes. "By the grace of the Führer, who, like God the Father, reigned over great and small, she had been raised to this exalted post, while in her native Swabia she would have been, perhaps, a waitress" (*Playing* 136). Fénelon also tells of an occasion when one of the head guards, in a moment of boredom, summoned a thousand women from their barracks, divided them into groups of a hundred, and sent some to their deaths, letting the others live. "What sheer delight, this power!" Fénelon exclaims (*Sursis* 253). Or as another inmate, Anna Pawelczynska, observes, "Acceptance of a job in Auschwitz [was] especially alluring because it satisfied a need for daily experiencing one's own dominance and strength, the right to decide life and death, the right to dispense death personally and at random, and the right to abuse one's power over the prisoners" (19).

The guards reserved a special fury for those inmates who were not quick enough to show their submission, who failed to lower their eyes or, even worse, to carry out a command. But what makes the camps a special case is that the guards' desires for supremacy encounter no obstacle of any sort, legal or moral; each guard is thus tempted to demand greater and greater submission of others (the only limit being that of absolute submission, or death). The guards do not have to justify anything to anyone; they are entirely free and sovereign. Drunk with their own power, they feel they belong to a race of supermen. It is to this state of mind that the inmates refer when they speak of "corruption by power." Vladimir Petrov, who escaped from Kolyma, observes that "Almost unlimited power over living beings, deprived of nearly every right, inevitably awakens the specific instincts of arbitrary tyranny, absolute intolerance of any opposition from these 'lower creatures,' and complete irresponsibility in dealing with them" (Conquest 73).

Between those who are only guards and those who are only inmates stands a host of intermediates occupying what Primo Levi has called the "gray zone" (a zone that in totalitarian states includes the entire population to one degree or another). These prisoner-guards (the kapos of the Nazi camps, and their Soviet equivalents), often recruited from the ranks of ordinary criminals, are all the more keen to exert their power knowing that they themselves are at the mercy of the real guards, the militiamen or the SS. Slaves to those above, tyrants to those below, they use their sovereignty in one direction to compensate for their lack of freedom in the other. It is they who are most bent, therefore, on demonstrating their power over others, as is plain in any number of accounts.

An enjoyment of power that requires the physical torture or death of the other exists only in extreme circumstances, in the camps or during colonial conquests, where the forces of the colonizers enjoy a similar "freedom of action." One wonders therefore whether this kind of will to power—absolute in that it does not stop short of death to achieve its satisfaction—is of the same kind as that which one encounters in daily life. Jean Améry thinks not: "The dominion of the torturer over his victim has nothing in common with the power exercised on the basis of social contracts," he argues. "It is not the power of the traffic policeman over the pedestrian, of the tax official over the taxpayer, of the first lieutenant over the second lieutenant" (*Mind* 39). His claims do not fully convince me. If the examples he cites point to a difference between the two situations, it is because these examples are of hierarchical relations rather than power relations. The two are compatible but distinct; thus we find it a perversion of a hierarchical relation when a military superior takes pleasure in demanding proof of submission from his subordinates, or when a tax collector mentally tortures taxpayers instead of simply collecting their taxes, or when a traffic policeman humiliates pedestrians instead of asking them to obey the traffic laws. The hierarchical relation has become a power relation.

Political life in totalitarian states represents an intermediate zone between the world with which we are all familiar and the world of torture and death that reigned inside the camps. The story of Chaim Rumkowski, the president of the Jewish Council in Lodz, is a well-known example. Irresistibly attracted to power, then intoxicated and corrupted by it, Rumkowski created in the ghetto a caricature of the totalitarian German state and indulged in practices befitting the camps themselves. Yet he reflects back to us an image of ourselves, exaggerated, to be sure, but not distorted beyond recognition. "Like Rumkowski," Primo Levi writes, "we too are so dazzled by power and prestige as to forget our essential fragility. Willingly or not we come to terms with power" (*Drowned* 69).

Albert Speer, a politician and not a subaltern guard, was courageous enough to recognize the role his desire for power had played in his life. "When I analyzed the complex of motives which so surprisingly led me back to this intimate circle [of Hitler's closest associates], I realized that the desire to retain the position of power I had achieved was unquestionably a major factor," he writes. "I had been bribed and intoxicated by the desire to wield pure power, to assign people to this and that, to say the final word on important questions, to deal with expenditures in the billions. . . . I would have sorely missed the heady stimulus that comes with leadership" (342). Power here is an end in itself. Vasily Grossman says of Lenin: "All his talents, all his will and his passion, were directed to one purpose—to seize power. To this end, he sacrificed everything." And yet, as Grossman points out, Lenin himself did not profit personally. "He did not seek the power he won for himself" (*Forever Flowing* 203, 204). The aim of power is, then, neither money, nor the good life, nor the flattery of one's subordinates. The aim of power is power; the enjoyment it offers is not of the material sort.

It would be going too far to say that politics, especially in democratic countries, is nothing more than a power game (at least without unduly stretching the meaning of the term *power*), yet the ambition that Speer describes is a familiar one, certainly recognizable to any politician today. As for the pleasure to be taken in making someone else feel that he or she is in your power, that pleasure, too, is not restricted to the political domain, narrowly defined. One finds it in all sorts of social relations. Who has not seen the pleasure an imperious receptionist or policeman or maître d' can take in subjecting others to the power of office? Nor are intimate ties exempt. The enjoyment of power is found everywhere, although it would be obscene to equate the murders of the concentration camps with a humiliation suffered in the course of a dinner party.

People who enjoyed their power over others in the camps by making them suffer had no particular distinguishing characteristic. A number of inmates have observed that these people had no idea what to do with their power at first, although they learned with stunning rapidity. "Some of us made a rather grim little game of measuring the time it took for a new *Aufseherin* to win her stripes," Germaine Tillion writes (69). "And one young woman, who kept saying 'Excuse me' to everyone on the day she arrived at Ravensbrück, took only four days to start enjoying the submission of others. Another, who wept when she started work as a guard at Birkenau, also became exactly like her colleagues in just a few days" (Langbein 397). It is not that these young women were of a particular type; in other circumstances, they would never even have made the discovery that it was possible for them to partake in the enjoyment of power in these sorts of ways.

ORDINARY VICES AND ORDINARY VIRTUES

Much like my catalog of the ordinary virtues, my list of ordinary vices was arrived at in a largely intuitive fashion. There is no reason, therefore, to consider it exhaustive. These are simply the traits I encountered the most frequently in my readings on life in the camps. Unlike the virtues, the vices do not form a complex hierarchy among themselves. It is true that self-depersonalization and the enjoyment of power pull in opposite directions: in theory, one cannot consider oneself a nonentity and at the same time derive pleasure from the submission of the other. Yet if one acts unconsciously and has fragmented one's personality, it becomes perfectly possible to combine the two in practice. In all probability, this was what people like Eichmann and Höss did. Though they liked to see themselves as the simple executors of orders, cogs in a machine, they surely took no less pleasure in controlling the lives of millions. And the dovetailing of depersonalization and fragmentation is exactly what produces the perfect technocrat: it is as important to him to separate his private feelings from his public behavior as it is to forget that he is dealing with human beings.

It seems there is no place for Satan in this roster of ordinary vices that helped pave the way for one of the most extreme manifestations of evil the world has ever known, or for such notions as human homicidal instincts. The novelty of totalitarian crimes lies less in the fact that heads of state could conceive of such projects—there have surely been others, throughout history, who have fantasized about exterminating substantial portions of humanity—than in the fact that these men were able to realize their projects, an accomplishment that required the collaboration of thousands and thousands of individuals acting on the state's behalf and at its behest. The essential question, then, concerns not the project itself so much as the conditions of its realization. The key factor is the transformations that all these thousands of individuals underwent so that they could suspend their usual responses to fellow human beings. These transformations proceed from two sources—ideological indoctrination and the need for efficiency. The guards did what they did because they were told it was their duty to do so, that this was how they could contribute to the good. Even if they did not believe it, they had every interest in acting as if they did. Then, having consented to perform the tasks asked of them, they could rely on habits of mind that made accomplishing those tasks all the easier: compartmentalization, professionalism, and internal fragmentation—each of these bound up with the others—as well as instrumental thought, which abolishes the distinction between persons and things.

People living in democracies are accustomed to ideological pluralism (and also to public access to many different sources of information). That is why in these countries the danger of fanatical indoctrination is smaller, although not altogether nonexistent, as is demonstrated by the flourishing of the extreme left a few years ago and the extreme right today. As for professionalism and instrumental thinking, we are certainly acquainted with them too, but, unlike fanaticism, they are traits we also admire. That is why I have lingered much longer on this point than on indoctrination techniques. In democratic societies, fragmentation and depersonalization do not kill, of course, but they threaten our humanity nonetheless.

Something about the appearance of an evil as extreme as that of the concentration camps remains puzzling, however. The enigma, moreover, is not limited to totalitarian situations but is found in our own lives too. To pose the question somewhat provocatively, if all of us can understand intuitively the urge to kill or the pleasure one might take in the act of torture, why are there so few killers and torturers among us? If indeed the enjoyment of power over another is the most effective way to exercise sovereignty and prove to ourselves that we exist, how is it that only a few of us actually cross that boundary and kill or torture? Must we infer that in spite of everything there really are two categories of human beings? I have no precise answers to these questions. This same enigma underlies totalitarian crime: we may understand how ordinary vices and the totalitarian regime facilitate the proliferation of evil, but not why or how an individual living under such a regime decides one day, of his own free will, to beat an infant to death.

The ordinary vices are to a certain extent an inversion of the ordinary virtues. Dignity is, above all, internal consistency; fragmentation is its absence. Both have to do with the individual taken in isolation. Caring leads us to see others as the end of our actions; depersonalization transforms all subjects, both self and other, into a means. The enjoyment of power over others is thus a particular (but crucial) instance of depersonalization as well as a most rigorous inversion of caring. In one case, *I* am a means and *you* are an end; in the other, *I* am the end and *you* are the means. The life of the mind has no negative counterpart, but we have seen how easily it can turn against itself and against the world it is meant to understand and beautify. This is the well-known theme of the sorcerer's apprentice, a theme that today's physicists and biologists bring to mind when they lose sight of the humanity they are supposed to serve.

TOTALITARIAN HEROISM?

Totalitarian ideologies have never claimed to draw their inspiration from the ordinary virtues, whereas they have unfailingly promoted the cult of the hero and tried to bank on the traditional respect for heroic values by claiming those values as their heritage. Ample evidence attests to the conflation of the two orders, the totalitarian and the heroic. To what extent is this conflation justified?

Communist propaganda was particularly effective in developing an elaborate cult of heroes various and sundry. First among them were the men and women who had fallen in battle, fighting for the victory of the regime; their names were given to towns and streets and schools in posthumous recompense. Next were all those living individuals on whom the regime wished to confer distinction. In the former Soviet Union, they composed two categories: Heroes of the Soviet Union (for military or political exploits) and Heroes of Socialist Labor (for excellence in the achievement of production quotas). The head of state, of course, constituted a category all his own. Dead and mummified, he was venerated in a mausoleum; while still alive, he was praised in millions of images, songs, poems, and novels, the tangible incarnation of perfection in every domain. This cult of the hero was practiced at school, at work, and in all public places, with the full participation of the media.

Nazism did not attain quite this level of perfection, but the ideology of the hero figured crucially there as well. "In those days [Hitler] seemed to me," Speer remembers, "like a hero of ancient myth who unhesitantly, in full consciousness of his strength, could enter upon and masterfully meet the test of the wildest undertakings." In a note he adds, "And, in fact, nine months previously I had had bas-reliefs portraying the legend of Hercules installed on the new Chancellery" (163). Hitler (or, for that matter, Stalin) as Hercules—is there any legitimacy to the comparison?

It is true that Hitler established a cult of courage and that his own political acts were often audacious. Life was obviously not his supreme value, and during his last meeting with Speer a few days before the collapse of the Third Reich he said, "Believe me, Speer, it is easy for me to end my life" (480). The ordinary SS man liked to advertise his intimacy with death, right down to the emblems and color of his uniform. The faithful servant of the Communist ideal was no less prepared, if we can believe the propaganda, to sacrifice his life if called on to do so. The struggle against the enemy is implacable: loyal commissars, party secretaries, or just plain rank-and-file Chekists all died for their ideal, whether in the civil war or in the war with Germany, in the course of the collectivizations or while working on socialist construction projects. Innumerable novels ply this theme with greater or lesser skill, thus offering a heroic ideal to their young readers.

(*As a child, I must have read Vera Ketlinskaya's* Virility *at least a dozen times. All I remember of this novel is that it is about some young and ardent Komsomols who are building a new city in Siberia and are surrounded by hideous enemies—Chinese, or maybe Japanese, spies. Fortunately, the good Cheka officers are watching out.*)

We saw how the classical hero has an abstract ideal and pursues it single-mindedly; he is faithful to his king and loyal to his comrades and community in the name of that ideal, not for their own sake. In the totalitarian state, the relationship between the moral ideal and the obligations that devolve from it is not so very different. The servants of the regime fight to realize abstract goals (the triumph of Communism or the Soviet state, the supremacy of the Aryan race or the German state), not to secure the welfare of those they know and love. As a result, individual lives are subordinate to the advancement of these goals, and (as we saw with the "idealism" of Eichmann and many others) the end justifies any and all means. Notice that these goals, though abstract, nonetheless remain particularist: the victory of a country or a class.

There is also the question of loyalty. In the totalitarian ethic, loyalty to the leader is a fundamental obligation. The cults of both Stalin and Hitler are notorious in this respect. The motto Himmler chose for the SS, for example, proclaimed, *"Meine Ehre heisst Treue,"* my honor is called loyalty, a phrase from one of Hitler's speeches indicative of the special place this quality occupies in Nazi thought. Loyalty toward others engaged in the same struggle and blind submission to the leader go hand in hand. In the Soviet Union, party members protected one another, for all of them enjoyed the same privileges. In his description of the "paramilitary groups" that prefigured the SS units, Höss recalls, "Each of us had to take an oath of loyalty to the leader of his group. This leader personified unity; without him, the group would cease to exist. This is how we created an esprit de corps, a feeling of solidarity that nothing could shatter" (35–36). This certainty of being able to count on their comrades in adversity, the willingness to die for them are qualities that fill the future Nazis with pride and arrogance. Highly esteemed in wartime, these qualities are extended under the Nazi regime to the totality of existence. The strong sense of solidarity among members of a group makes it easier to exclude all those who do not belong to it and who thus become its enemies, external or internal.

Earlier we saw that the traditional hero refuses to bow to the weight of circumstances. The Polish generals in the Warsaw Rising of 1944 sought to compensate for a dearth of weaponry with their soldiers' blood and spirit of self-sacrifice. Like the heroes of that revolt, the leaders of the totalitarian state believed that in sufficient quantity the human will could triumph over reality. During the first German offensive, Stalin tried to stop the enemy advance with offerings of Russian blood, his orders to his soldiers making clear that they were better off dead than defeated. Stalin made them pay for his own errors—his blind faith in the pact with Germany, his distrust of his officer corps (which led to the massive purges), and his general incompetence. The Nazis, for their part, refused throughout the final phase of the war to acknowledge their imminent defeat, for it contradicted their desires. "They did not want to acknowledge the legitimacy of their doubts," Höss writes, describing his colleagues' attitude in the spring of 1945. "It was impossible that our world was destined to perish—so we had to win" (234). Göring showed evidence of the same type of thinking as far back as September 1943. When informed that American combat planes had been shot down over the territory of the Reich, he insisted on the impossibility of such a thing, became irate, and finally blew up at the bearer of the news, shouting, "I officially assert that the American fighter planes did not reach Aachen" (Speer 290).

Hitler himself never capitulated to reality. "So-called experts and men who by rights should have been leaders repeatedly told me: 'That isn't possible, that won't do!' " he declares in the spring of 1942. "I cannot resign myself to such talk! There are problems that absolutely have to be solved. Where real leaders are present, these problems always are solved and always will be solved. . . . I repeat: For me the word 'impossible' does not exist" (223–24). The will of the true hero always prevails over reality, Hitler proclaims as the Allies advance. And as Speer notes, "Hitler had again and again asserted that our lacks would be balanced out by miracles of courage from the moment the German soldier was fighting on German soil" (424).

Lastly, much like the classical hero, his counterpart under totalitarianism needs stories to immortalize his glory. Hence the well-known predilection of these regimes for monuments in granite or steel; hence also their leaders' need to surround themselves with poets. The number of poems, novels, paintings, and symphonies dedicated to the glory of Stalin is beyond counting. When Göring declared that for him the demands of historical greatness took precedence over more immediate ethical considerations, he was still thinking of the need for tales of glory. After all, without them, where would the sense of grandeur come from? For this same reason Hitler wanted bronze plaques put up to commemorate the extermination of the Jews (Gilbert, *Psychology* 89).

In his famous speech to Nazi dignitaries at Poznan, Himmler draws a portrait of the ideal SS man. Of the dozens of requisite attributes he mentions, only two—that the man be a good worker and someone with initiative—have no direct relationship to the classical heroic virtues, although they do characterize that modern avatar of the classical hero, the "efficient manager." All the other qualities Himmler mentions belong either to the hero or to the saint: the SS man must be courageous, ascetic (avoid corrupting influences such as alcohol), and, above all, loyal, faithful, and of course a good comrade. How could the SS not feel themselves heirs to the heroic tradition?

Obviously these claims of heroic filiation are not to be taken at face value. The actual operations of the totalitarian regime represent not just a departure from the traditional concept of heroism but a perversion of the values it embodies. The pseudoheroes of totalitarianism imitate the form of the heroic act, seeking to clothe themselves in the trappings of heroism, the better to conceal an altogether different reality. For one thing, there is the brutal contrast between the content of official propaganda and the typical practices of totalitarian regimes. If we go by what the novels and films tell us, the camp guard was as incorruptible as a saint, whereas in fact corruption was rampant both within the camps and in the world outside. Those held up as exemplars of self-denial enjoyed numerous material advantages. With the enormous power of the state behind them, moreover, they had little occasion to prove their courage. Even their loyalty wasn't worth much since it was directed toward leaders whom the party could from one day to the next unmask as enemies of the regime.

The Nazis, one might recall, loved to claim their heritage in the *Nibelungentreue,* and indeed in many traditional epics, the hero owes allegiance to his king. But it is because the king is himself the incarnation of an ideal; he personifies honor. In classical heroism the opposite of the SS motto I spoke of earlier is true: one does not honor loyalty, one is loyal to the concept of honor. What the totalitarian regime calls loyalty is really nothing other than the ordinary vice of submission.

Furthermore, the claim to heroic prestige rests on a logical ruse.

Having expanded the idea of war to cover all conflicts and even dis-
agreements (or simply the failure to kowtow swiftly enough), the totalitarian regime equates repression and extermination with national
defense. But isn't it a complete perversion of the concept of heroism
to treat as one and the same the soldier who dies defending his country and the state security officer who tortures alleged enemies of the
state in an underground cell?

The most subtle transformation in the notion of heroism is the
displacement of the toughness and sacrifice demanded of oneself onto
others. The hero and the saint will brave tempests and adversity without feeling sorry for themselves or complaining about their sufferings;
they are willing to sacrifice themselves to achieve their goals. Totalitarian pseudoheroes know only one form of sacrifice, that of others,
while they themselves take pride in having enough fortitude to watch
the ordeals of their victims without trembling! Himmler's Poznan
speech is explicit on this point: the difficult thing is no longer the act
of dying but that of killing; it is only his agents we ought to pity. The
extermination of the Jews, he says, "is the hardest and most difficult
thing in the world. . . . For the organization assigned to that task, it
was the most demanding job they'd ever done" (Himmler 167–68). In
exterminating the Jews, the SS sacrifice themselves; for the good of
their people, they accept this particularly arduous assignment that
only the toughest can perform. Indeed, they are all the more admirable because their glory, the hero's usual recompense, must wait. They
sacrifice themselves in secret so that future generations might live in
happiness.

The result of these various perversions of heroism is that Nazi
practices stand as the very opposite of the chivalric or even the Prussian tradition. Hitler never missed an occasion to point this out; his
references to the chivalric tradition are filled with scorn. He will not
spare an enemy too weak to fight or make it a point of honor to save
women and children. Nor will his guards. Much the same is true in
Communist regimes: once power has been seized, the new rulers
cannot rid themselves of their "heroes of the revolution" quickly
enough. If people were more compassionate in the Soviet Union than
in Nazi Germany, we have not Communism but the Russian tradition
of charity to thank. Yet the idea of a code of honor is incompatible

with that of total war, and total war is what totalitarian empires aspire to. The pseudoheroism cultivated in these regimes maintains a homonymous relationship with classical heroism: similar forms refer to different meanings. Heroic virtues perhaps do not always merit respect, but one cannot confuse them with totalitarian practices. Nor can one imagine Colonel Okulicki a guard in a concentration camp.

FACING EVIL

Nonviolence and Resignation

TO IMITATE OR TO REJECT

Commenting on Eugen Kogon's *The Theory and Practice of Hell,* Germaine Tillion speaks of the dilemma faced by inmates and former inmates of the camps, namely, whether to imitate or reject the model provided by their guards. "Should we adjust to their criminal behavior?" Tillion asks. "Should we make some sort of compromise with it, in order to save a few lives and values which, without this compromise, would be sacrificed? In other words, do we have to *get our hands dirty*? . . . Or should we struggle tirelessly to avoid contamination by the shame of a shameful enemy? (What good is there in destroying an enemy if, in the process, we take on his hated characteristics?)" (229). Tillion declines to pursue this line of thinking, for the actors in the drama had doubtless already made their choice, rendering the question a purely academic one. But if it is too late to raise the issue in the heat of the moment, all the more reason to use our distance from it now to ponder the matter in more general terms. Should one fight the enemy with his own methods and run the risk of handing him, in our triumph, this dark, covert victory—that we have become just like him? Is it right for us, in Borowski's words, "to conspire so that there are no more conspiracies, to steal so that there are no more thefts, to kill so that no more people are killed?" (*Monde* 144–45). There is another part to this question: Does a refusal to use the enemy's own weapons to fight him mean, in effect, that we are abandoning the struggle altogether?

In exploring one of the two paths of which Tillion speaks, that of refusing to imitate the enemy's behavior in any way whatsoever, I begin with the remarkable story of Etty Hillesum. A word of caution, however: in seeking to extract something like a doctrine or a code of conduct from her writings, I am in a sense misrepresenting her. It is not that her journal lacks insight or depth; it is simply that what impresses and attracts one most in her journal is the human being and writer, not the creator of a doctrine. There is nothing of the professional philosopher in this young woman (she was twenty-seven years old at the beginning of the German occupation of Holland and died two years later), who supported herself as a private tutor and dreamed of becoming a writer. Yet she offers us the rare example of someone who achieves a moral understanding at the very moment the world is collapsing around her. In the midst of the deepest despair, her life glitters like a jewel. She does everything in her power to reestablish harmony in her immediate surroundings, first by looking after those closest to her, then by going to work at Westerbork, the Dutch transit camp. At no time does she preach at us, however, for what she asks of others she demands first of herself. She has taken to heart Marcus Aurelius's precept that one ought not to talk about the good man but to be him, and in her journal she writes, "All I need do is to 'be,' to live and to try being a little bit human" (*Interrupted* 38).

One might imagine that with her quest for inner perfection came a certain scorn for concrete, material everyday life. Not at all; her embrace of the ordinary is perhaps her most engaging quality. Reading the pages she left behind, we feel in the presence of someone whom we would want to spend time with, to count among our friends, to love. Etty could find the words to express her attachment to the simplest acts—giving a lesson, darning stockings, or drinking a cup of cocoa—and to the people around her, her family and friends. This combination of virtue and love of life—an almost sensual one—makes her an exceptional being. Yet she also feels she must rationalize her conduct, and so she turns to arguments that she finds in books and that arise in conversations with others. It is this rationalization that I would like to examine here, keeping in mind that her life cannot be fully accounted for in this way; but it is precisely because the arguments she uses are not entirely her own that Etty Hillesum interests me.

In her journal, Etty transcribes a conversation she had with her friend Jan Bool in the streets of Amsterdam in February 1942: "I no longer believe," she tells him, "that we can change anything in the world until we have first changed ourselves" (*Interrupted* 71). Later, in one of her last journal entries, from September 1942, she reiterates her credo in an imaginary conversation with her good friend Klaas: "We have so much work to do on ourselves," she writes, "that we shouldn't even be thinking of hating our so-called enemies" (179). Her fellow inmates believe otherwise, however. Here is the way she describes one of them, a man from Westerbork, to Klaas: "He hates our persecutors with an undying hatred, presumably with good reason," she says. "But he himself is a bully. He would make a model concentration camp guard" (178). Klaas listens but apparently does not agree with her that one must change oneself before setting out to change things in the world. "And you, Klaas," Etty continues in this imaginary dialogue, "give a tired and despondent wave and say, 'But what you propose to do takes such a long time and we don't really have all that much time, do we?' And I reply, 'What you want is something people have been trying to get for the last two thousand years, and for many more thousand years before that, in fact, ever since mankind has existed on earth' " (179–80). Solzhenitsyn makes much the same observation, but in a different context: "To beat the enemy over the head with a club—even cavemen knew that" (616).

Etty's "program"—if I may call it that—has two imperatives: forswear hatred of the enemy and fight evil in oneself rather than in others—that is, with moral, not political, means. "It is the only thing we can do, Klaas," she writes. "I see no alternative, each of us must turn inwards and destroy in himself all that he thinks he ought to destroy in others" (180). When she is suddenly ordered one morning to appear before the Gestapo, she manages to overcome her initial feelings of outrage despite the waiting, interrogation, and calculated abuse. "And that was the real import of this morning: not that a disgruntled young Gestapo officer yelled at me, but that I felt no indignation, rather a real compassion" (72). It is not the enemy but hatred itself that must be defeated: "True peace will come only when every individual finds peace within himself," she writes, "when we have all vanquished and transformed our hatred for our fellow human beings of whatever race—even into love one day, although perhaps that is asking too much" (123).

If we hate the enemy the way he hates us, all we are doing is adding to the world's evil. One of the worst consequences of the occupation and the war, Hillesum maintains, is that the victims of the Nazis begin to become like them. "If we allow our hatred to turn us into savage beasts like them," she writes, "then there is no hope for anyone" (143). Someone who sees no resemblance between himself and his enemy, who believes that all the evil is in the other and none in himself, is tragically destined to resemble his enemy. But someone who, recognizing evil in himself, discovers that he is like his enemy is truly different. By refusing to see the resemblance, we reinforce it; by admitting it we diminish it. The more I think I'm different, the more I am the same; the more I think I'm the same, the more I'm different . . .

In one of her gripping letters from Westerbork, Hillesum describes what it is like to be in the camp and then realizes, like Marek Edelman, that she has perhaps not said what she is expected to say: "This is a very one-sided story. I could have told quite another, filled with hatred and bitterness and rebellion." Though she never stops fighting the injustices of the camp, hatred remains her chief enemy: "The absence of hatred in no way implies the absence of moral indignation. I know that those who hate have good reason to do so. But why should we always have to choose the cheapest and easiest way? It has been brought home forcibly to me here how every atom of hatred added to this world makes it an even more inhospitable place" (*Letters* 36).

Hillesum goes to Westerbork voluntarily at first, as a worker, then as a detainee, but always driven by the same desire, to contribute to the world's goodness, not its hatred, and to care for others around her. In her journal, when she reflects on what life will be like after the war, she knows that what she has fought against will not necessarily have disappeared. " 'After this war [she recalls someone telling her], two torrents will be unleashed on the world: a torrent of loving-kindness and a torrent of hatred.' And then I knew: I should take the field against hatred" (*Interrupted* 177). That war, the war against hatred, was the only war Etty Hillesum ever agreed to wage. Before that day could arrive, however, her turn came and she was packed into a train for Auschwitz, where three months later, in November 1943, she died. But her writings continue the fight today in her stead. She is not the only one to have chosen the second of Germaine Tillion's alternatives; in the Russian camps, Ginzburg and, later, Ratushinskaya echo Hillesum's words. Primo Levi, too, will write, "From violence only violence is born, following a pendular action that, as time goes by, rather than dying down, becomes more frenzied" (*Drowned* 200).

Usually we react with skepticism to this sort of counsel, equating it with the idea of nonresistance to evil. Like Klaas, we always feel it's too late; when danger looms before us, we know we cannot avert it with gestures of goodwill. And we are not necessarily wrong. If Hitler's armies are streaming across borders, nothing is gained by making peace proposals. If Stalin decides to put to death all the peasants in the Ukraine, they cannot protect themselves by pitying him. There are times when taking up arms is the only appropriate response; not all phases of history are equally responsive to moral (as opposed to political or military) action, which is often better suited to peacetime than to war. Yet moral action can perhaps be more effective than we think. I would like to recall two true stories that illustrate this hope, that show the possibility of dampening with a simple act of kindness the pendular movement Primo Levi speaks of.

The first story comes from Auschwitz. An SS guard there named Viktor Pestek approaches various inmates with an offer to help them escape. He has a plan: he will get hold of another officer's uniform and the two of them will leave the camp together, as if everything were perfectly normal. The inmates are wary of the offer, suspecting a trap. Finally, one of them, a man called Lederer, accepts, and the escape succeeds. Later, Pestek returns to Auschwitz to arrange more such escapes, but this time he is caught and executed. Why did he take such risks? It seems that while fighting on the Russian front he had taken part in a punitive action against a village suspected of concealing resistance fighters. Pestek was wounded during the attack and left behind by his comrades. The following day several members of a Russian family found him hiding in their barn. Pestek was thirsty; instead of finishing him off, they led him to the stream. "He never forgot that these people had saved his life when they had absolutely no reason to spare a uniformed SS man whose unit had just massacred their entire village" (Langbein 417).

The second story concerns another SS officer, a man named Karl, who after the war signed on with the French Foreign Legion and was sent to Algeria. Once there, he worked in the prison infirmary. The prisoners, to their surprise, found in him a man of the utmost delicacy and discretion. He adjusted the records so that their treatment would last as long as possible, and he spoiled them by fixing them tasty dishes—fruits, biscuits, eggs, hot chocolate. Karl's kindness also had an explanation: when he was taken prisoner on the Russian front, he was first put into solitary confinement, then sent to Siberia; there he became so ill that all he wanted was to die. "He finally came under the care of a Russian woman doctor, who took charge of his care and who changed his mind in that regard. Later, in Algeria, doing the job of a nurse and watching over his chocolate, he confided [to one of his charges]: 'I would just like to do the same for you' " (Tillion 235–36).

ACCEPTING THE WORLD

However admirable acts like these may be, and even if we grant, as I am prepared to do, that they sometimes have a more significant effect than they are usually credited with, Hillesum's reasoning is not entirely persuasive. Did the man at Westerbork who hated the Nazis really turn into someone like them? To assume that he did suggests not only a conflation of the real with the virtual but also a failure to acknowledge any difference between attack and defense, between degrees of evil, or between the various means of power that different people have at their disposal. In fighting Hitler (and hence for justice) we are not imitating him: he is fighting for injustice. Sometimes hatred is not only justified but necessary. It is true that one can lack both the distance and the information necessary to know whether the enemy is one's double or an incarnation of evil. Still, the distinction is crucial: Can we put the rebels in the Warsaw ghetto on the same plane as the SS because both threw bombs? Is it right to stop ourselves from hating the Communist commissars who built the gulags, the Nazi functionaries who built the concentration camps? Must we be tolerant of evil? If we are to cure ourselves of hatred once victory is ours, must we also stop abhorring those responsible for the suffering and death of millions of human beings? As we struggle against the hatred inside ourselves, do we not risk forgetting about the struggle against the hatred incarnated by totalitarian regimes? It would seem that for Hillesum the struggle against the evil within us *takes the place of* the struggle against the evil around us instead of serving as a preparation for that struggle. The two parts of her "program"—to refuse to hate the enemy and to begin by fighting the evil inside oneself— scarcely exhaust our options. She says nothing, for instance, about a struggle that could be intransigent and still require neither demonization of the enemy nor collective guilt nor a Manichaean outlook. Might not a position like Hillesum's even facilitate the spread of evil? Would the "moral indignation" of which she speaks have been enough to stop the advance of Nazism? It is an important question, for it concerns not only Hillesum but all resistance to evil.

Hillesum apparently gives little thought to the prospect of a military victory against Hitler. "I don't much believe in help from the outside," she writes, "nor do I count on it. . . . No one should put his trust in that sort of help" (*Interrupted* 161). It is not a question of pessimism here; she is simply skeptical of this kind of solution in general. If she declines to put her hopes in the Allied landing, it is not because she doesn't believe in it but because she expects nothing from it. She does not share the opinion of those "who have not yet abandoned all political hope. I believe," she says, "that we must rid ourselves of all expectations of help from the outside world" (151). Hillesum maintains this outlook with regard not only to the general course of events but to her own life as well. She refuses to join a resistance movement or even to take steps to protect herself. She will not hide or flee. "I simply cannot make active preparations to save myself," she writes. "It seems so pointless to me and would make me nervous and unhappy" (152). It is not that she has deluded herself about either her own destiny or that of her people, for on July 3, 1942, she writes, "What is at stake is our impending destruction and annihilation, we can have no more illusions about that. They are out to destroy us completely, we must accept that and go on from there." And yet instead of trying to prevent this horror, she contents herself with the following rule: "Even if we are consigned to hell, let us go there as gracefully as we can" (130). But why?

Hillesum's arguments can be seen as spanning three different registers, the first being *indifference* toward everything outside the self. The only thing that counts is the world we carry inside; suffering caused by external factors is of no importance. "It is never external events," Etty writes, "it is always the feeling inside me—depression, uncertainty, or whatever—that lends these events their sad or menacing aspect" (118). If only one can defeat this internal menace, the serenity achieved will serve as "a dark protective wall" (113) against which external dangers will break apart like the ocean's waves. "Yes, we carry everything within us," Hillesum continues. "The externals are simply so many props; everything we need is within us" (131). These "externals" are, in fact, so unimportant that Hillesum goes willingly to Westerbork: "If you have a rich inner life, there probably isn't all that much difference between the inside and outside of a camp" (74). An extraordinary declaration, which, without denying that the reality of the camps is an evil, makes it possible to maintain that the difference between good and evil in the world beyond the self is without importance.

Sometimes, however, Hillesum rejects this argument, that the self must be indifferent to the world, and instead posits a necessary harmony between self and world. Here, her argument reaches its second register, the one most amply represented in her journal: rather than being a matter of indifference, evil can be *acceptable*. As she stresses repeatedly, this does not mean that she has resigned herself to evil, that she has sunk into impotent despair. Her incredible activity—caring for others, writing—proves the contrary, if proof were needed. "It is not as if I want to fall into the arms of destruction with a resigned smile," she writes. "And surrender does not mean giving up the ghost, fading away with grief, but offering what little assistance I can wherever it has pleased God to place me" (150, 142). On the other hand, her surrender is not the same thing as resistance or revolt, both of which she associates in her journal only with hatred of the enemy. "I am not bitter or rebellious, or in any way discouraged. I continue to grow from day to day. . . . I have come to terms with life" (131). And again, praying: "I am deeply grateful to You for leaving me so free of bitterness and hate, with so much calm acceptance, which is not at all the same as defeatism" (159). What does this "calm acceptance" mean, this capacity to accept all things serenely?

Here, Hillesum turns to a line of reasoning that she believes she has drawn from Christianity but that seems to me more properly associated with stoicism or quietism or, in the Eastern tradition (to which Hillesum also refers), Taoism. The world must be accepted as it is, she argues, with all its joys and sorrows (not that they are one and the same thing), for together they create the world's totality and its beauty. "Living and dying, sorrow and joy, the blisters on my feet and the jasmine behind the house, the persecution, the unspeakable horrors—it is all as one in me and I accept it all as one mighty whole" (130). Everything that is is good. "Whatever happens is for the best," she writes. "I accept everything from Your hands, oh God" (161, 169). The only thing Hillesum cannot accept—and I wonder if this exception does not call the coherence of her doctrine into question—is the human will, the desire to change the way of the world, to banish evil and keep only the good. "When one has once reached the point of experiencing life as something significant and beautiful," she writes, "even in these times, or rather precisely in these times, then it is as if everything that happens has to happen just as it does and in no other way" (170). Nor does Hillesum have any particular sympathy for reformers: "I am rather gratified when I find that yet another well-laid plan turns out to have been nothing but vain speculation," she writes (188). For Hillesum, to accept one particular aspect of life and reject another is tantamount to following one's pleasure and whims, and this, she argues, is what makes life absurd. But might one not reject the camps and the extermination of the Jews for reasons other than our pleasure and whims? Why does everything have to happen just as it does?

In Amsterdam, signs of misfortune multiply around her: deprivation, denunciations, arrests. Hillesum reacts to this upsurge in violence and evil not by rejecting it but by absorbing it into the preestablished harmony of the universe. She allows it to grow outside of her, while within herself she transcends it by finding meaning in it. The worse the situation becomes, the more frequently she repeats in her journal such things as Yes, life is meaningful, or Yes, life is beautiful. "I have already died a thousand deaths in a thousand concentration camps," she writes, "and yet I find life beautiful and meaningful. From minute to minute" (127). And again: "beautiful and meaningful. Yes, even as I stand here by the body of my dead companion, one who died much too soon, and just when I may be deported to some unknown destination" (172). And "I am a happy person and I hold life dear indeed, in this year of Our Lord 1942, the umpteenth year of the war" (123). Nothing can shake her resolve: "That is my attitude to life and I believe that neither war nor any other senseless human atrocity will ever be able to change it" (115).

Perhaps Etty Hillesum's secret is that she managed to transcend the idea of her own personhood, which is to say, the usual recourse to one's self as one's point of reference, as the measure of all things. "We have to find the courage to let go of everything," she writes, "only then will life become infinitely rich and overflowing" (144). As her self begins to dissolve into the universe, she begins to think in the name of the universe itself: "I was able to feel the contours of these times with my fingertips" (177). She sees herself as "the thinking heart of the barracks" (169), indeed, of the entire camp; she sees herself from the outside, a tiny particle of the universe, useful but in no way central. This is precisely the reason she can write such amazing sentences as this one: "People often get worked up when I say it doesn't really matter whether I go or somebody else does" (150). Even though she is speaking here about people being sent to their deaths, she no longer makes distinctions between herself and others (and she seems to have ignored as well the possibility there was for her—and for others—to avoid going to Auschwitz).

Hillesum wishes to become one not only with other human beings but with all forms of life: "We have to become as simple and as wordless as the growing corn or the falling rain," she writes. "We must just be" (145). This universalization also bears on everything around her; she reproaches herself for giving only to a few and not to everyone. For each day is a condensation of all of life, and each place the equivalent of any other. "We are 'at home' in every place on earth," she insists, "if only we carry everything within us" (176). Thus it is that Hillesum can aspire to her own special goal. It is not that of the humble believer who prays that God will come to her aid, nor is it that of the enterprising atheist who will try to help herself; Hillesum's goal is to help God, to keep Him inside her, and so in the world. "That is all we can manage these days," she writes, "and also all that really matters: that we safeguard that little piece of You, God, in ourselves. And perhaps in others as well" (151).

In the wake of this acceptance of the world as a whole, Hillesum can (at certain moments only, it is true) take her argument to its third and ultimate register and declare her *preference* for suffering. Westerners, it seems to her, have found it especially difficult to accept suffering and find strength in it, to accept death as an integral part of life. The source of the suffering is unimportant; whether it is the Inquisition or the pogroms, Ivan the Terrible or Hitler, wars or earthquakes, "all that matters is how we bear it and how we fit it into our lives" (129). Hillesum herself accepts suffering as part of human life and considers it her personal role to persuade others to do the same by helping them and caring for them (though not by seeking to eliminate the causes of their suffering). And because in these times of trouble the camp remains the purest incarnation of suffering, Hillesum decides of her own free will to go there.

At Westerbork, Hillesum is happier than she has ever been. She is sorry only when she has to leave; her departure feels to her like the loss of a privilege. "I should so much like to go back on Wednesday," she writes "if only for two weeks" (187). The first two months she spent there were "the richest and most intense months of my life, in which my highest values were so deeply confirmed. I have learned to love Westerbork" (174). So much happiness, however, ultimately makes Etty Hillesum a stranger to us, even if we can understand the excitement she feels as she confronts the obstacles that must be overcome. It almost seems as though she would have the misery around her increase so that her personal development might proceed more swiftly. "How is it," she asks, "that this stretch of heathland surrounded by barbed wire, through which so much human misery has flooded, nevertheless remains inscribed in my memory as something almost lovely?" (177). There is indeed a mystery here, and as readers we find ourselves wishing that Hillesum, too, could *suffer* from this suffering instead of constantly transmuting it into beauty or a wellspring of happiness.

I have quoted at length from Etty Hillesum's writings because they fascinate me; she was, without question, an extraordinary human being. Still, I do not believe that the path they trace is advisable for everyone. In her most exalted moments, there is something superhuman—and therefore, inhuman—about her: she does not altogether belong to this world. True, she prefers ordinary virtues (caring) to heroic virtues (war), but she goes much further. Instead of trying to do something about the causes of evil, she is content to be "the balm for all wounds" (196). She lives not in resignation but rather in joyful acceptance of the world and thus of evil as well.

Even though I may not believe in the possibility of a world without evil or suffering, I do not agree that we should welcome every evil and every suffering as though they were fated to be, as though they were all part of cosmic harmony, providential design, or the cunning of reason. Of course, we must make room in life for death, but the deaths that took place in the camps do not belong in the same category as those that come with old age or incurable illness. Hitler was not a natural disaster. The notion of a world without suffering may be utopian, but still I am grateful to those who have contrived to find ways so that people might suffer less and to those who are struggling to eliminate the causes of those evils that are not ineluctable. We needn't be utopians to oppose certain kinds of death and seek to mitigate certain kinds of suffering. Totalitarianism and the camps were not "necessary" in any cosmic or historical sense. Evil is not only painful; very often it is also absurd and, for that very reason, unacceptable.

The position Etty Hillesum defines for herself is not one of resignation, but the result is similar: in the end, her fatalism and passivity lent themselves to the murderous project of the Nazis. And this is why, despite her uncontestable nobility, I cannot commend her position to the downtrodden of this earth.

POLITICS OR MORALITY

It is not enough, however, to maintain that nonresistance to evil is politically ineffective. Indeed, there can come a time when resignation is preferable to resistance or at least equally justifiable. The question is, how can one tell? In his autobiography, *I Cannot Forgive,* the resistance fighter Rudolf Vrba describes his devastating confrontation with Fredy Hirsch, a German Jew who took care of the children deported to Auschwitz from Terezin. Vrba learns through the camp's underground that the extermination of these children (and their families) is imminent. He thinks the adults of the group who are strong enough physically should revolt: they have nothing to lose, and they may be able to inflict some losses on the guards. The Terezin inmates hold Hirsch in high esteem; if he agrees to lead a revolt, Vrba argues, it will surely take place and achieve some measure of success. A terrible argument ensues, with Vrba trying to convince Hirsch to put himself in charge of the rebellion and Hirsch objecting that if he does he will be party to the sacrifice of the children in his care. "But they'll die anyway!" Vrba argues. "Yes," Hirsch replies, "but at least I won't have betrayed them."

Fredy Hirsch was a Zionist, a physical education teacher who was very popular in Terezin. After his transfer to Auschwitz, he became the *Lagerkapo* of the "family camp" and was responsible for seeing to the children's education. He told the camp authorities that the children might perhaps learn German—an absurd proposal, all things considered, but one that may have appealed to the officers' German pride—and under this pretext he arranged for them to use their own barracks as a school. The children did indeed learn a bit of German, and many other things as well: they drew, made toys, and, under Hirsch's direction, even staged a performance of *Snow White*, which the SS in attendance received with warm applause. Later, a second barracks was put at their disposal, this one for the youngest children. Hirsch took care of everything, and the children adored him.

(We need not wonder what the drawings of these children looked like. At Terezin, before their deportation to Auschwitz, the children drew a lot, and several thousand of the pictures have been preserved. I saw them in Prague, in the synagogue, a narrow building, now a Jewish museum, perched above the old cemetery. The vast majority of the children who made these drawings died in Auschwitz. Some of the drawings look like those made by children everywhere: butterflies, a black cat, flowers, a house. Others are more disturbing: here, nothing but three tiers of beds, the people on them piled one on top of the other; there, a burial. Or a stack of skeletons. Or a hanging, with a six-pointed star on the chest of the dead man. The children who drew these pictures, with whatever pencils or crayons they could find, were Fredy Hirsch's young pupils.)

Hirsch asks for an hour to think over Vrba's proposal. When Vrba returns, he finds Hirsch sprawled on the floor, foam coming out of his mouth; he committed suicide by swallowing Luminal. Vrba thinks for a moment about trying to save him but decides against it. And so he resigns himself: the family camp will be exterminated without any effort at revolt, a prospect made all the more painful by the fact that Vrba's first love, Alice Munk, who was introduced to him by Hirsch, is among the condemned. What happened next comes to us through the account of Filip Müller, a *Sonderkommando* survivor. There was indeed no revolt, but when the prisoners from Terezin reached the door of the gas chamber, they began to sing.

Hirsch's suicide calls to mind that of Adam Czerniakow, the president of the Jewish Council in Warsaw, who killed himself when he saw that he could do nothing to prevent the deportation of the children of the ghetto to Treblinka. There is a difference, however: Czerniakow committed suicide at a time when not everything had been decided. The inhabitants of the ghetto still had some possibility of choice, albeit a minute one. By dying without telling his people what lay in store for them, Czerniakow did nothing to awaken their resistance, which was their only chance of surviving; it is for this reason, as we have seen, that Edelman and Ringelblum reproach him. Hirsch, on the other hand, killed himself when he saw that his survival would be of no help to the children. Had he agreed to Vrba's idea, the rebels might have killed a few SS men at best, before being shot down themselves. Hirsch knew that if he remained alive, he would have to accept Vrba's proposal, for he was the only one who could lead the revolt. Yet had he accepted, not only would he have failed to save a single one of those children to whom he was so devoted but he would have *chosen* to abandon them to their fate by involving himself in what, under the circumstances, could only have been a symbolic struggle, one that they neither would have understood nor could have been helped by. Lucidly, then, he chose suicide.

In the streets of the Warsaw ghetto, Pola Lifszyc and Mordecai Anielewicz took two different paths: Lifszyc voluntarily boarded the train for Treblinka so as not to abandon her mother; Anielewicz attacked German patrols and threw himself into the adventure of the insurrection. Lifszyc responded to evil by acting in the purely private sphere; Anielewicz chose the arena of public action. It is he who hastened, if only by a little bit, the defeat of Nazism. Lifszyc, by her submission, contributed—again, only slightly—to the efficiency of the extermination process. Should we blame her for her resignation and praise him for his resistance? We cannot begin to answer this question until we have separated the moral from the political. From a political point of view, Anielewicz's position is uncontestably preferable: Nazism had to be fought, and in the extreme conditions of the ghetto, fighting Nazism meant firing on German soldiers. Upon escaping from Auschwitz, Rudolf Vrba knew what he had to do: he joined the resistance and continued fighting the SS. In doing so, he felt the same childlike excitement Marek Edelman describes, the thrill that comes from firing on the enemy. "I was running now," Vrba writes, "and tears of happiness were coursing down my cheeks. I was running forwards, not backwards. . . . We burst through the door into a fiery chaos and sprayed the room with bullets" (261). Vrba was right to help speed the collapse of a hateful regime and to call on all his heroic virtues to do so. Morally speaking, however, Pola Lifszyc's ordinary virtue seems to me to have the edge on Anielewicz's courage; nothing is nobler than the act of caring for others. In certain extreme cases, then, no reconciliation between the moral and the political is possible.

This is not to say, though, that a noble soul is all it takes to triumph over evil. The most effective barrier to the political fact of totalitarianism is itself political: an active democracy concerned with both individual freedom and the advancement of the common good, tolerant of criticism and transformation from within but at the same time intransigent toward democracy's real enemies. Moral actions, however, occur on a different plane, even if in certain conditions they can also have a political effect (I am thinking here of dissidents in the Communist countries). Moral actions do not lead, as one might hope they would, to a better regime, but they do embody a dimension of existence that is no less essential. They improve the individual and contribute to the general happiness in an ultimately more positive way than the mere elimination of an external danger might. Moral actions bring about what even the best political regime can allow for but can never create: they make our lives more humane.

Forms of Combat

TO ACCEPT OR TO RESIST

As a person, Etty Hillesum was exceptional. The position she espoused, however, was not. It was shared, in effect, by members of Agudat Yisrael, an influential organization of orthodox Jews in the Warsaw ghetto who refused to take up arms or defend themselves; they were among the Nazis' earliest victims. Others tried to find meaning in the absurd and thus make it tolerable: now as before, they said, God demands more of the Jews. Or: this incredible suffering heralds the coming of the Messiah. Instead of fighting or going into hiding, many chose to surrender so as to bring themselves into conformity with the laws of men as well as those of the cosmos. "No one escapes his destiny" was the fatalistic reply frequently heard by resistance leaders. Thousands of miles separated Etty Hillesum from Eugenia Ginzburg, but they came to similar conclusions. "In those years, the mid-fifties," Ginzburg writes, "I was deeply convinced that the world was rational and that there was a higher meaning in things, convinced that God perceived the truth, though he might be slow to speak" (*Within* 397–98). These various ways of accepting and rationalizing distress leave no room for resistance of any kind.

People have often drawn unwarranted conclusions from these observations. We have already examined one of them, which sees the passivity of the victims as a uniquely Jewish reaction and tries to explain it in terms of Jewish traditions or a Jewish national character;

we have seen why this explanation is unsatisfactory. Another conclusion focuses on the victims' passivity at the threshold of death in the Nazi extermination camps. Zalmen Gradowski, a member of the *Sonderkommando* at Birkenau, who buried his manuscript to ensure its survival, was obsessed with the thought. "Instead of fighting like wild animals," he says, "the victims for the most part came down from the trucks peacefully and passively" (Roskies 560). With all due respect for a witness of this kind, I regard as misplaced Gradowski's regret that the victims did not die fighting. Once arrested and selected, the victims no longer had any chance of escape; in terms of relative strength, they were at an overwhelming disadvantage, even if the numbers themselves—hundreds of thousands of victims versus only a few hundred guards—suggest otherwise. Under such conditions, to die calmly seems to me no less honorable than to go down fighting "like wild animals." The young rabbinical student who stood at the door to an Auschwitz gas chamber and cried, "We must submit to the inevitable," did nothing shameful (Müller 161–62); his action is as worthy of respect as the rare instances of successful resistance in these circumstances. In fact, this is why the inmates agreed not to reveal the truth about the camps to the next victims; it would have done them no good to know and would only have made their deaths more cruel.

But as the case of Czerniakow illustrates, the question takes on a very different meaning with reference to the period prior to the arrests and roundups, when the future victims still had some freedom of action, however limited. As we know, bitter accusations were leveled against the Jewish Council for having done nothing to prevent the imminent catastrophe. Although any judgment of our own benefits from the clarity of hindsight, it seems evident that if those who were being hunted down had tried to escape rather than hastened, like Hillesum, to obey the summons, they would have had a better chance of surviving. While there is still time, one must act. If there is any lesson at all to be learned from the resistance to Nazism, it is that one. In the face of Hitler, the pacifism of the 1930s was reprehensible, and we can't help but sympathize with future partisan Misha Gildenman's defiance of his elders, who could think of one thing only, to say their prayers for the dead. "A voice cried out in me," writes Gildenman,

" 'Not with prayers will you assuage our grief for the rivers of innocent blood that was spilled—but with revenge!' As soon as the Kad-
dish was over, I banged the table and cried out: 'Listen to me,
unfortunate, death-condemned Jews! . . . Know that sooner or later
we are all doomed. But I shall not go like a sheep to the slaughter!' "
(Suhl 260). Taking steps to assure one's survival is already a first act of
resistance.

Of all the historians and eyewitnesses of this period, perhaps no
one has argued more forcefully for the necessity of resistance than
Bruno Bettelheim. He regrets, he says, that, once sentenced to death,
the prisoners did not choose to die "like men," and he makes much of
the famous story of the dancer who killed as SS officer right at the
door to the gas chamber (*Heart* 264–65). Bettelheim's judgment here
strikes me as both unrealistic and unfair. His analyses seem pertinent,
however, when he turns his attention to the period preceding the
arrests. Those who refused to acknowledge the danger of Nazism,
who consoled themselves by maintaining that people were fundamentally good and the world fundamentally harmonious, unwittingly abet-
ted the spread of evil. For Nazi persecution did not take its extreme
forms at the very start; on the contrary, it progressed only insofar as it
failed to meet with resistance.

Bettelheim is particularly harsh in laying out what he calls "the
ignored lesson of Anne Frank" and in attacking what he sees as a cult
of admiration for a family of Dutch Jews who tried to deny the gravity
of the situation and continue living as they had before the disaster, in
the comfort of intimacy and family love. "Hers was not a necessary
fate," Bettelheim argues. "Anne, her sister, her mother, may well
have died because her parents could not get themselves to believe in
Auschwitz." Had their attitude been less passive, they might have
saved themselves. Bettelheim declares his admiration for the Warsaw
ghetto insurgeants: they, at least, knew how to die fighting (*Surviving*
248, 250, 257).

*(March 1990. Bruno Bettelheim has just committed suicide. Numerous
concentration camp survivors, some famous, others not, preceded him
in that choice, but I'm not sure that it had the same meaning for
everyone. What I see in Bettelheim's case, above all, is a brutal illus-*

tration of the precepts he systematically applied to others: the neces-
sity of human autonomy and will, of taking one's destiny in hand, of
not letting oneself become the plaything of forces beyond one's control,
of choosing one's life and therefore also one's death. At the age of
eighty-seven, he must have dreaded the moment when he would no
longer be able to carry out this act, however much he wanted to. And
so he made certain his will would be done by killing himself twice over
—with a drug overdose and by asphyxiation. No one can accuse him
of not taking his own ideas seriously.)

Jean Améry, who chose to end his life a dozen years earlier, and
doubtless for reasons similar to Bettelheim's, also believed that the
ghetto uprising marked the beginning of a new era in the history of
mankind. In addition, he had no qualms about espousing, in the name
of the revolt, the notion of vengeance. Militarily, the Warsaw uprising
was altogether absurd, Améry wrote, "and can be justified only morally, as the realization of *humane vengeance.* . . . It was reserved for
few to discover their authenticity in battle and in genuine revenge."
According to Améry, the Warsaw ghetto uprising "was the avenging
establishment of justice, the chance to create a new kingdom of man
on earth" (*Humanism* 26–27, 35).

THE TEMPTATIONS OF REVENGE

Even if we accept the necessity of combat, the dangers it holds for all
who fight, including those whose cause is just, cannot be ignored;
moreover, one wonders whether vengeance is ever a legitimate substitute for justice, as Améry suggests it is. If the only change is that those
who were hunted become the hunters, then the new kingdom he
speaks of will not be so new after all. One is reminded of those stories
about resistance fighters who became as hardened as their enemies
(and who found it difficult to reintegrate themselves into civilian life
after the war).

Once the war was over, those who fought against, or suffered at the
hands of, the enemy had to face the question of what their attitude
toward the defeated enemy should be. Viktor Frankl recounts an epi-

sode typical of the times. The day after their liberation, he found himself walking with a comrade beside a field of green oats. Suddenly, his friend began stomping furiously all over the growing stalks. Frankl "stammered something about not trampling down the young crops. [My] friend became annoyed, gave me an angry look and shouted, 'You don't say! And hasn't enough been taken from us? My wife and child have been gassed—not to mention everything else—and you would forbid me to tread on a few stalks of oats!' " (144). This futile and, moreover, harmless rage is an example of choosing to adopt an attitude similar to that of one's tormentors: I was the victim of violence, and therefore I now have the right to inflict violence. "The only thing that had changed for them," Frankl says, "was that they were now the oppressors instead of the oppressed. They became instigators, not objects, of willful force and injustice." And yet, Frankl continues, "no one has the right to do wrong, not even if wrong has been done to him" (143, 144).

Breaking a few stalks of oats rarely brings satisfaction, and so one dreams of a total reversal of roles. Inmates ask one another what they will do after the liberation, provided there is one. "I'm going to buy myself a machine gun," one woman in Auschwitz exclaims, "and I'm going to kill every single German I can find!" (Fénelon, *Sursis* 308). Others, adopting the language of their oppressors, dream of an immediate extermination of the "vermin" by the Allies. "They can use flamethrowers," one suggests (373). When the English liberate Bergen-Belsen and arrest all the SS men, the former prisoners cry out, "You must kill them! You must kill them all!" (19). Such reactions are fully understandable. "For those who have suffered unjustly," Borowski explains, "justice is not enough. They want the guilty to suffer unjustly as well. For them, that is justice" (*Monde* 181).

Of course, it makes a difference whether these dreams of revenge are nurtured by a former inmate or by a powerful statesman. We know, for example, that Henry Morgenthau, Jr., secretary of the Treasury of the United States during the war years, drew up a plan whereby former Nazis, government functionaries, and German soldiers would be deported and forced to work in Allied countries. Certain Nazis and their families would be sent to "remote corners of the globe" (a problem arose as to what to do with children under the age of six). As for the major war criminals, "the high officials of the Nazi party and state," Morgenthau proposed that their names be put on a list to be turned over to the Allied military forces, "who would use [it] to identify and immediately shoot captured prisoners" (Smith 23–24). The British had a similar plan, but ironically, it was the Russians who insisted the most vehemently that there be a trial. Given their experience, they must have had no doubt whatsoever about the outcome.

Hannah Arendt criticized many aspects of the Eichmann trial but basically approved of the death sentence the court imposed, justifying it with the following judgment, which she proposed in place of the one the court pronounced: "And just as you supported and carried out a policy of not wanting to share the earth with the Jewish people and the people of a number of other nations . . . we find that no one, that is, no member of the human race, can be expected to want to share the earth with you. That is the reason, and the only reason, that you must hang" (*Eichmann* 279). If that is truly the only reason, then in my opinion Eichmann should have been allowed to live. I do not understand the argument that, because he excluded certain human beings from the ranks of the human race, we in turn should exclude him. Why repeat his actions? In what way is that an improvement on the law of "an eye for an eye"? Some people have expressed satisfaction at knowing that Eichmann's ashes were scattered over the ocean so that no trace of them remained; but was this not also the fate of his victims, whose ashes were tossed into the water, and with the same intention in mind?

During the Auschwitz trials in Frankfurt, Rudolf Vrba, one of those who managed to escape the camp, argued that the death penalty should be reinstituted on an exceptional basis so that such serious crimes could be appropriately punished. It is not that he seeks revenge, he says; rather, he wants to help Germany recover its dignity. "It is not merely a question of punishing criminals, for what punishment could fit the crime, but of purging a nation's conscience in public," Vrba explains (269). But isn't it a dangerous idea to want to purge a country of its undesirable elements by putting them to death —even if that very country had just done the same thing a few years before?

(During the years 1968–69, the Vincennes campus of the University of Paris became the base of activity for a group of Maoists, veterans of the events of May 1968. The leaders of this group were two brilliant Parisian intellectuals, both of whom I had once known. As I left class one day, I was brought up short by a strange procession: a completely naked man, hairy and bearded, was trying to push his way out of a small but hostile crowd that was being led by my two old friends. Before he was let go, someone smeared tomato sauce or some other colored liquid on him; it was a symbolic lynching. The victim, I subsequently learned, was François Duprat, a militant right-wing ideologue who would be killed several years later in an explosion, the origin of which has never been determined. Why he had come to Vincennes, bastion of the extreme left, I do not know. Was it to spy? Was he seeking a confrontation? Whatever the facts, the sight of this naked man surrounded by a hissing crowd made me feel profoundly ashamed. "This makes you fascists!" I blurted out to the friend I knew best. "No," he said, smiling calmly, "he's the fascist." The devastating effects of "revenge" on the avenger—in this case, for an offence that was probably nonexistent although theoretically possible—had never been so clear to me as they were that day.)

Is vengeance ever justifiable? Primo Levi has studied this question with the scrupulous honesty that characterizes all his writings. In *If Not Now, When?*, a work at once fictional and autobiographical, he recounts the journey of a group of Jewish partisans during World War II who make their way from Byelorussia to Italy, passing through Poland and Germany. When a comrade is murdered in a city in Germany, Mendel, the protagonist of the story, joins in a retaliatory action. "Had that revenge been just?" he asks. "Does a just revenge exist? It doesn't exist, but you're a man, and vengeance cries out in your blood, and then you run and destroy and kill. Like them, like the Germans" (304).

Mendel thus allows himself to be caught up in an act of revenge. But though he may take some comfort in having avenged a completely senseless death, the effortlessness of his action continues to plague his conscience. "Blood isn't paid for with blood," he says. "Blood is paid for with justice. Whoever shot Black R. was an animal, and I don't want to become an animal. If the Germans killed with gas, must we then kill all the Germans with gas? If the Germans killed ten of ours for one of theirs, and we do the same, we'll become like them, and there will never be peace again" (305). Persecuting the persecutors does not erase the debt; the debt in fact is increased.

Mendel (or Levi) reasons, as Etty Hillesum does, that vengeance is reprehensible because it makes us no different from those on whom we wish to avenge ourselves. This realization, however, does not lead him to pacifism and acceptance of the world as it is, much less to a desire for reconciliation with those who tortured him, an unsavory fraternization between victim and executioner, or to Christian forgiveness. To refuse vengeance means neither to forgive nor to forget: these alternatives leave no room for justice. Despite his renunciation of vengeance, despite his profound disgust for killing, Mendel decides to fight and thus to kill. "We will fight until the end of the war," Gedaleh, his superior, declares, "because we believe that making war is a bad thing, but that killing Nazis is the most just thing that can be done today on the face of the earth" (215). Mendel chooses this course of action not out of a taste for fighting but because he respects justice even more than he does life. To hate evil is legitimate, then, and at this precise moment in history, Nazism incarnates evil, as do those who have made themselves part of the Nazi apparatus or have not at least demonstrated their dissociation from it. Fighting against Nazism does not mean answering evil with evil. It means working to eradicate evil itself.

THE VIRTUE OF THE RESCUERS

As Levi points out, avenging the evil one has suffered (and in the process being contaminated by what one reproves in the enemy) and refusing to fight evil altogether (and accepting the world as it is, without aspiring to change it) are not the only alternatives. One can also take a stand against evil and fight it out of a sense of justice, not hatred. That is the route chosen by any number of soldiers, partisans, and resistance fighters. It is also the route chosen by those whose resistance to evil was no less consequential for being nonviolent.

Nonviolence does not mean nonresistance to evil. Consider the men and women of Eastern Europe who came to be known as "dissidents": their nonviolent actions—including their efforts to repudiate lying and expose the truth—proved to be among the most effective means of combating Communist totalitarianism in a later stage of its existence. What I would like to discuss here, however, is a different form of nonviolent combat—in this case, against Nazism—as it was practiced by the "rescuers," individuals who devoted themselves during the war to saving people in mortal danger, Jews especially, by taking them into their homes and hiding them. Their acts are particularly instructive because they fall between the categories of the ordinary and the heroic. I focus on the example of three groups of rescuers—in France, in Poland, and in Holland—whose deeds are by now well known.

On the one hand, the rescuers do not look on themselves as heroes. Long after the war, when people sought them out to congratulate them and tell them that they were heroes, they fiercely denied it. Why? First, because, unlike heroes, they believed that the life of the individual is the supreme value and they did not make a cult out of death. Second, because, unlike heroes, they never sought out self-sacrifice and they took only calculated risks. Their work was saving human lives; consequently, avoiding Borowski's paradox, they refused to sacrifice any life so that another might be spared. The rescuers were unarmed and did not even know how to shoot, although they knew very well who their enemy was. They refused to make war, which meant that their relations with other members of the resistance, the saboteurs and the maquis, were strained. Magda Trocmé, the wife of the Protestant minister who organized the rescue of Jews in the village of Chambon-sur-Lignon in the Cevennes, years later explained her actions: "Helping the Jews was more important than resisting Vichy or the Nazis" (Hallie 128). This antipathy to warfare accounts for the reaction of another rescuer to a soldier whom he had rescued and who later said to him, by way of commendation, "Without ever firing a shot, you give a new dimension to the term 'war hero.'" "I don't much like the sound of that term," the rescuer replied. "Any way you twist it, it still glorifies war" (Stein 91–92).

Rescuers do not fight for abstractions. Their actions are not about duties or ideals, which for the most part they seem unable to formulate. Rescuers concern themselves with flesh-and-blood human beings, people who must be helped in ordinary, everyday ways. Magda Trocmé insists not only that she is not a heroine but that she is not even an especially good Christian. All she did, or so she says, was to open her door when someone knocked and share her food with others who were hungry (Hallie 154). As her daughter Nelly explains, "Her dedication was not because of religion; it was because of people" (156).

Thus, unlike heroes, the rescuers do not see themselves as exceptional people. They shun praise; they did what they did, they say, because for them it was the most natural thing in the world. What surprises them (or surprised them at first: one can be surprised only so many times) is that others failed to do likewise. The rescuers do not feel as though they have performed a great exploit; besides, with them it is a question not of a single deed, like slaying a dragon or blowing up an enemy machine-gun nest, but of a multitude of banal acts—pulling up potatoes or setting the table or emptying chamber pots—that are repeated day after day, sometimes over the course of years, and that consequently are difficult to shape into a satisfying narrative. Thus, rescuers have trouble understanding why historians are interested in them; they avoid fame and publicity to the point of not wanting their real names used in the books written about them. In their rejection of celebrity, in their refusal to have their stories told, they have generally met with success. Whereas every country recognizes and applauds its great war heroes, those responsible for death and destruction, no one builds monuments to the glory of the rescuers. To my knowledge, there is no city in France with a Magda Trocmé Avenue.

On the other hand, the rescuers' attitudes are not the same as those we associate with the ordinary virtues, especially the virtue of caring. As every rescuer knows, there is a difference between risking one's life for a Jewish family one does not know and preparing meals for one's own children. The rescue action involves danger and is undertaken in behalf of people who, even if they can be identified individually, nonetheless remain strangers (rescue actions are akin to charity in this respect). The act of caring, however, involves not strangers but one's own family or friends and, except in times of extremity, rarely puts the carer at risk. The father-in-law of one of the rescuers, who reproached his son-in-law for his activities, makes this very point: you have a wife and child, he says; you must take care of them first. You must provide for their needs in these difficult times and not risk their lives for people who mean nothing to us. "I will risk nothing for a stranger," the father-in-law adds (Stein 65). Being a stranger is, of course, a temporary condition. Once settled in a rescuer's home, the newcomer soon ceases to be an outsider; in fact, he may even come to have the same reaction as the father-in-law. The first person to be hidden thus warns his rescuer against taking in any new refugees: "Where will it end, Tinus, I ask you, where will it end? Is your home going to become a private club for illegal Jews?" (268). The rescuer is someone who opens his door to strangers, and even if this welcome has its limits (in France rescuers saved French Jews, in Holland Dutch Jews; foreign Jews had a much harder time), the difference between the act of rescue and the ordinary virtue of caring is clear.

In more positive terms, the rescuer's action requires not only the courage and capacity for self-sacrifice of the hero (or saint) but also— as in the logic of caring—exclusive concentration on the well-being of others. The rescuers did not stop the war or even the genocide. At best, the individual rescuer managed to save one or two or perhaps a dozen families, but frequently these were the only families to survive. They risked their lives for people they did not know but were suspicious of "idealism," of grand designs, for these can turn into deadly practices: good ends accommodate themselves too easily to evil means. They pursued a goal that was plainly not a matter of debate: they acted to save human lives. As one rescuer concludes, "To stop the war just like that because it's not rational to kill is not a reasonable expectation. . . . But if you say, 'I am going to save the life of one person in addition to my own' or 'I'm going to hide one family' . . . then you have a chance for a victory that makes sense" (Stein 69). This lesson in modesty is worth heeding.

The rescuers' acts managed to avoid both hatred and resignation. Indeed, for one to become involved in a rescue, it is not enough to be morally upright, unwilling to betray others, and uncompromising in the face of evil; one must also believe that the way of the world can be changed in some way. In the end resignation and indifference to the fate of others amount to one and the same thing. The rescuer, then, is an interventionist, an activist, someone who believes that the will of the individual can have an effect. But at the same time the rescuer refuses to pursue the struggle by emulating the enemy, by mirroring his hatred. As one rescuer puts it, "We will not apply to them their own laws" (Stein 94). The rescuer knows that the "enemies" are human beings, that, like him, they are neither saints nor monsters: the good person does not ignore evil, but he hates the system, not the individuals who serve it. The rescuers who fought the Germans did not hate them. "Jews or Germans—it made no difference to me, as long as I could see them as human beings," one rescuer says. "I didn't allow myself to fall into the trap of seeing an enemy in every German" (184). "I always separated the Nazis from the Germans," adds another (227). And a third concludes, "If we were to close our eyes to all Germans and treat them all as if they had a shameful disease, how would that make us different from the Nazis?" (298). The people who saved the Jews also know Germans they esteem. If there is a paradox here, it is only an apparent one. Those who, alone among a generally docile population during the war, took great risks to save others are the same people who later, surrounded by a liberated population bent on vengeance and purification, intervened to prevent young women having their heads shaved or German soldiers being lynched.

In no nation are rescuers a particularly numerous category of individual, and yet these are not exceptional people. How does one explain their scarcity, then? What character traits, political or religious convictions, socioeconomic or professional backgrounds favor these admirable activities? Nechama Tec tried to answer these questions by studying a fairly wide sample of Polish rescuers, who, at least in numbers, constitute the single largest group of rescuers from any nation. Her results are fairly negative: there is no set of characteristics by which to predict with certainty whether a given individual will act to save the life of someone in danger. Tec's research does suggest, however, why there were so few rescuers: the act of rescue requires certain qualities that are somewhat at odds with one another. As a rule, rescuers are not conformists, in other words, people who allow their neighbors' opinions or the law to dictate their conduct. Instead, they see themselves as outsiders, free spirits who balk at conformity. It is not that they reject the concept of law. On the contrary, they are quite able to distinguish between good and evil; they have keen consciences, whose dictates, moreover, they tend to follow. At the same time, they are not lovers of principles, content to cherish abstractions. Not only are they universalists who in their willingness to help people they do not know, recognize the common membership of all in the human community; they are also individualists, in that they defend not ideals but people of flesh and blood.

It is probably for this reason that the rescuers are usually couples: it is hard for any one person to combine all the requisite qualities. One of the partners, for example, will embody the morality of principles. He or she will decide that the right thing to do is to help all those who are in need, not just family or friends; he or she will also be the one to take the first step and decide to intervene instead of waiting in resignation. The other partner will be swayed by the morality of compassion: he or she will not think about noble principles but feel the humanity of those in need. Without forcing himself (or herself), he will see to the daily needs of those who must be helped, their food and shelter. Without this second person, there is no act of rescue; without the first, there would have been no one to save. Both partners are indispensable because their actions are complementary.

In a great many cases (although not all), the first role is played by a man, the second by a woman. Typically more comfortable in the public arena, men are the ones to take the initiative in receiving those in need and organizing the aid networks. As a result, they are frequently away from home and are not involved in taking care of their "boarders." The women, who often preside over the private domain, may at first object to this invasion of their home life but go on to see to their boarders' daily needs with patience and ingenuity. I will not go over again the reasons underlying this division of labor; suffice it to say that it is the combination of these two types of qualities that make acts of rescue more likely and thus prompt us to see the complete moral being in the couple, not in the individual.

André Trocmé, the pastor of Chambon, and his wife, Magda, are a good illustration of this rule. When they met, they each had their own kind of moral aspiration: he practiced his ascetic love of God; she

confined herself to tender concern for those around her. Their encounter changed both of them. "Magda saw that if he gave way to
[mystical feeling], his life would be one of ecstasy and bliss, but without action," Philip Hallie writes. "Instead of helping others, he would
embrace them in ineffectual passion" (67). At the same time, Magda
decided that her direct interactions were no longer enough, that she
would also believe in the higher ideals in which her husband found
inspiration. To the very end, the two of them were complementary
rather than alike. André thinks about God, Magda about her neighbor. André dreams up vast projects, Magda makes them real. Without
this collaboration, there would have been no haven for Jews in
Chambon and several thousand more would have died.

The rescuers' acts can in fact be doubly beneficial. Not only do they
protect the lives of possible victims, they also prevent potential executioners from doing evil and even prompt them to change from within,
as they respond to good with more good. The Trocmés' actions apparently convinced certain members of the Vichy police to collaborate
with the couple rather than with the Gestapo. The people of
Chambon were thus regularly informed of impending roundups. Even
the commandant of the German garrison in the neighboring city of
Puy was clearly moved by the Trocmés' nonviolent struggle to save
human lives; in fact, he claims that he himself kept the SS from
dismantling their entire operation. Years later, he tells André Trocmé,
"I told Metzger that this kind of resistance had nothing to do with
violence, nothing to do with anything we could destroy with violence.
With all my personal and military power, I opposed sending his troops
to Chambon" (245). Does this mean that the war against Hitler could
have been won by persuasive example? I don't think so, any more
than did the rescuers of Chambon: these methods work only in certain circumstances, when one can be sure of making personal contact
with the "enemy." Where tanks rumble and airplanes empty their
bomb bays, such resistance makes no sense. In those conditions,
nonviolence is suicide.

The rescuer's rewards lie solely in what his or her action accomplishes; beyond that, there are few bonuses. To have strangers in the
house for months, sometimes years, is not always pleasant, particularly
as the rescuers tend to be people of modest means. Even aside from

the risks that the host family incurs, there are all the small inconveniences of daily intimacy, the inevitable envy and jealousies, the multiplication of household tasks; all these problems, moreover, have to be resolved on the sly. In addition, the people one rescues are not necessarily likable (it's not a requirement; if it were, the rescuers' act would be a simple matter of ordinary caring): this girl from a wealthy family demands breakfast in bed; that young man insists that his girlfriend be allowed to visit him; another refuses to eat anything that isn't kosher. Once the war is over, the rescuers are hardly overwhelmed by expressions of gratitude from the people whose lives they've saved. In the first place, those who have been saved still find themselves in precarious circumstances, having lost family and worldly goods, no longer feeling they belong to the country they once called home and not yet having found a new one. And then it has always been true that those who receive tend to want to forget the period when they were powerless and reduced to depending on others. To evoke those times rekindles the memory of their humiliation.

It may come as a surprise to learn that after the war the fate of the rescuers was rarely a happy one. Of course they still feel they acted justly, but even so, many succumb to depression. Only a few are able to resume their prewar lives as if nothing had happened. With keener moral sensibilities than most other people, they often develop reactions similar to those of the survivors; they feel guilt and shame. They came too close to too great an evil not to feel threatened within themselves: If others could act in this way, what is to prevent me from doing so one day? Aren't they human beings, too, just like me? And if others died but not I, isn't it because, in spite of everything, I acted selfishly? Such reactions, however, do not make the rescuers particularly indulgent toward their compatriots, whose cowardice and indifference they have observed throughout the long years of occupation. These compatriots, for their part, tend to regard the rescuers with hostility, seeing them as a living reproach, proof that they themselves could have behaved differently. Often former rescuers choose to emigrate to distant lands that did not experience the same degree of evil, countries like Canada, Argentina, and Australia; having behaved differently from their compatriots in a time of crisis, the rescuers find it hard to reintegrate into their community when those days are over.

Once settled elsewhere, however, they find that countries, like individuals, resemble one another, that each is an unequal mix of good and bad, that the majority is always conformist, and that the righteous are few and far between.

As positive as they are, the stories of rescue are not, then, a source of optimism, precisely because they demonstrate that people who are capable of such acts are very rare, almost as rare as the great heroes and saints (although more likable than either), and also that no one can guarantee how he or she might one day act. The survivors all suffer from the same certainty: they know that if similar acts of persecution were to begin again tomorrow, despite all the official demonstrations of sympathy for the victims and condemnation of the oppressors, the rescuers would be as rare as they were before. Their good neighbors who now greet them every morning would once again turn away. "Facing people I meet," writes Charlotte Delbo, "I wonder, 'Would he have helped me walk, that one? Would he have given me a little bit of his water?' I examine all the people I see. . . . Those about whom I know from the very first glance that they would have helped me walk are so few" (254). The righteous are, and will always be, exceptional. And yet the ordinary virtues are not rare. Each and every one of us, usually at a fairly young age, discovers a moral sense within himself, though few would be willing to risk their lives to save the life of another, or the lives of their children to protect the sons and daughters of a stranger. As one rescuer, a woman, put it: "There is no good news about the Holocaust" (Stein 85).

The Perils of Judgment

Nothing in modern times comes closer than the concentration camp does to being an incarnation of evil. Yet, as we have seen, the perpetrators of this evil were neither monsters nor beasts but ordinary people, rather like us. Today, our response to this evil must take both of those facts into account. First of all, we must not abandon the principles of justice: the guilty must be judged, each according to his precise acts and responsibilities. (In Germany, the passage of years has now all but eclipsed this issue, but in the former Communist countries, it could not be more timely.) Second, we must refuse to establish a radical discontinuity between "them" and "us," to demonize the guilty, and to look upon individuals or groups as perfectly coherent and homogeneous.

This refusal need not take the form of any sort of "pardon." Simon Wiesenthal's *The Sunflower* expressly invites us to reflect on our attitude toward evil and to ask whether, under certain circumstances, it should be forgiven. I would not put the question this way. Once again I find myself in agreement with Primo Levi, who, although he refuses to be described as a "forgiver" (which is what Améry called him) and rejects the notion that the guilty should be absolved because they, too, had their moments of kindness and remorse, maintains his firm belief in our common humanity.

Some former inmates, as we have seen, cannot help thinking in terms of revenge, which is certainly understandable. All the more remarkable, then, is the fact that most of those who address this issue explicitly reject summary judgments or Manichean positions. Yes, they say, some acts are monstrous. Their authors are not monsters, however, and it would be regrettable if we succumbed to indignation and ignored the complexities of such individuals, their inconsistencies. Even many of the camp guards belong to what Levi calls the "zone of gray." Good people have their moments of cowardice, and executioners are not strangers to mercy. As Ella Lingens-Reiner concludes, "It seems right to me not to pass over those little acts of kindness in silence" (16).

What is true of individuals is even truer of groups: none is perfectly good or entirely bad (which is not to say that they are all the same). Joe Siedlecki, a survivor of Treblinka, sees it this way: "In Treblinka, some of [the guards] were animals, but some of them were good too. . . . Then, of course, there were the terrible ones . . . animals, sadists. But there were such people amongst the Jews too" (Sereny 188). Hermann Langbein, another survivor and a historian of Auschwitz, made a tally of every instance of an SS member's offering aid to the inmates, occasionally even helping them to escape (of course, there were not many such instances). And Primo Levi made it a rule always to point out exceptions to whatever the prevailing stereotype about group behavior happened to be at the moment. "In telling this story after forty years," Levi writes, "I'm not trying to make excuses for Nazi Germany. One human German does not whitewash the innumerable inhuman or indifferent ones, but it does have the merit of breaking a stereotype" (*Moments* 92). Typically, he would introduce one of his counterexamples with words like these: "And right here, as a breath of fresh air and to prove how alien I am to global judgments, I would like to recount an episode: it was exceptional, and yet it happened" (*Drowned* 169).

These survivors were not content merely to declare that one ought not to exclude from the circle of humanity those whose acts one deplores or hold the crimes of individuals against the group to which they belong; they also acted on that principle. Gitta Sereny in her book of interviews brings to the fore several examples: Richard Glazar, a Treblinka survivor, sent his son to study in Germany after the war; not all his former fellow inmates approved. Stanislaw Szmajzner, a survivor of Sobibor, who testified for the prosecution at Stangl's trial, "allowed press photographers to take pictures of him with Frau Stangl" after the hearing in Düsseldorf. "I agreed to it," Szmajzner says, "because I had nothing against Stangl's family and I was aware of how hard all this was on them" (Sereny 130). Joe Siedlecki married a German who had converted to Judaism in order to marry him; here again, not all his friends understood. And yet the explanation is clear: these three survivors refused to imitate the Nazis, who made no distinction between the group and the individuals who belonged to it, condemning each on the basis of the other.

We would do well to keep in mind the attitudes of these victims as we approach the thorny question of how to judge evil.

AGENTS OF EVIL

To begin with, we must distinguish between legal guilt and moral responsibility. From the standpoint of justice, the men and women who actually committed the crimes and who alone are properly the concern of the judicial system must not be confused with the bystanders, the passive spectators who are responsible at most for not coming to the aid of those in danger and thus who need answer not to the courts but to history or their own consciences. Karl Jaspers made this distinction immediately after the war in *The Question of German Guilt.* If I dwell on it here, it is because we are dealing with totalitarian regimes in which this boundary, clear enough elsewhere, tends to blur. In a totalitarian system, all are involved in maintaining the status quo and thus all are responsible; at the same time, all are subjugated and act under constraint. The totalitarian situation is of course unique, yet that fact does not make personal responsibility a moot question. Even inside the camps, in that most extreme situation, it was still possible to choose between good and evil. All the more reason, then, for this choice to continue to exist outside the camps, though perhaps not as accessibly as in a democracy.

In a brilliant chapter on informers in his book *Forever Flowing* Vasily Grossman juxtaposes different points of view on this subject.

He begins by sketching a portrait of four Judases and then imagines their public trials and the clash of prosecution and defense. The first Judas was subjected to overpowering pressures—prison, camps, torture—to which he succumbed. The second Judas fell victim to his fear of the immovable state colossus, against which his efforts could never have succeeded. The third Judas chose unconditional surrender, while the fourth Judas suffered from an impoverished childhood. Although Grossman refrains from judging his characters, he ultimately inclines toward general absolution. In each case it is held that "the state alone bears all the guilt" (79). Grossman concludes, "They are not guilty, they were forced to do it by grim, gloomy, leaden forces" (83).

Yet the state has no life outside the people who incarnate it; dark forces need human arms to do their bidding. To presume subjects to be so submissive is to have a very sorry opinion of them indeed; in effect, Grossman damns his characters with such excuses. Human beings are never *entirely* unable to choose. However great the pressures, the individual remains responsible for his actions; otherwise, he renounces his humanity. Still, when these pressures are truly great, our judgment of the individual must take them into account. For to the extent that human beings are the sum of their actions, and have no essence apart from those actions, we cannot say that only actions are affected by evil and individuals are not.

"Perhaps we are guilty," Grossman adds, "but there is no judge who has a moral right to raise the question of our guilt. . . . Among the living, there is no one who is innocent. All are guilty, including you, Comrade Prosecutor, and your defendant, and I, who am now considering the defendant, the prosecutor, and the judge" (80, 83). Today, after the collapse of Communist totalitarianism, the question is timely: should the guilty be judged? And if so, where are the innocent judges who will judge them? Grossman's argument is ill-considered, however: courts dispense justice in the name of principles accepted by all, not because the just, and only the just, have the right to condemn the guilty. In confusing legality with morality, Grossman is mistaken. Justice demands of judges only that they rigorously carry out its principles; their personal virtue is of no concern. It is true that the pressure exerted by the state may constitute an extenuating circumstance and that the extremely widespread practice of certain crimes may, in time, argue for a general amnesty. Still, at least at first, the truth must be established and justice rendered. Clemency is a welcome thing, but it must come later; there is a vast difference between being lenient and concealing the truth. In France, after the liberation in 1944, the literary world was torn by an impassioned debate pitting those calling for justice (which often meant getting even) against those who sought charity (and hence pardons for the collaborators), Vercors and Albert Camus against François Mauriac and Jean Paulhan. Yet their positions were not mutually exclusive: even a decision to pardon needs to be made with open eyes and full knowledge of the facts. Justice is not just a question of meting out punishment; it also involves bringing the truth to light.

Furthermore, in a world as compartmentalized and specialized as ours, the question of responsibility has to cover everything from words to deeds, that is, from first formulations to final execution. That there were so many who took part in the commission of evil does not make them less responsible. It is true that the courts are charged only with the determination of legal guilt and that not every accomplice is guilty in the eyes of the law, which punishes decision makers, not those who by their words inspire the ultimate decisions. Thus, alongside legal judgments, a place must be made for moral judgments, which can be expressed only by social consensus; moral responsibilities are real and cannot be ignored simply because they fall outside the purview of the law. One may not share the indignation of Hermann Kesten, who thinks that in Germany "the 'writing-desk' murderers were much more dangerous and abominable than the actual torturers and executioners" (Wiesenthal 153) and that therefore writers and intellectuals like Ernst Jünger, Gottfried Benn, Martin Heidegger, and Carl Schmitt should have been punished more severely than concentration camp commandants Höss and Stangl. Nonetheless, one cannot ignore the role, and hence the responsibility, of certain currents of thought in the rise of totalitarian regimes. Anti-universalism (the privileging of a race, class, or nation), hyper-determinism (which, in the end, means a denial of morality), and conflictualism (which sees in warfare the supreme law of life) all played a part, and real crimes were committed in their name.

At the Nuremberg trials, two positions were in evidence: some of the accused denied all wrongdoing, laying the blame for their misdeeds on the state or the führer; others, notably Speer, considered themselves guilty. Speer drew a distinction between two sorts of crimes—those for which he was personally responsible (the use of camp prisoners as forced labor in armament factories, for example, and hence their deportation) and those for which he was responsible only by complicity, as a member of the country's ruling circle. Eichmann, at his trial, acknowledged his guilt only in the second sense, except that he did not belong to Germany's ruling class. Speer was all the more willing to accept his share of responsibility for Hitler's crimes, of which he did not stand accused, inasmuch as it left in the dark crimes of which he was more directly guilty; he reproached himself for having been part of the Nazi state, not for having committed any specific act. (This is his strategy throughout his book as well.) Nonetheless, during the trial itself, Speer took responsibility for both types of crime, which is probably what allowed him to survive spiritually.

The vastly more common position, though, is that of the erstwhile agents of evil (officers and guards) who refuse to acknowledge any responsibility whatsoever. In the courtroom, as well as in the forum of public opinion, most of them pleaded not guilty. "Not one of those who served in Hitler's 'machine' used the simple phrase 'I am sorry' in defending himself," wrote psychoanalyst Alexander Mitscherlich after attending the trial of members of the Nazi medical corps (18). Yet for the health of the social group, acknowledgment of the crime by its perpetrators is no less important than is its punishment. We should therefore examine the various arguments that these individuals and their apologists advance in their defense, arguments that, however mutually contradictory, are nevertheless often put forth simultaneously. Like the man whose neighbor accuses him of having broken a kettle he borrowed, the defendants say that the kettle isn't broken and that, besides, they never borrowed it in the first place. And furthermore, the hole was already there when it was lent to them.

The first defense, then, is usually to deny the facts and declare that nothing of the sort ever took place. Yet even the most systematic efforts to destroy all the traces inevitably fail: decades later, witnesses speak out (the first eyewitness account of the massacre at Katyn has just been published, fifty years after the fact), buried manuscripts are unearthed, and even the remains of the dead make their contribution to the establishment of the truth (in 1990 Bulgarians began disinterring skeletons that provided evidence damning for the victims' executioners, many of whom are still alive and enjoying their privileges). And so, with the failure of the first argument, a second one is needed. It goes like this: I had no idea. When real, this ignorance tends to be a matter of more or less conscious and deliberate effort. Stangl, the commandant of Sobibor, then of Treblinka, preferred not to see what was happening. "At Sobibor, one could avoid seeing almost all of it," he says. "It all happened so far away from the camp-buildings" (Sereny 114). A former SS guard at Treblinka says much the same thing: "I didn't *want* to see anything. Yes, I think several people felt like I did. But that was the most positive thing one could do—you know, play possum" (Sereny 167). Of course, when people like him played possum, it made it that much easier for others really to be killed.

Speer describes in detail his successive refusals to take account of news or information that might have disturbed him. During the summer of 1944, his friend Karl Hanke, the *Gauleiter* of Silesia, confided in him. "He advised me," Speer writes, "never to accept an invitation to inspect a concentration camp in Upper Silesia. Never, under any circumstances. He had seen something there which he was not permitted to describe and moreover could not describe" (375–76). Speer acceded docilely to Hanke's request: he chose to ignore the truth about Auschwitz. By not knowing, he could continue to do his part for the German war effort with perfect peace of mind. Speer is correct, then, in concluding that "in the final analysis I myself determined the degree of my isolation, the extremity of my evasions, and the extent of my ignorance" (113). He also writes the following: "Being in a position to know and nevertheless shunning knowledge creates direct responsibility for the consequences" (19).

Those who can pretend neither that these things never happened nor that they were unaware of them resort to a third argument: I was just obeying orders. We have already seen that this defense implies a degradation of self worse in some sense than the crime itself, for the person availing himself of such a defense is essentially declaring himself less than human. Legally speaking, moreover, committing a crime under orders remains a crime.

The fourth and final argument is the one children use: Everyone else is doing it. Victims often remark that the executioners were ordinary people, "people like us," and with anguish they conclude, "We, too, then, are guilty." The executioners make the same discovery and find it immensely gratifying: "We're no different from everyone else," they say, "and therefore we are innocent." Such was Göring's strategy at Nuremberg. He did not deny what had happened, nor did he dodge his responsibility under the pretext that he was following orders. Instead, he drew parallels between the history of Germany and that of other countries. "The British Empire [was] not built up with due regard for principles of humanity," he said. "America has hacked its way to a rich Lebensraum by revolution, massacre, and war" (Gilbert, *Nuremberg* 202). As for the Soviet Union, its totalitarianism was no less fierce than that of Hitler, who, moreover, often found the Soviet version a source of inspiration. No country can wage war on the basis of humanitarian principles, and none has managed to eschew war, particularly not the victorious Allies. "When it is a question of the interests of the nation . . . then morality stops. This is what England has done for centuries" (370).

Other defendants at Nuremberg did not hesitate to use the same argument. "They are trying to pin the murder of 2,000 Jews a day in Auschwitz on Kaltenbrunner," Hans Frank, the Nazi governor-general of Poland, points out, "but what about the 30,000 people who were killed in the bombing attacks on Hamburg in a few hours?" To which Reich minister Alfred Rosenberg adds, "They were also mostly women and children." "And how about the 80,000 deaths from the atomic bombing in Japan?" Frank continues (265). Alfred Jodl, the chief of Wehrmacht operations, concedes his responsibility for the bombing of Rotterdam; it was as bad, he says, as the Allied bombardment of Leipzig, which took place after the war had already been won. If some are judged but not others, he implies, it is not because the latter are in the right but because they were on the winning side. Or as Göring put it, "The victors are the judges."

This sort of argument, that might makes right, cannot simply be brushed aside. One can rejoin, of course, that a crime is not excused by the existence of similar crimes. True enough, but inasmuch as one crime is punished and not the others, it is obvious that might has something to do with it. At the Nuremberg trials, the sight of Stalin's representatives condemning those of Hitler surely bordered on the obscene, since until that time each side tended to emulate the other, that is, when they weren't collaborating directly. The Soviet camps were perhaps less "advanced," but they predated those of the Nazis and were larger, every bit as deadly, and just as full after the war as before. The response to Göring, Frank, and Rosenberg is that the Jews were never at war with Germany, and thus they cannot be compared to casualties of war (the same is true of the "internal" enemies of the Soviet Union, China, and Cambodia). But does war justify the murder of children? It can also be argued that there are degrees of crime and that the extermination of an entire group of human beings by the state apparatus, an extermination based on pseudo-racial criteria, is particularly grave, almost unique. On the other hand, Nazi officials stood trial for other crimes in addition to those of the concentration camps; they were also charged with bombing cities to terrorize civilian populations, and in this practice they were in greater company.

There is an element of incontestable truth in Göring's contention. The crimes of the major colonial powers, especially England and France, were vast in number, and those of the Communist regimes were no less serious. In all wars, the rules of humanity get trampled on, and the bombings of Leipzig and Hamburg, not to mention Hiroshima and Nagasaki, go far beyond what any conventions of war should allow. Yet I draw the opposite conclusion from Göring's: instead of justifying the crimes of the Nazis, this kind of comparison should prompt us to think about the other crimes—"our" crimes, in the same sense as the Nazi crimes were "German"—and to condemn them as well. One cannot remake history and undo what ought not to have been done, but one can at least reestablish the truth about what happened and keep that truth alive in the collective memory. It confers no moral distinction on the French or the Americans or any other peoples for them to remember the crimes of the Germans while repressing the memory of their own, even if in this particular instance their own crimes were less grave. "It appears to be symptomatic of a certain modern mentality," John Glenn Grey writes, "to marvel at the absence of guilt consciousness in others while accepting its own innocence as a matter of course" (173). One cannot remake the past, but today, in the present, we must remember what the cost of another war would be. And it can be made clear that in the future even "legal" crimes will be punished. For the time being, although supranational justice remains but a solemn hope, the idea can still serve as a guiding principle. Rather than criticize the legitimacy of Nuremberg, as Göring does, I would like to see a Nuremberg in permanent session, one that would try all crimes against humanity, which others besides the Nazis have committed, too.

ONLOOKERS

Let us now cross the boundary dividing the active participant from the passive spectator and thus the notion of legal guilt from that of moral responsibility. The mere drawing of this boundary is critical, and concentration camp survivors themselves often refer to the distinction in rejecting the idea of a collective guilt that would condemn a whole nation as executioners. Etty Hillesum once again has the merit of having insisted on this distinction at the very moment she was being made a victim. "If there were only one decent German," she writes in 1941, "then he should be cherished despite that whole barbaric gang, and because of that one decent German it is wrong to pour hatred over an entire people" (8). Shortly after the war, Jaspers argued the absurdity of condemning, legally or morally, an entire people. Only individuals have a will, he declared, and thus only individuals can be held guilty; to say that "the Germans" or "the Europeans" or even "the Christians" are guilty of the Holocaust is nonsensical. Camp survivors do not dispute this position. "Whoever accepts the doctrine of the guilt of a whole people," Bettelheim writes, "helps to destroy the development of a true democracy, which is based on individual autonomy and responsibility" (*Heart* 288). Primo Levi is more vehement: "I do not understand," he says, "I cannot tolerate the fact that a man should be judged not for what he is but because of the group to which he happens to belong" (*Drowned*

174). Once again, to deny the capacity of the individual to wrest himself away from the influence of his origins or environment is to strip him of his humanity.

The guards in the gulags and the concentration camps were firm believers in the notion of collective guilt. Buber-Neumann recalls that in the Soviet camps all Germans were automatically considered fascists, even if they were in fact Communists who had fled the Nazi regime. Things were no different in the German camps: the individual amounted to no more than his group identity. Each time a protest over what was being done to the Jews arose in any corner of the world, Eicke responded by terrorizing Jewish prisoners: in his eyes, they were collectively guilty. Hitler himself believed at first that all Jews were guilty and then, toward the end of the war, that all Germans were, too (because they were losing their battles). This perverse notion of group solidarity extended to far more arbitrary assemblages: a boxcar of prisoners or an entire barracks. This is why ten prisoners were shot for every one who escaped, one hundred for every act of resistance; each member of the group was held responsible for the actions of any one of them. Bettelheim is thus quite right to conclude that "when we select a group of German citizens, show them the concentration camps, and say to them, 'You are guilty,' we are affirming a fascist tenet" (*Heart* 288).

Jean Améry, another survivor who endured terrible suffering, disagrees. In his book *At the Mind's Limits*, he inveighs against Jaspers and defends the idea of collective German guilt. He knows full well that there were exceptions, for he himself met good Germans, but he nonetheless considers his thesis a valid statistical approximation. When the train full of deportees crossed Czechoslovakia, he says, helping hands reached out to it; when it stopped in Germany, there were only stony faces. Consequently, "as long as the German nation . . . does not decide to live entirely without history," Améry says, "it must continue to bear the responsibility for those twelve years" (76). Yet if what Améry has in mind is legal responsibility, then we must point out that only individuals, and not "the Germans," can be judged and found guilty. And if the question is one of historical responsibility, then we must allow the comparison between Germany's history and that of other countries and recognize that Germany, unfortunately, is not the only nation with cause for self-reproach. Améry dismisses such comparisons, arguing, for instance, that the term *totalitarianism* is a camouflage for German crimes. To be sure, an individual cannot help feeling resentful seeing his unique experience grouped together with others and transformed into an example of something more commonplace. That is his right, and it has to be respected. But it is also our obligation to make clear that there is a difference between justice and resentment.

Onlookers, as a matter of principle, are not liable to prosecution under the law, but they can still be held morally responsible. They do not constitute a homogeneous group, however, and it might be better to envision them as spread out across a number of concentric circles according to their degree of distance from those who took an active role in the commission of evil. In the *first circle* are the close personal relations—the families and intimate friends—of those who are judged legally responsible. These people cannot really take refuge in claims of ignorance, for they had, as it were, front-row seats. And so they turn to other arguments, one of the most common being that they were sorry indeed about what was happening but could do nothing to help. "It is dreadful," someone with firsthand knowledge of what was going on in Treblinka tells Franz Stangl's wife, "but there is nothing to be done" (Sereny 137). Or as the wife of an SS guard in the Sonnenstein "euthanasia institute" puts it, "It was awful, of course, but what could *we* do?" (106). A basic fatalism is compounded by the fear of retribution. What's the point of protesting, the argument goes, when it won't help the victims and will bring about the protester's own demise? This two-tiered argument is a typical one among people living under totalitarian regimes, for not only do these regimes depend on the individual's fear for life and limb, they also present the course of history—in other words, the life of society—as something inexorable, no more subject to human volition than a process of nature is. Such an idea is entirely in keeping with the hyperdeterminism of these regimes' philosophies. In reality, neither part of the argument stands up to scrutiny: a regime will sometimes modify its position in the face of widespread protest, and the expression of disagreement does not necessarily entail the death of the protester. But what the totalitarian regime cannot bring about in reality it brings about in the mind of its subjects; therein lies its strength. That said, we must not forget that acts of protest do carry certain risks, and morally speaking, while it is legitimate to encourage others to run such risks, one may not reproach them for not doing so (such reproach one can level only at oneself).

Gitta Sereny had the excellent idea of interviewing at length not just Stangl but also his wife, Theresa. How could she accept the fact that her husband made his living sending people to their deaths, Sereny asks. By doing her best to ignore it, Frau Stangl replies. By not asking him embarrassing questions. By accepting his awkward explanations, his claims that he was involved with administrative tasks exclusively, not with the killings. ("Of course I *wanted* to be convinced, didn't I?" Theresa Stangl admits to Sereny, thirty years after the fact [137].) By likening the victims to the soldiers who had died on the front lines. By refusing to believe that women and children were being killed, too. This response to the world, a process psychologists call accommodation, was necessary for Frau Stangl if she was to continue living in peace and tranquillity. She herself says so clearly enough: "That was how I wanted, how I needed, how I *had* to think in order to maintain our life as a family and, if you like . . . my sanity" (348). Theresa Stangl preferred comfort to truth, but in this she was not alone.

What responsibility do those in this first circle of intimates bear? As we have seen, the men and women who played an active role in carrying out evil often lived a fragmented existence, their lives split into a public and a private realm, with no communication between the two; they could be good spouses and excellent parents. Stangl, in particular, wished to be an exemplary father to his children, seeking thereby to compensate for his dissatisfaction with his work. What would he have done had his wife insisted he choose between her and his work? Sereny raises this question with Frau Stangl, who understands the implications of her answer: if she says that she thought her husband would have changed jobs, she would be admitting responsibility for what happened, because she could have stopped it. Her reaction is revealing. After pondering the question a long time, she replies that if she had confronted her husband with the alternative, Treblinka or herself, "yes, he would in the final analysis have chosen me." Yet a few hours later, in the middle of the night, she changes her mind and sends Sereny a letter with the opposite response. Sereny draws the obvious conclusion, "that the truth can be a terrible thing, sometimes too terrible to live with" (361, 362). In countless cases, family or close friends could have helped prevent the killings but did not choose to do so.

In the *second circle* around the active perpetrators of evil one finds their compatriots, those who, without knowing them personally, belonged to the same community. Former inmates generally felt that the civilian population around them remained indifferent to their fate, and there is no reason to doubt their impressions. Inmates of the Nazi concentration camps in Germany and the countries of Eastern Europe were often from countries other than the ones where they were interned, but in the Soviet Union, as in Bulgaria, where inmates were on home soil, the civilian population was no more helpful. The explanation generally given by those who did nothing was ignorance: we did not know what was going on inside the camps. This explanation has been scrutinized from all possible angles. Certainly it contains an element of truth: secrets, often quite closely guarded, are intrinsic to the totalitarian state. Frequently, the agents of evil themselves lack a complete picture of the action in which they were engaged. But on the other hand, the camps were not hermetically isolated from the rest of the country. Many of them were work sites and thus part of the general economic scene; some contact with the outside population was inevitable. Moreover, there were too many inmates and thus too many guards for the news not to travel from friend to friend and neighbor to neighbor until it was known everywhere. If people truly did not know what was happening, it was because they did not want to know; one cannot, however, hold each person, individually, guilty of this neglect.

(With the arrival of press freedoms in Bulgaria in 1989, people began talking a lot about the massacres of 1944, immediately after the Communists seized power. "How could you have condoned this?" I asked my father. "How could you have declared your solidarity with the Communists who were responsible for this slaughter?" "We knew nothing about it," my father answered. "It happened in the villages,

and in the capital we heard nothing about it." Yet he also told me that
his own mother, who lived outside the capital, had begun to look at
him with fear in her eyes ever since he joined the party. One of my
mother's best friends, I also seem to recall, was the wife of a former
prime minister who was shot dead during that period. Had my father
really tried to find out what was happening around him? Would I
have, in his place?)

The accounts of survivors abound in examples of willful ignorance
on the part of those who were in a position to know. Long after the
war, Primo Levi began a correspondence with a man named Müller
whom he'd known at Auschwitz; Müller was not a guard but a chemist. Levi asked him what his reactions were to what he saw, and
Müller answered that he saw nothing. He may not have been lying.
"At that time, among the German silent majority," Müller wrote to
Levi, "the common technique was to try to know as little as possible,
and therefore not to ask questions" (*Periodic* 221). The facts "were
stifled by fear, the desire for profit . . . blindness and willed stupid-
ity" (*Drowned* 16). As another witness explains, "They didn't want to
look, you know. They hastened to buy what they had to buy and
hastened back into their houses" (Lanzmann 50–51). And Eugenia
Ginzburg writes, "When I look back on that frightening time, I marvel
at people's willful blindness. How could we have failed to ponder over
what was so obvious?" (*Within* 282). Ginzburg realizes that, like everyone else—victims as well as witnesses—she, too, had acceded to
her own deception. Clearly, one of the lessons to come from this
experience is that the desire to believe is more powerful than the
desire to see. The prisoners needed to believe in the possibility of
survival in order to hope; thus they "forgot" what they saw and heard
and felt. The onlookers needed to believe in the harmlessness of the
measures directed against their neighbors so that they could go on
living undisturbed by what they had seen; thus what they saw at Kolyma did not enter their field of awareness.

(The new opposition press in Bulgaria has called attention to another
period as well, 1959–62, when the fact that there were no more "fas-
cists" at hand meant that other internal enemies had to be found. So it

was nonconformist young people who were hunted down, in particu-
lar those who danced and dressed "as they did in the West," which,
for men, meant in tight trousers. Police raided nightclubs and asked
the men to take off their pants without touching their shoes; those who
couldn't were hauled off to police stations, where they were savagely
beaten. At the second "infraction," they were subject to administrative
detention and sent without trial to a special camp, a rock quarry in
Lovech. Half the detainees died there, thanks to the guards' excellent
care. I was not a child at the time; I was in my final years at the
university. In fact, I often went dancing. I was never subjected to one
of those humiliating roundups. Could it be that the police took care in
choosing which places to raid? I knew nothing about Lovech. Did I
try to know? Not at all. I was too pleased with my own small privi-
leges to risk losing them by sympathizing with the victims of the re-
gime. Like everyone else, I knew there was a camp on the island of
Belene, but it never posed a problem for me: I considered its existence
no more unnatural than that of prisons.)

The parallel Eugenia Ginzburg draws between the blindness of the
onlookers and that of the victims themselves is crucial to any reading
of the accounts of survivors. Primo Levi talks about the "voluntary
blindness" of the German populace, yet he uses the same term in
describing his own attitude on the eve of his arrest in Italy: "If we
wanted to live, if we wished in some way to take advantage of the
youth coursing through our veins, there was indeed no other resource
than self-imposed blindness" (*Periodic* 51). "Our ignorance," he
writes, "allowed us to live" (129). Examples abound of warnings
brushed aside, of information deliberately ignored. Gitta Sereny tells
of a young man who travels secretly to Treblinka to find out what has
happened to the Jews who were taken there; afterwards, he returns to
Warsaw and describes what he saw. "This young man besought the
ghetto elders to believe him and . . . finally they said he was over-
wrought and needed a rest which they would arrange for him in the
ghetto clinic" (257). In Elie Wiesel's *Night*, when Moshe the Beadle
returns to the village with his terrible news, "people refused not only
to believe his stories, but even to listen to them. . . . 'He's just try-

ing to make us pity him. What an imagination he has!' Or even, 'Poor fellow, he's gone mad' " (4–5).

This attitude existed inside the camps, within the very sight of death. Filip Müller gives its guiding principle: "If you want to live," he says, "you are condemned to hope" (Lanzmann 69). For Louis Micheels, it is "one of the many forms of denial without which life would be unbearable" (34). Survivors all use the same words: "I didn't believe it," they say, or "I couldn't believe it." In *Ravensbrück*, Margarete Buber-Neumann describes coming upon some inmates who had been transferred from Auschwitz to Ravensbrück. She didn't believe a word of what she heard, she says. She thought they had completely lost their minds. Richard Glazar sorted through clothing belonging to people who had arrived at Treblinka along with him and says, "I think I still didn't think. It seems impossible now, but that's how it was" (Sereny 177). Even in the shadow of the crematory ovens and at the doors to the gas chambers, this same denial of reality recurred again and again, for reasons that are not hard to understand. "We should commit an immense historical error were we to dismiss the main defence mechanisms employed by the victims . . . as mere symptoms of blindness or foolishness," writes Louis de Jong. "Rather did these defense mechanisms spring from deep and inherent qualities shared by all mankind—a love of life, a fear of death" (54). We believe what we want, not what we see.

Yet isn't it an outrage to attribute the same psychological process to both victims and onlookers, when the consequences were so different? I think not, to the extent that in denying reality both victims and onlookers acted from the same motive: they were protecting their own well-being (or at least they believed they were). Still, if victims and onlookers used the same psychological strategy, the fact remains that their situations were entirely dissimilar. The danger the victims denied was one that threatened them directly, whereas the onlookers ignored a danger that threatened their neighbor. For this reason, the same psychological process has a different moral significance in each case: one may regret the willful blindness of the victims, but one cannot reproach them for it. The same cannot be said of those who stood by and watched and who thus can legitimately be blamed, if only in the eyes of history, for failing to come to the aid of persons in danger.

Opinions on this subject are divided. Some survivors bitterly accuse the onlookers of indifference. Without it, they say, the agents of evil, always few in number, could not have committed their crimes. "Knowing and making things known was one way . . . of keeping one's distance from Nazism," writes Primo Levi, who, notwithstanding his reluctance to subscribe to the notion of collective guilt, adds that "the German people, as a whole, did not seek this recourse, and I hold them fully culpable of this deliberate omission" (Afterword 201). Others find the reproach unjustified, for it means demanding exceptional qualities of ordinary people. As Bettelheim writes, "Certainly one can blame the average German for not having been one of those heroes, but how often has there been a people whose average citizen is a hero? . . . We cannot ascribe blame to the unarmed onlookers of the crimes of the Gestapo as long as we do not charge the unarmed onlookers of a holdup who do not stop the gunmen from assaulting the cashier" (*Heart* 286).

Set forth this way, the issue seems a bit too abstract. Levi ignores his own distinctions between legal and moral, collective and individual guilt, while Bettelheim doesn't especially illuminate the situation in which everyone finds himself swept into criminal complicity. Ginzburg's reflections on the subject are more useful: "When you can't sleep," she writes, "the knowledge that you did not directly take part in the murders and betrayals is no consolation. After all, the assassin is not only he who struck the blow, but whoever supported evil, no matter how: by thoughtless repetition of dangerous political theories; by silently raising his right hand; by faint-heartedly writing half-truths" (*Within* 153). For these things, the citizens of totalitarian countries are truly responsible.

(*I know what Ginzburg is talking about. I was still young at the time, but I remember that we kicked a student in my class out of the Komsomol just after Stalin's death because we thought the boy hadn't shown sufficient grief. A while later—and here my recollections are vaguer—his family, White Russians who had emigrated to Bulgaria after the revolution, was sent back to the USSR. Nothing more was heard of them. I learned recently, that this forced emigration was, in fact, a deportation. A few years after those events, as a university student, I was present—this time, in silent disapproval—at the expulsion of another comrade, for what sin I do not know. Both times I'd voted the way I was supposed to. If I had stayed in Bulgaria, I would have spent the next thirty years writing half-truths, trying to beat "them" at their own game, seeing who could outsmart the other. That is one of the most striking characteristics of totalitarian regimes: everyone becomes an accomplice; everyone is both inmate and guard, victim and executioner.)*

The *third circle* around the agents of evil consists of the populations of the subjected countries, like Poland and France, during the Second World War. We cannot shift onto the shoulders of these people a burden of responsibility properly belonging to the agents of evil, who, after all, were their enemies. Yet one wonders whether some of these populations did not show a marked complacency toward what was taking place on their soil. The question has been raised in particular about the Poles, who witnessed the extermination of the Jews in the Nazi death camps close at hand. Doesn't their indifference, often ascribed to their traditional anti-Semitism, make them guilty? As Marek Edelman says, in some situations "your enemy is not only the one who kills you but also the one who is indifferent. . . . Not to help and to kill are the same thing" (*Au sujet* 271).

The impassioned debate surrounding this question makes it quite clear that the truth is complex. Anti-Semitism played a part, as did greed and fear; in the end, non-Jewish Polish onlookers not only accepted the unacceptable but also took more pity on themselves than on their Jewish neighbors. At the same time there were many instances of mutual aid and kindness, even though the Poles themselves lived under the Nazi menace and were persecuted by the occupying Germans with particular severity. The following example illustrates the situation well. During the occupation, an "Aryan" Polish couple hid a Jewish woman. One day the husband, who had never shed his anti-Semitism, decided to denounce the woman and so be rid of her. Threatened by a friend of his wife's, however, he gave up his plan and left home. After the Warsaw uprising of 1944, with the general evacuation of the city's population, the Jewish woman was obliged to leave her hiding place. In an effort to protect her, the Polish woman "lent" her baby to the Jewish woman, as the Germans were less suspicious of mothers with children. And what if, because of her gesture, the Polish woman had lost her child? "Irena would not have harmed him," the mother replied. "She would have taken good care of him" (Tec 55). Betrayal and caring could dwell together beneath the same roof. Forty years later, Walter Laqueur concluded that the attitude of the Polish people during this dark period was far from the worst. "A comparison with France," he writes, "would be by no means unfavorable to Poland" (107).

The comparison with France is not unwarranted: their differences notwithstanding, both countries were occupied by the Nazis and both had substantial Jewish populations. Yet those who accuse Poland typically tend to extoll France. "It would have been impossible to have death camps in France," Claude Lanzmann states categorically. "The French peasants would not have stood for it" (*Au sujet* 249, 232). Statements like this will remain forever unverifiable, of course, but certain facts about France should not be overlooked. The racial laws promulgated by Vichy, for example, were more rigorous than the Nuremberg edicts, and the deportation of Jewish children was undertaken on French, not German, initiative. As for the spontaneous sympathy of the local population, let me quote from a recent study of the transit camps set up for Jews in the area of Orléans. A woman who as a little girl had been arrested in the roundup at Vel d'Hiv describes what took place: "Buses came to take us to the Velodrome, which meant a long ride through the capital in broad daylight, under the largely indifferent, sometimes surprised gaze of the Parisians." A police report states with obvious relief, "For the most part, the people watched indifferently as the convoys of prisoners passed by" (Conan 21, 77).

A woman who lived near the camp remembers the moment when the guards separated the mothers from the children. "Screams, such screams that we asked ourselves what was happening," she recalls. The curiosity, however, stopped there. "I remember that we passed right by the imprisoned people," another neighbor reports, "without our teacher saying anything at all to us about them" (97, 124). The subprefect, a man who until recently still held a civil service position, recalls nothing at all, even though the transfers of prisoners from one French camp to another were organized and escorted by the French gendarmerie and were carried out with the same cattle cars that soon after would take these children to Auschwitz. The French, I think, ought to be grateful to Eichmann and his colleagues for having chosen Poland as their extermination ground, a choice made for "practical" reasons and not at all because the French would have refused to collaborate in the endeavor or because they would have been troublesome witnesses. Had the decision been otherwise, we might have learned yet again that, as Napoleon said, the word *impossible* is not French. One can blame onlookers for their indifference, but not one population more than the others.

It is true, however, that two European countries, Denmark and Bulgaria, proved exceptions to the rule, for the Jews in these countries were not deported. In Denmark, the Nazis met with a blanket refusal to collaborate on the part of the entire population, which was in fact busy organizing itself to ensure the successful flight of their Jewish minority into neutral Sweden. In Bulgaria, the deportation of Jews from territories newly acquired from Greece and Yugoslavia was allowed to take place; as for Jews of Bulgarian nationality, they were registered, their property was expropriated, and they were assigned to live in designated areas outside the capital, but they were never deported beyond the country's borders. The reasons for these relatively happy outcomes are identical in each case: the absence of deepseated anti-Semitism in the population and the willingness of a few politicians to make courageous decisions and stand by them. In Denmark, the king, the prime minister, the director of the civil service, and the bishop publicly announced that they would oppose any discrimination against the Jews; many people of lesser prominence also took an active role in the rescue operations. In Bulgaria, the king, the vice president of the National Assembly, the metropolitan of Sofia, and even the minister of the interior spoke out openly against the deportations. There, too, many individuals in the general population helped the Jews hide and survive.

Can one conclude from all this that the Danes and the Bulgarians are intrinsically better than other peoples? That they are made of finer stuff? As far as the Bulgarians are concerned—a subject on which I may be said to have a less than disinterested view—I do not think this is true (moreover, recent persecutions of the Turkish minority in Bulgaria show that exclusionary and discriminatory sentiments are not altogether unknown among the Bulgarian majority). I believe instead that the Danish and Bulgarian experiences represent a fortunate confluence of circumstances. Geography and politics played a part, as did tradition and sociological factors, but nothing decisive would have happened had not a few politically influential individuals had the courage of their convictions and stood by what they believed at the risk of losing their jobs or even their lives.

In the *fourth* and final circle are the populations of the free countries, the enemies of the dictatorships under which these crimes are committed. These populations are free not only because they do not live under the menace of totalitarianism but also because they have multiple sources of information at their disposal, which allows them access to the truth if they desire it. We know today that news of the Nazi death camps leaked out early on; it is the subject of Walter Laqueur's *The Terrible Secret*. As for the Soviet camps, there was never any lack of information about them, even as early as the 1920s. We also know that outside intervention, when it did take place, proved rather effective. And yet intervention against the Nazi camps was nearly nonexistent, and against the Soviet gulags it came very late. The question is why.

The answer as it pertains to the extermination of the Jews is particularly sinister: the Allies feared that Hitler might take them at their word and send them several million Jews instead of proceeding with the exterminations. A document from the British Foreign Office dated March 1943 and addressed to the American government states, "There is a possibility that the Germans or their satellites *may change over from the policy of extermination to one of extrusion,* and aim as they did before the war at embarrassing other countries by flooding them with alien immigrants" (Wyman 105). In October 1943, a document from the U.S. State Department says in turn, "There are grave objections to a direct approach to the German Government to request the release to us of these people. . . . The net result would be the transfer of odium from the German to Allied Governments" (Wyman

189; see also 46). The Canadian government used similar arguments. The officials and representatives of the Allied governments preferred to let the Jews die on somebody else's soil rather than be saddled with them at home.

In the case of the Soviet camps, the reasons are different. The governments of the West did not so much fear inundation by a tide of undesirable immigrants as they feared discomforting the Soviet government itself and—even more, perhaps—the Communist sympathizers in their own countries. The latter were a small minority, of course, but because they were heavily represented among intellectuals, they knew how to make themselves heard. In France, despite efforts after 1949 by several survivors of the Nazi camps, including David Rousset and Germaine Tillion, to prove the ongoing existence of the gulags, public opinion remained skeptical. During the course of a libel action brought by Rousset, Communist Party members, citizens of a democratic country though they were, argued: It isn't true because it isn't possible. After some ten people had presented irrefutable testimony, a Communist Party deputy named Marie-Claude Vaillant-Couturier, who had been deported to Auschwitz, told the court that even to ask the question of whether a Soviet gulag system existed was an affront, "because I know there are no concentration camps in the Soviet Union" (Rousset et al. 194). Others, Sartre among them, conceded that the facts were true but refused to discuss them. They didn't wish to demoralize Billancourt, the Communist working-class suburb of Paris, they said. Thus both groups fought, in effect, to maintain the camps; consequently, both bear responsibility for them. It was not until the mid-1970s, with the publication of Aleksandr Solzhenitsyn's books, that the left-wing French intelligentsia changed their tune.

A further example of this kind of resistance to the truth is evident in the fate of a book by another survivor of the gulags, Gustaw Herling. Published in Polish in 1951 and translated into English, with a preface by Bertrand Russell, A World Apart was turned down by every French publishing house, including the respected Editions Gallimard, despite the persistent intercession of Albert Camus, one of the few people in the world of French letters to denounce the Soviet camps, an action that earned him some powerful enemies. To all intents and purposes, whatever concerned the Soviet Union was subject to censorship. Czeslaw Milosz's *The Captive Mind,* published in 1953, was virtually ignored by the French intelligentsia; at the time, Milosz recalls in a preface written in 1981, "the majority of French intellectuals resented their country's dependence upon American help and placed their hopes in a new world in the East, ruled by a leader of incomparable wisdom and virtue, Stalin. Those of their compatriots who, like Albert Camus, dared to mention a network of concentration camps as the very foundation of a presumably Socialist system, were vilified and ostracized by their colleagues" (v).

The intellectuals of the free country of France became willing accomplices to the Communist camps by preventing the disclosure of information about them, information that would also have been a means of combatting them. But Kolyma is a long way from Paris, some will say; you can't compare this situation to that of the German people, who claimed to know nothing about Buchenwald and Dachau, German camps on German soil. Perhaps not, but the Parisian intellectuals of the forties and fifties were not living in a totalitarian country. Nor did they have the excuses of people in Weimar or Munich. No repression would have come down on them had they told the truth.

This journey through the circles of complicity with evil leads, I'm afraid, to a rather somber conclusion: even if one can find exceptions to the rule, most onlookers, whether close or distant, let events take their course. They knew what was happening and could have helped but did not. Everywhere and always there were people who showed concern for the victims, but the bulk of the population proved, incontestably, indifferent. Whatever contrasts existed between various countries (apart from Denmark and Bulgaria) were slight and ultimately of little consequence for those concerned, although those who suffered the rejection of a particular population may understandably feel otherwise. Germans and Russians, Poles and French, Americans and English—all were equal in this respect. They might not all bear the same responsibility because circumstances in each country were different, but all of them allowed things to happen. The misfortune of others, it seems, leaves us cold if in order to alleviate it we have to sacrifice our own comfort.

Of course, we need not have looked as far as the concentration camps to learn this truth. Acts of injustice take place all around us every day and we do not intervene to stop them. In Rumania and Bulgaria, certain populations continued to be deported until 1989; in what was formerly Yugoslavia, such deportations are still taking place. One could go on. We have resigned ourselves to wars, both present and future. We have grown used to seeing extreme poverty all around us and not thinking about it. The reasons are always the same: I didn't know, and even if I had, I couldn't have done anything about it. We, too, know about deliberate blindness and fatalism, and here totalitarianism reveals what democracy leaves in the shadows—that at the end of the path of indifference and conformity lies the concentration camp.

Must we each, in consequence, take upon ourselves all the suffering in the world, ceasing to sleep peacefully so long as there remains somewhere in the world even the slightest trace of injustice? Must we think about everyone and forget nothing? Of course not. Such a task is beyond human strength; it would kill anyone who undertook it before he or she could take even the first step. Forgetting is perilous, but it is also necessary. Only the saint can live in perfect truth, renouncing all comfort and consolation. We can, however, set ourselves a more modest and accessible goal: in peacetime, to care about those close to us, but in times of trouble, to find within ourselves the strength to expand this intimate circle beyond its usual limits and recognize as our own even those whose faces we do not know.

Telling, Judging, Understanding

There are no longer any camps in Germany or even, it seems, in Russia, although some still remain in China and perhaps elsewhere. We have a different battle to fight, and it is far from over. It is taking place in our memories of the past, in the judgments we bring to bear on it, and in the lessons we draw from it.

To revive the stories of the camps today actually means to continue a struggle begun while they were still in operation. The proper functioning of concentration camps requires that neither the inmates—or witnesses—nor even the guards have precise knowledge of what is going on; therefore, the first weapon against them is the collection and diffusion of information. We know how meticulous the Nazis were in guarding the secret of the "final solution" and how systematically they worked to erase all traces of their deeds. As for the Communist regimes, their entire existence was predicated on the pervasiveness of state propaganda, on the impossibility of the population's gaining access to any kind of free press.

It is no accident that Stalin and Hitler waged a war of information alongside their wars of conquest. The distinctive feature of totalitarianism is that it attempts to control the life of society in its totality, to make everything and everyone dependent on the will of those who wield power. In the totalitarian regime, not only does might make right, it also makes truth. The existence of an autonomous truth, whether embodied in universal principles or in a knowledge of facts, is inadmissable, for it represents an island of independence over which the powers that be have no control. The idea that the will to power and not empirical knowledge or the common consensus of free individuals should control and shape the interpretation of facts is a cornerstone of the totalitarian philosophy. Truth is to be nothing more than the consequence of that will. That is why those in power cannot tolerate any loss of control over information. Totalitarian countries may indeed have constitutions and laws, but it is often exceedingly difficult to gain access to them; under the totalitarian regime, the adage "Ignorance of the law is no excuse" becomes something like "Knowledge of the law will not be tolerated." Factual information, like data or statistics, is simply unavailable (I remember how in Sofia the telephone book was one of the hardest books to get one's hands on). With regard to the camps, therefore, the decision whether to keep silent or speak out is never a neutral one. "If we remain silent," Bettelheim says, "then we perform exactly as the Nazis wanted: behave as if it never did happen" (*Surviving* 97). Or in the words of Auschwitz survivor Sarah Berkowitz, "Silence is the real crime against humanity" (43).

It must be said, however, that the inmates and, later, many of their contemporaries waged a tenacious battle for information and truth and in the end won their victory. Of course, "in the end" may be longer than a single human life, and lives, moreover, are sometimes cut short by the struggle itself. Yet victory is possible because once truth is established, it is indestructible, whereas lies and dissimulations must be constantly renewed. And since, as Pasternak wrote, the entire system is based on lies, it will collapse once the truth is known (this is one of the things the recent experience of glasnost has taught us).

Circulating information about the camps obviously no longer carries any danger (it can even be commercially profitable). Nevertheless, this knowledge still encounters resistance today. In many cases, the resistance is all too comprehensible; for example, former guards (there are few left from the Nazi period but many from the Communist regimes) have everything to gain from their files' remaining unopened. For related reasons the search for truth is often opposed by the far right and by the Communist parties, two different "negation-ist" schools, "assassins of memory," as Pierre Vidal-Naquet has called them. On the other hand, former prisoners themselves can also offer resistance, but of course from entirely different motives. Often they maintain that the study of their unique experience devalues or trivial-izes it; they believe that no one who has not actually experienced what they themselves went through can possibly understand it.

The most powerful and insidious resistance, however, comes nei-ther from survivors nor from the opponents of democracy but from the rest of us—ordinary individuals who, belonging to neither of these groups, are outside parties, as it were. We would rather not hear the accounts of these extreme situations. They disturb us. Primo Levi describes a recurring dream, a nightmare, that he had at Auschwitz. In this dream he leaves the camp, returns home, and proceeds to tell in detail the horrors that befell him. As he speaks, he realizes none of those who are present is listening to him. They are talking to one another. In fact, they hardly notice he's there; worse, they get up and leave without saying a word (*Survival* 54). After his liberation, he continues to have this dream and discovers he is far from unique; other survivors tell him they have dreamed the same dream. Sadly, it contains a significant element of truth. While the camps were still in existence, there was no dearth of accounts about them, neither in the neutral countries nor among the Allies; nor were accounts of the gulags a rare thing during the days of Stalin and his successors. Yet people refused to believe what they heard and finally stopped listen-ing altogether, for if they had listened they would have had to radi-cally rethink their own lives. Some troubles are best ignored, it would seem.

Even after the camps were closed down things remained the same. We all have our own problems; we are all in a hurry. Don't we already know these stories by heart? And besides, we tell ourselves, these extreme situations have nothing to do with us. If we belong to the workaday majority, our lives are still relatively easy, no matter how many emotional disappointments or spiritual frustrations we encoun-ter. Wars happen elsewhere. Great disasters are reserved for others. Our own lives unfold quietly, far from the extremes. And yet one thing we've learned from the recent past is that there is no break between extreme and center, only a series of imperceptible transitions. If, in 1933, the German people had understood that Hitler was going to exterminate every Jew in Europe, he would not have won the election as he did. Each concession agreed to by a population that is in no way extremist may be insignificant by itself; taken together, however, such concessions lead to nightmare.

Yet if we were willing to admit that totalitarianism is a possibility for any of us, that Kolyma and Auschwitz "happened" to people like us and that one day we could find ourselves in the same situation, we would find it hard to continue leading the untroubled lives we know. We would have to change how we see not only the world but ourselves as well. The fact is, however, that the task is too onerous. Truth, it seems, is incompatible with inner comfort, and most of us prefer comfort. The manuscripts buried in the ground at Auschwitz and in Warsaw escaped the notice of the guards, withstood the damp, and with great effort were finally deciphered; but there is still no telling if they will succeed in breaking through the new wall of indifference that we have erected around them. I do not think we can change this state of affairs, nor do I even wish we could. I do believe, however, that from time to time we need to disrupt it.

To conclude that we must recount the past or recover the memory of it does not go far enough, however. It is imperative that we do both, but we cannot stop there, for reasons having to do with the very nature of memory, its limitations. Memory cannot reconstruct the totality of the past—that would be both impossible and undesirable. It can only reconstruct a selection of those elements we consider worth remembering, and never more than that. The defenders of totalitarianism choose certain segments of the past and cover up the others; their enemies fight this selection—by proposing another one in its place. Neither wants simply to restore the past; both want somehow to make use of it in the present. There is, however, no necessary correlation between how we tell the past and how we use it; that it is our moral obligation to reconstruct the past does not mean that all the uses we make of it are equally legitimate.

The peoples of what was once Yugoslavia, for example, often give the impression that the reason they are now at war is a matter of memory—of the suffering they inflicted on one another during World

War II, not to mention other, even more distant calamities. Thus the Serbs claim they're fighting the Muslims because they cannot forget their struggle against other Muslims (the Turks), which took place centuries ago. At the very least, they are using this excuse to block any reasons that might encourage them to stop the war. Discovering and telling the truth about the past is perfectly legitimate, but it does not justify wars of aggression.

How, then, do we distinguish between the good and bad uses of "recovered" memory? Should we mourn the disappearance of a strong collective tradition that selects certain facts and rejects others? Or else resign ourselves to the infinite diversity of individual cases? Of course not. We can, for instance, apply standards of good and evil to the acts that people use their memories to justify; we can opt for peace over war. We can also—and this is what I wish to propose— distinguish between various forms of reminiscence. The recovered event can be read either literally or paradigmatically. *Either* this event is preserved in its literalness, meaning that it is mine, unique, and inimitable: I, the person to whom the event happened, determine what caused it and what its consequences are; I discover all the people who can be linked to the initial perpetrator of my suffering, and then I condemn them in turn; I also establish a continuity between the person I was and the one I am now, between my people's past and present, and I spread the consequences of the intial trauma over all the moments of existence. *Or* the event is perceived as one instance among others of a more general category, in which case it can be used as a model by which to understand new situations and new perpetrators; in other words, it becomes an exemplary, or paradigmatic, memory, one that teaches us certain lessons. The associations it evokes for us are analogical; they are defined by relations of similarity, and the task at hand becomes not to reinforce one's identity but to determine whether the analogies are justified.

As a first step, then, we can say that literal memory is a potentially risky endeavor, whereas exemplary memory is truly liberating. Not all lessons are good, of course, but they can all be evaluated according to certain universal and rational criteria that underlie human dialogue. This is not true of literal memories, for they have no common measure of comparison.

I use the word *memory* in both cases because literal and exemplary memory alike are concerned with the past. In ordinary usage, however, literal memory is simply "memory," while exemplary memory goes by the name of "justice." Justice involves generalizing from the particular and applying abstract principles to concrete offenses, which is why it is embodied in impersonal laws, interpreted by anonymous judges, and rendered by jurors who do not personally know either the offender or the victim. Of course, victims can suffer when they see themselves and their stories reduced to so many illustrations of the same rule, for from their perspective what happened to them is absolutely unique, and they may feel that the perpetrators of crimes against them are not punished severely enough. But that is the price of justice, and it is no accident that justice is not administered by the victims. It is this dis-individuation, if you will, that allows the law to function. The past must serve the present, just as memory—or forgetting—must serve justice, otherwise we remain prisoners of the past.

The first duty of the witness is to tell, so that the truth can be established. The task of the judge is to judge, and, in so doing, uphold the principles of justice. But even these things are not enough. Ultimately an effort must also be made at all costs to understand. If we are content to tell the event without trying to relate it to other events that have occurred in the past or are taking place now, we turn it into a monument. This is better than ignoring it, of course, but that doesn't mean it's enough. Our memory of the camps should become an instrument that informs our capacity to analyze the present; for this to happen, we must recognize our own image in the caricature reflected back at us by the camps, regardless of how much this mirror deforms and how painful the recognition is. Only then can we tell ourselves that, at least from the viewpoint of humanity, the horrible experience of the camps will not have been in vain, that it contains lessons for us, who think we live in a completely different world. The act of telling events of the past without seeking to understand them and without allowing them to be compared with other events, past and present, amounts to a consecration of the horror. To reject that consecration does not mean we wish to turn this page of history. Instead, it means that we have finally decided to read it.

The objection perhaps will be raised that understanding and judging are mutually exclusive, that he who understands also accepts and that he who judges cannot be involved. I couldn't disagree more. If I try to understand a murderer, it is not to absolve him but to prevent others from repeating his crime. Furthermore, if I understand nothing, I cannot be a good judge: the impersonality of the law must not lead to the depersonalization of those it condemns. Both the objective causes of an act and the subjective intentions of its perpetrator must be allowed to influence our judgment.

Through the different facets of our being we are all of us witnesses, judges, and interpreters. Thus the responsibility I am speaking of here belongs to all of us, not just to specialists, professionals, historians, judges, or scholars. So that we may be spared the horror of repeating the past, we must not hesitate to set about reconstructing it yet again.

PRIMO LEVI

It goes without saying that to reconstruct the past, particularly one as fraught with evil as the past that is the focus of this book, is not a simple matter. The fact that witnessing, judging, and understanding are necessary does not make these tasks any less complicated or, indeed, less dangerous for those who undertake them. To grasp some of the problems encountered by those who speak of the camps and seek to draw lessons from them, I propose looking at a few of the many works about the concentration camp experience. The authors whose works I discuss—Primo Levi, Claude Lanzmann, and Gitta Sereny—represent, in my view, something like a range of possible responses to the challenges faced by those who would understand the past.

Primo Levi is no doubt the best known of all the witnesses to the Nazi camps. Levi was an aspiring resistance fighter when he was arrested in Italy, but it was as a Jew that he was deported to Auschwitz, where he remained for a little over a year, until his liberation by the Soviet army. Back home again, in 1947, he wrote his first book of meditations on the world of the concentration camp, entitled *If This Is a Man*. The work remains the masterpiece of concentration camp literature. Explaining how he came to write it, Levi said that in the beginning he felt compelled to write out of an inner need that he could not silence, a need composed of the obligation to bear witness, the desire for vengeance, the hope of purging himself of unbearable memories, and an appeal to the sympathy of his contemporaries. He wrote feverishly, but the pages still did not come together as the book we know today. Levi wanted to "become a man again, a person like everyone else," he writes in *The Periodic Table* (151), but he couldn't quite manage to do it until he met his wife. The fact of being loved transformed him, freed him from the clutch of the past; recognized in the gaze and in the desire of another, Levi was confirmed in his humanity. At last he could distinguish himself from the man he had been before and see him from the outside. "My very writing became a different adventure," he says, "no longer the dolorous itinerary of a convalescent, no longer a begging for compassion and friendly faces, but a lucid building, which now was no longer solitary" (*Periodic* 153). The atrocities of the past were not forgotten, but now they formed the stuff of a communicable reflection, a story that reached out even to those who had not undergone the same experiences. Primo Levi the writer was born: "Onto my brief and tragic experience as a deportee," he writes, "has been overlaid that much longer and complex experience of writer-witness, and the sum total is clearly positive" (Afterword 216).

Levi's position with regard to his experience of the camps is characterized by a double transcendence: he is beyond both hatred and resignation, which may explain, among other things, why his book came and went relatively unnoticed during the period directly following the war, a time when people preferred the security of clear-cut positions and radical solutions (I am not sure this era is entirely behind us). Jean Améry's calling Levi a "forgiver," a label both inaccurate and unfair, tells us less about Levi than about Améry, who seems to believe that vengeance and forgiveness exhaust the possibilities. Levi disagrees: "I never forgave our enemies of that time," he writes. "I demand justice, but I am not able, personally, to trade punches or return blows" (*Drowned* 137). If the enemy has not changed radically, he says, then "it is our duty to judge him, not to forgive him," though, Levi points out, "one can try to salvage him, one can (one must!) discuss with him" (*Periodic* 222–23). By agreeing to talk to the enemy, we are refusing to allow the first ostracism—the one that excluded us —to be followed by a new but comparable one, aimed this time at him. Levi distrusts such replications: "I am not a Fascist or a Nazi," he states. "I believe in reason and in discussion as supreme instruments of progress, and therefore I repress hatred even within myself: I prefer justice" (Afterword 196). Levi, then, overlooks neither aspect of his project: "The [oppressor] is to be punished and execrated (but, if possible, understood)" (*Drowned* 25). Indeed, his message to the Germans who survived the war is, "I would like to understand you in order to judge you" (174).

Levi's books have come from this effort to understand and to judge. Several are devoted to the camp experience, especially the first, *If This Is a Man (Survival in Auschwitz)*, and the last, *The Drowned and the Saved*. By the variety of questions they raise and the quality of Levi's thought, these works represent an accomplishment unparalleled in modern literature. What I retain from them, above all else, is Levi's rejection of Manicheanism, whether in reference to groups (the Germans, the Jews, the kapos, the members of the *Sonderkommandos*) or individuals. In the world there is not just white and black, he writes, "but a vast zone of gray consciences that stands between the great men of evil and the pure victims" (*Moments* 127). We have already seen how alert Levi is to exceptions that defy stereotypes. His interpretations are cautious, his judgments subtle. His interest in the ordinary, the everyday, may well account for these qualities in his work. Unlike Jean Améry, Levi never suggests that his intellect and creativity set him apart from those around him; instead, he finds human virtue in the most ordinary acts (recall that he recited *The Inferno* to someone who had probably never heard of Dante).

Everything would be clear and simple had Levi not taken his life in 1987. This act, as he himself said of Améry's suicide in 1978, "like other suicides admits of a cloud of explanations" (*Drowned* 136). To be sure, all suicides of survivors—whether Améry's or Bettelheim's or Borowski's—do not mean the same thing, but it is difficult not to want to look for meaning in them. Some explanations are too singular or too personal for there to be any interest in discussing them publicly, but I cannot believe that there is no relationship between Levi's suicide and the position he finally arrives at regarding the concentration camp experience. Perhaps the cause of his suicide lies elsewhere, but even if all we can say about his position is that it did not block his suicidal impulse, we still have an obligation, I believe, to reread his work more attentively in the light of his final act. Should the apparent serenity that graces so much of his writing be qualified by certain less visible—and more somber—conclusions?

It is worth noting that the great majority of survivors have fallen victim to depression and trauma. The rate of suicide among this group is abnormally high, as is the prevalence of mental and physical illness. Levi often speaks to this issue, explaining the survivors' anguish as rooted in a feeling of shame, a diffuse and insurmountable guilt for having lived through what they did. This feeling bears no direct relationship to the kind of guilt with which the courts are concerned; in fact, as a rule, the legally guilty feel they are innocent while those who are truly innocent live in guilt. As Martin Walser, who attended the trial of the Auschwitz guards in 1963, observes, memories of the camps are far more devastating to the victims than to their tormentors (Langbein 488).

The shame of the camp survivor has several components, the first being the *shame of remembering*. In the camps, the individual prisoner is deprived of his will. He is made to perform acts that he not only disapproves of but also finds abject, that he does either because he is ordered to or because he has to so as to survive. Améry compares this feeling to that of a victim of rape; logically, it is the rapist who ought to feel shame, but in reality it is the victim who does, for she cannot forget that she was reduced to powerlessness, to a total dissociation from her will. Often, even in the eyes of the inmates, the guards emerge as the true victors, for they succeeded in transforming normal individuals into human beings prepared to do absolutely anything in the name of one single thing, survival. Levi describes the feeling in the chapter of *Survival in Auschwitz* entitled "The Last One." A man is about to be hung from a gallows in the middle of the roll-call square for having supported the *Sonderkommando* revolt at Birkenau; he is the "last man," because everyone else, all those present at his hanging, have already had their spirit broken. They can no longer rise up in revolt. In fact they dare not express any solidarity with the victim when, before the trap door opens, he calls out to them, "Comrades, I am the last one!" (135). Levi makes the point again, recounting the final days before the liberation, when he was in the camp infirmary: "The work of bestial degradation," he writes, "begun by the victorious Germans, had been carried to its conclusion by the Germans in defeat. It is man who kills . . . it is no longer man who, having lost all restraint, shares his bed with a corpse" (155–56). It is unbearable to recall having been reduced to existing only to eat, to living in one's own excrement, to fearing all authority, just as it is unbearable to recall the time when one did not do all one could to defend one's dignity, to care for others, or to keep one's mind alive. Even if one had tried, one would surely have often failed. This shame of having been the object of humiliation and insult is indelible. Améry, who was tortured in Gestapo prisons, writes, "Whoever has succumbed to torture can no longer feel at home in the world. The shame of destruction cannot be erased" (*Mind* 40). Through the experiences of the former inmates, we discover our own imperfection; simply to read their stories is to acquire the inner conviction that we would not have been any better than they.

A second form of shame, specific to those who came out of the camps alive, is what is called *survivor's guilt*. Camp officials would often use the tactic of deciding on the precise number of victims in advance; anyone who escaped deportation or extermination knew therefore that someone else would be taken in his or her place. Yet the survivors share this shame in a much more general sense as well. The camp is a place where everyone has to fight for the extra spoonful of soup, the extra mouthful of water; that means someone else has one spoonful less, and in these conditions, such losses can kill. If only I'd shared with him, each survivor thinks, he wouldn't have died: every survivor believes that he is living in the place of someone else, someone who died. It is not "the best" who survive but rather those who cling the most fiercely to life. "The worst survived, that is, the fittest," Levi writes, "the best all died" (*Drowned* 82). The survivor thus has nothing to be proud of. It goes without saying that this self-accusation is usually unwarranted; nonetheless, it is widely shared. I was no better than the others; why should I be alive when they are dead? "It's the impression that the others died in your place," Levi writes, "that you're alive gratis, thanks to a privilege you haven't earned, a trick you've played on the dead. Being alive isn't a crime, but we feel it like a crime" (*Not Now* 295).

The third kind of shame, the most abstract, is the *shame of being a human being*. Members of the species to which we ourselves belong have committed atrocities, and we understand that we cannot protect ourselves from the implications of that fact by calling those persons madmen or monsters. No matter how we look at it, we are all cut from the same cloth. Levi has this feeling from the moment of his liberation: he returns to Italy, feeling "guilty at being a man, because men had built Auschwitz" (*Periodic* 151). Already in *The Reawakening* (1963), he speaks of "the shame . . . that the just man experiences at another man's crime; the feeling of guilt that such a crime should exist, that it should have been introduced irrevocably into the world of things" (2). Shame, first because the survivor could not prevent this evil from occurring (how far we are from the ideas of Etty Hillesum!), then because the survivor belongs to the same species as the perpetrators of it, because no man is an island. Jaspers calls this "metaphysical guilt": "That I live after such a thing has happened weighs upon me as indelible" (32). Yet one need not know anything about metaphysics to feel this guilt. Lorenzo, the silent bricklayer who saved Levi's life and the lives of many other Italians at Auschwitz, felt it and died of it. He committed a sort of passive suicide, letting the desire to live ebb away until it left him altogether. He had seen evil too closely to continue believing in and holding on to life. Lorenzo was not a prisoner; he was a witness and a rescuer. But, as we have seen, rescuers, too, are often victims of the "survivors' disease" (*Moments* 118). And given that all of us are witnesses in one way or another, no one can consider him- or herself immune to the malady. Rudolf Vrba foresaw just this possibility in describing how he felt immediately after his escape: "There were times when we wondered whether we would ever be happy again, or whether Auschwitz, scene of so much death, was immortal and would live in our minds until we, too, died—and then live on to haunt those who understood" (254).

Compounding these various forms of overwhelming shame are the more recent disappointments that came with liberation, with life lived in freedom. Home at last, the survivors could not help expecting some sort of gratification after the inhuman suffering they had endured.

None came. Desolation reigned outside the camps as well; everyone was in a hurry to bandage his own wounds and forget yesterday's misfortunes. The survivors, those shades returned from the dead, symbolized a past people wanted to forget. Even beyond this personal frustration, the survivors often found the world a deeply disappointing place, at least in relation to what they had hoped for, and they had hoped for much. They had been subjected to extraordinary pressure; they had endured extraordinary suffering. They expected, on their return, that they would find the world changed by this exceptional experience. "We had experienced one extreme, that of absolute evil," Grete Salus, an Auschwitz survivor, explains, "and we thought that afterwards we'd experience the opposite extreme—absolute good" (Langbein 452). It was not like that at all. Everything continued much as before: people shut up in their own small and egocentric worlds, opportunists seizing opportunities, injustices abounding, new wars threatening. Those who died in the camps had died for nothing; having failed to change the world, the survivors felt they had betrayed their dead comrades. Despite the quietist ideals she so cherished, Etty Hillesum already predicted this possibility in 1942: "If all this suffering does not help us to broaden our horizon, to attain a greater humanity by shedding all trifling and irrelevant issues, then it will all have been for nothing" (*Interrupted* 161). But now the former inmates found themselves surrounded by people who wished only to suppress the memory of the camps or, if they did consent to preserving that memory, simplified and schematized it to the point of caricature until it fit into one of the available stereotypes—cops and robbers or angels and demons.

Or else a different reaction set in. While in the camps, the inmates had had to marshall all their energies, to live beyond their capacities. Now, back in the normal world, they experienced a kind of general collapse. Life in the camps had been arduous in the extreme, and precisely because of this, there had been something exalting in it. After the intensity of this experience, everything seemed colorless, futile, false. The usual illusions and consolations had little to offer those who had made the journey back from hell. Even the sensation of being alive diminished, until it often simply disappeared. This is what those survivors meant who, not long after their liberation, found themselves saying, It's horrifying, but I miss the camps; a part of me has remained behind, and now something inside me is dead, even if it doesn't show. In the third part of *Auschwitz and After*, entitled *The Measure of Our Days*, Charlotte Delbo transcribes numerous anguished monologues; "I am dead" is the leitmotif that runs through most of them. "I'm not alive," says "Mado" (Madeleine Doiret). "I see myself from outside this self pretending to be alive. . . . I'm living without being alive. I do what I must. . . . I just don't feel myself living. My blood circulates as though it flowed through veins outside my body. . . . I died in Auschwitz but no one knows it" (257, 258, 262, 267).

In daily life after the war, one did not often encounter the absolute. There was something disproportionate in the contrast between the intensity of life in the camps, even if that life had been miserable, and the mediocrity of happiness outside (assuming one could attain it). One woman, who had witnessed the slaughter of her husband and children and survived the ordeals of both Auschwitz and Ravensbrück, found herself in New York in 1952. She had remade her life. "My [new] husband's been working this whole time in a sports jacket factory, and we manage all right. We have a nice three-room apartment with all the conveniences. We read the *Post*, and from time to time go to a show" (Trunk 293). How can one compare two incommensurable values? And yet there is no cause for regret in this: life can't always meet the heroic requirements of the absolute. We should take life as it comes, with all its little misfortunes and its simple joys. It's just that it isn't always easy.

The former inmate thus has many reasons to feel depressed, and these reasons sometimes lead to suicide. Levi knew all about this. "The ocean of pain, past and present, surrounded us," he wrote in his final book, "and its level rose from year to year until it almost submerged us" (*Drowned* 86). This is a terrifying admission, particularly in the fragility of that "almost." And yet these general considerations shed little light on Levi's suicide. Former inmates generally fall into two categories: there are those who keep silent and try to forget and those who choose to forget nothing and speak out so that others, too, might remember. Levi belongs incontestably to the second group, and its attitude, so much healthier than that of the first, gave him some

measure of protection from the "survivors' disease": he knew its
symptoms only too well. It seems to me, then, that if we are to interpret his decision we must look beyond those traits he shares with
other survivors and consider the unique aspects of his story.

Levi's meditations center on two subjects, the inmates and the
guards. Proportionally, the attention he devotes to one or the other of
these two preoccupations varies with the years. In the beginning, Levi
writes in an effort to reintegrate himself into the human community;
his own experience as an inmate is at the center of his attention,
although his interest in the guards continues to run parallel to his
personal story. "I cannot say I understand the Germans," he writes in
1960, in his preface to the German edition of *If This Is a Man*.
"Something one cannot understand constitutes a painful void, a punc-
ture, a permanent stimulus that insists on being satisfied" (*Drowned*
174). The subject of the guards assumes an increasingly large place in
Levi's thought. His project, moreover, is to understand and to judge,
and since the dispensation of justice in a formal sense was a task that
could be left to others, to the professional judges, the major preoccu-
pation of his final years becomes that of understanding the Germans.

This project, however, draws Levi onto a dangerously slippery
course. We know his views; on the one hand, these were not monsters
but ordinary people; on the other hand, an entire nation—rather than
just this or that particularly active individual—was guilty, not of the
extermination itself but of cowardice and silent complicity in not having sought to know and consequently not having tried to prevent what
was happening in its midst. Mightn't the missing conclusion to this
syllogism be, If the others are like me and if they are guilty, then I
must be guilty, too? Wouldn't this then add another measure of guilt
to whatever burden was already on Levi's shoulders? An absurd conclusion, of course, an erroneous deduction, but our unconscious
minds favor that kind of mistake. Levi himself likens the process to
that of "dogs studied by neurologists, conditioned to react in one way
to the circle and in another way to the square, so that when the square
became rounded and began to resemble a circle, the dogs were
blocked and presented the signs of neurosis" (183). In his effort to
understand, Levi may well have internalized the desire of others to
destroy him. And in his effort to see the human side of his would-be

killers, he may have run out of resources with which to fight the death sentence they passed on him. In other words, he forgot his own warning: "Perhaps one cannot, what is more one must not, understand what happened," he writes, "because to understand is almost to justify" (Afterword 213).

One almost regrets Levi's committment to his project of understanding the enemy (for his sake, not for ours: as readers we are only enriched by his accomplishment). The project is more than admirable, but the former victim may not be the most suitable person to carry it out. Do we ask parents who have watched their children be killed to investigate the psychology of the murderer? In this respect, the incomprehension of other former inmates is clearly healthier, at least from the standpoint of their own well-being. Better for them to hate their enemies, as Rudolf Vrba does, than to understand them. "There's no point trying to understand the SS," Jorge Semprun says bluntly. "It is enough just to exterminate them" (71). The statement is appropriate because it is Semprun who says it, during the war.

Perhaps Levi realized that there was something impossible about his effort to understand the Nazis. Each time the hint of a real encounter appeared on the horizon, he panicked. A German friend sends him Albert Speer's book ("I would gladly have eschewed this reading," he comments) and later gives Levi's book to Speer, promising to send Levi Speer's reactions; Levi is thrown into turmoil. "These reactions, to my relief, never arrived," he writes. "If I had been forced . . . to answer a letter from Albert Speer, I would have had some problems" (*Drowned* 196). A peculiar reticence on Levi's part? I don't think so. Getting to know a Nazi in a deep and meaningful way would have forced Levi to see him in all his humanity, and had he done so, he would have had no weapons left to defend himself against the Nazis' intention to destroy him. The episode with Dr. Müller, which Levi describes in *The Periodic Table*, is rather similar: Levi first met this Müller, a German chemist, in Auschwitz, at a time when one of them belonged to the master race and the other to the race of slaves. Many years after the war their paths cross again, through a business connection. Levi sends him the German edition of *If This Is a Man,* and asks "if he accepted the judgments" in it (*Periodic* 218). Müller replies by asking if he might pay Levi a visit. Levi is frightened; he has no desire to see this man and so avoids answering. When news of Müller's sudden death reaches him, Levi feels great relief. And he is right: it is not his job to play the role of investigator of the German mind.

At the same time, I am not convinced that Levi's project vis-à-vis "the Germans" was simply to understand them, as he said it was. "I hope that this book will have some echo in Germany," he writes, again in his preface to the German edition of *If This Is a Man*, "because the nature of this echo will perhaps make it possible for me to better understand the Germans" (*Drowned* 174). The echo came, as the final chapter of *The Drowned and the Saved* tells us, but it brought no comfort. In *The Periodic Table*, Levi defines his intentions more precisely. "To find myself, man to man, having a reckoning with one of the 'others' had been my keenest and most constant desire since I had left the concentration camp" (215). He calls this hoped-for moment "the hour of colloquy" (*Drowned* 168), but what he goes on to describe does not seem much like a dialogue. He does not really want to hear what the others might say in trying to defend themselves. What he wants to hear is only a particular kind of echo, a balm for his pain; he wants his interlocutor to be cornered by irrefutable facts and to confess his crime. These things amount to retribution, not dialogue, even though hate does not figure into it. Levi seeks not just to understand the others but also to convert them.

Convert them to what? To a better humanity, it seems. Everyone must begin by admitting his guilt and then transform himself internally to prevent another Auschwitz from happening in the future. "Every German must answer for Auschwitz, indeed every man," Levi argues, "and after Auschwitz it is no longer permissible to be unarmed" (*Periodic* 223). Henceforth, all must prefer truth to comfort and be willing to help one another. If Levi takes his own demands literally, he cannot help but feel despair: clearly, he has set too high a hurdle. Humanity (for it's a question of humanity now, and not just the Germans) has not reformed itself. As Levi is the first to notice, humanity has already distorted and repressed even this very recent past. It is still and always the innocent who feel guilty and the guilty who feel innocent. This is no doubt why Levi feels the ocean of pain rise higher and higher with each passing year. It becomes agonizingly clear that, no matter what the fate of any given individual, humanity has not improved and still refuses, on the whole, to hear the lesson of Auschwitz. About that, there can be no illusion.

Just as Levi overestimated his ability to understand the enemy without suffering the consequences of that understanding, so did he underestimate the weight of the world. His books have done more perhaps than any others to alert us to the dangers that lie in wait, but the battle to improve humanity is never definitively won; we must continue to wage it because the fight is just, not because we will see its results. I wonder if Levi did not sometimes transpose the democratic political ideals of reasoned debate and voluntary participation into the realm of individual psychology. If so, his expectations were bound to be frustrated. As he has taught us well, human beings will allow themselves to be guided by darker, more obscure motivations and will follow pathways more torturous than those suggested by sound reasoning; only reluctantly do we use the "supreme instruments of progress." To refuse to admit such things leads to true despair.

SHOAH

The second work I want to examine is Claude Lanzmann's *Shoah* (1985). It is true that *Shoah* is a work of cinema and not a literary text in the strict sense (a transcription of the film has, however, been published as a book) and that visual images require a kind of analysis that literary textual analysis cannot provide. Nonetheless, I feel that the repercussions that *Shoah* has caused justifies its inclusion here.

Shoah is composed essentially of interviews with three groups of people: survivors of the concentration camps (Jews), onlookers (Poles), and former Nazis (Germans). The subject of the film, extermination, as well as the material from which the film draws, namely the interviews, clearly makes it a historical work, and yet the first thing that strikes one about the film is that it is not a documentary, at least not in the usual sense of the word, but rather—for lack of a better term—a work of art. Its aim is not to uncover new truths about its subject; in fact, it uses what historians already know. Most of the people interviewed had already testified elsewhere and in greater detail: Rudolf Vrba, Filip Müller, and Jan Karski had written and published books, as had Raul Hilberg, who has several to his name; Richard Glazar and Franz Suchomel were interviewed at length in Gitta Sereny's *Into That Darkness*. Moreover, Lanzmann by his own admission does not have much respect for purely factual documentaries. "As for memories, we can watch them on television every day," he says. "Guys with ties sitting behind desks and telling us things. Nothing could be more boring" (*Au sujet* 301).

Lanzmann's project is entirely different. "This is not a documentary," he states categorically (298). He aspires not to evoke the past with greater exactitude but rather to resurrect it in the present. Having chosen this goal, Lanzmann must also decide on the means with which to achieve it, and they are several. First, Lanzmann uses only those of his witnesses who do not limit themselves to reporting the facts but are willing to relive them before our eyes. He takes his subjects to the actual scenes of the crime (or to places that remind them of the original scenes) and then waits for their reactions. When necessary, he reconstructs the context. He rents a locomotive and puts Henrik Gawkowski, a former engineer on the transport trains to Treblinka, inside; he builds a beauty shop for Abraham Bomba, a former hairdresser. On other occasions, he asks provocative, even insidious, questions in order to expose unsuspected qualities in his interviewees. In other words, Lanzmann has made a film in which characters from long ago rediscover before the camera the intensity of their past experience.

The distance between past and present is abolished. Instead of filming the past, which is impossible (moreover, there is no archival material in *Shoah*), Lanzmann films the way it is remembered today. The film's emotional intensity is heightened by his personal involvement. "I needed to suffer while I made this film," he says. "I had the feeling that if I suffered, a kind of compassion would be transferred into the film, allowing the viewers to experience, in turn, their own suffering" (291). *Shoah* was a gamble and it paid off. By making us watch the same anxious faces, the same passing landscapes, the same trains over and over again, Lanzmann obliges us to share—to an infinitely more tolerable degree, of course—the anguish of the former passengers. The decision to produce a "work of art" rather than just another eyewitness account is responsible in the end for the film's overpowering effect on its viewers.

By defining Lanzmann's film as a work of art and not a documentary, I do not mean to deny *Shoah* its capacity to show us the truth about a historical period and the events that unfolded in it. *Shoah* deals in historical, not imaginary, facts; moreover, it offers us interviews that are real, not fictional; and finally (and above all), representational art aspires no less than documentary to reveal to us the truth about the world. When history serves as the point of departure for the poet's fictions, the poet can take certain liberties with the exact course of events so as to reveal their hidden essence: therein lies the superiority of poetry over history, as Aristotle pointed out long ago. Lanzmann is of the same opinion. "A film can be something other than a documentary," he declares. "It can be a work of art—and still be every bit as truthful" (243). That much is true. At the same time, a work of art is also a declaration of values and, as such, inevitably takes a moral and political stand. The choice of these values can be ascribed to no one but the artist: facts hold no lessons in themselves and their meaning is never transparent; it is the interpretation the artist gives to these facts that is responsible for the judgments embodied in a work. And here is where *Shoah* becomes problematic, not as a work of art but as an attempt to tell the truth about a certain world and as a lesson drawn from that world. The film succeeds in *telling* us the events of the past, and it does so with great power, but it also leads us to *judge* these events in so oversimplified a fashion that it does not always help us *understand* them.

Most of the reservations others have expressed about *Shoah* are confined to the Polish segments of the film. Except for Jan Karski, who fled Poland, the Poles whom Lanzmann chooses to show us are all anti-Semites. All of them remained indifferent to the suffering of the Jews, all use the same clichés in speaking about them, and in the end, all are pleased to be rid of them. Now, it is a law of art that what is not shown does not exist. Consequently, no matter what Lanzmann's intention, his message is clear: all Poles are anti-Semites. Without seeking to contest the existence of anti-Semitism in the Polish population, one may nonetheless find Lanzmann's assertion too schematic. The real situation was far more complex. In fact, *Shoah's* message is so simplistic that when the film was first released, the Polish government, wanting to defend itself against the film's image of their country, televised only the Polish segments, the effect of which was to make the bias too blatant to ignore. By not showing the exception to the rule he wants to illustrate, Lanzmann espouses—unintentionally, no doubt—the thesis of collective guilt. It is not true, then, as its author claims, that *Shoah* reveals "the true Poland, the *real* Poland," and that it omits "nothing essential" from its portrait of that country (244).

If we read the notes Lanzmann took during and after the filming, the reasons for his bias become clear. Poland was not a real country for him but, somewhat like the Poland of the men who led the Warsaw Rising, an abstraction or allegory, the land where the Jews died, "the perfect killing ground" (312). Immediately after his first visit to Poland, Lanzmann concluded that "a voyage to Poland is, first and foremost, a voyage in time"; later he says that "for me, it's the West that's human; the East frightens me" (213, 300). This allegorizing of the real Poland leads Lanzmann to focus exclusively on illustrating what he calls "my own obsessions" and to insist on the difference between the Poles and other human beings. According to Lanzmann, the French peasants, for example, would never have allowed death camps to be built on their soil—which means, therefore, that the Poles are guilty of having done just that. Lanzmann's surmise is unverifiable, but we might want to consider a historical detail that points out a less speculative parallel between the French and the Poles. Lanzmann reproaches the Poles for having rushed to the death camps in the wake of the exterminations "to sift through the earth in search of coins, jewels, and gold crowns they knew were buried there" (215). In France, when the Jews were imprisoned in the Loiret, the local peasantry came out, eager to help with the searches; some women actually tore off the inmates' earrings "when things weren't moving quickly enough." Others "distinguished themselves by raking through the contents of the latrines in search of rings, bracelets, and necklaces" (Conan 109–10).

The depiction of the Germans in *Shoah* is just as schematic, although as far as I know, the Germans have not criticized Lanzmann publicly. Except for the judges he interviews, who are on the bench today, everyone is invariably a Nazi, everyone pretended not to know anything about what was happening, and everyone secretly rejoiced at the fate of the Jews. In Lanzmann's notes the message of the film becomes explicit. "As for Germany," he writes, "the process of destruction could not have been carried out had it not been for the fact that it was based on a consensus of the German nation . . . [and] the active and patient participation of the entire German bureaucracy" (311). The postwar generation of Germans is not much better than its elders: "Fat and rich, Germany also has no past," Lanzmann says. "Her young men—those now between thirty and forty—are zombies" (312). Not only has Lanzmann selected his characters according to an obvious bias, but he edits out whatever they say that might in any way complicate his simple picture. Lanzmann interviews Richard Glazar at length, but he does not tell us that Glazar sent his son to study in Germany after the war (we learn this in Gitta Sereny's book). Nor does *Shoah* further our understanding of someone like *Unterscharführer* Franz Suchomel, also interviewed by Sereny. Lanzmann reserves his sympathies for the survivors of the camps. This is only natural, of course, but his hostility toward everyone else keeps us from understanding the mechanisms that enabled so many ordinary people to take part in these crimes. Lanzmann reassures us (and himself) by confirming the familiar oppositions: us and them, friends and enemies, good and wicked. For him, in the domain of moral values at least, everything is simple and straightforward.

Another problematic aspect of Lanzmann's film is his decision to disregard the will of the people being interviewed. His conversations with former Nazis could not have been filmed without some sort of deception (he did not tell them they were being filmed, for example, or they were promised anonymity). His interviews with former inmates and witnesses are coercive in other ways as well: Lanzmann presses on, refusing to stop the camera even when his subjects dissolve into tears and ask for a break. It is hard not to feel that these people are being just a little bit manipulated. Lanzmann's behavior gives the impression that their experience is less important to him than the result he wants to achieve, artistic or emotional. Artistically the film gains from these moments of emotional intensity, but the human beings in it are used as instruments. The lesson Lanzmann conveys in these scenes is that we need not pay attention to others' wills or wishes if they stand in the way of our objective. In any other circumstances, this practice, dazzling in its effect, might not have drawn notice, but because Lanzmann is trying to represent a world of which one of the most salient characteristics is the negation of the individual's will, one wishes that he had been somewhat more circumspect in his choice of methods.

To be sure, Lanzmann is aware of his vulnerability to this sort of criticism. The argument he offers in his defense is always the same: if I'd done it differently, the effect would have been much less compelling. He has been asked why he did not interview Wladislaw Bartoszewski, who took part in the rescue of Jews in Poland and knew quite a lot about the subject. Lanzmann replied that he'd met Bartoszewski and that "what he had to say was extremely boring. All he could do was talk; he was incapable of reliving the past" (231). Lanzmann has said that to produce a beautiful work of art one must forget about respecting the rules of polite society. Truth and morality thus must submit to this other objective of striking at the human heart, of creating a work of the greatest possible emotional intensity. Lanzmann seeks to resuscitate the horror rather than to have us understand it. In its own way, *Shoah* is an example of the kind of art Marek Edelman found so questionable, an art that sacrifices truth and justice to beauty. Is it an accident that Edelman himself, a survivor of the ghetto uprising, is nowhere present in the film?

As we have seen, there is clearly a moral dimension to the life of the mind and thus to the creation of a work of art; at the same time, there is something necessarily amoral about the creative act, since the artist can succeed only by freeing him- or herself from the external tutelage of dogma or doctrine. What concerns us here, however, is something different. Apart from these characteristics common to all great works, every work of art takes a position with respect to the values of the world, and *Shoah*'s position is one that revives a kind of Manicheanism, the thesis of collective guilt, and disrespect for the dignity of the individual. Therein lies the paradox of the film: even as it claims to take a stand against certain values, it perpetuates them.

Lanzmann has frequently stated his opposition to all efforts to understand the violence that occurred in the camps; he seeks instead to stage that violence, to reproduce it. "If there is one thing I consider an intellectual scandal," he says, "it is the attempt to understand *historically*, as if there were a sort of harmonious genesis to death. . . . For me, murder—whether the murder of an individual or mass murder—is an incomprehensible act. . . . There are moments when understanding is pure madness" (289). Later he adds, "Any discourse that seeks to deduce the causes of violence is the absurd dream of the nonviolent" (315). This is also why Lanzmann rejects all comparisons of the Holocaust with any past, present, or even future (!) event and why he defends the theory of its "unique singularity" (308). Yet even if death has no "harmonious genesis" and there are no premises from which it can be logically deduced, even if despite our efforts there will always remain something unintelligible in the Nazis' perpetration of Judeocide, there is still much to understand; and it is understanding, and not the refusal to understand, that makes it possible to prevent a repetition of the horror. The best way to allow the murders to happen again is to give up trying to understand them.

In a page of Lanzmann's book I find particularly troubling, he tells how he has made his own the lesson Primo Levi was given by an SS man at Auschwitz. *"Hier ist kein warum,"* Levi was told. "Here, there is no why." Lanzmann extrapolates: " 'No Why': a law that applies equally to whoever undertakes a program like this one," he says, referring to his own film (279). Primo Levi spent forty years after Auschwitz trying to understand why, so that he might fight the rule that harsh epigram conveyed, whereas Lanzmann prefers to make the "moral" lesson of the SS man his own. Elsewhere, when Lanzmann is asked by an interviewer if he believes the Nazis felt hatred, he impatiently brushes the question aside. These sorts of psychological considerations do not interest him (282). Later, however, he returns to the question, this time in relation to himself: in order to make his film, he says, he needed hate (though other things, too). Speaking of Suchomel, for instance, Lanzmann says he wished "to kill him with the camera" (287). Is it an accident that someone who refuses to understand murder should also want, albeit metaphorically, to kill? Lanzmann should have tried to understand, while Levi would have done well to hate. Unfortunately, their roles were reversed.

It might be said that my reservations about a work as powerful as *Shoah* are out of place. When the horror of the act has been so extreme and the pain so sharp, do we really need to ask ourselves so many questions and insist on subtle distinctions? Yet one can also argue the opposite, that it is in those who have delved most deeply into the knowledge of evil that one hopes to find the greatest wisdom. Lanzmann is right to hate evil as he does and to keep intact his "resentment" (to use Améry's word). But *Shoah* is not only an evocation of the past but also an act that is carried out in the present and that must be judged as such. The enormity of evils past does not justify a present evil, even if the latter is infinitely smaller.

INTO THAT DARKNESS

The last work I would like to take up, *Into That Darkness* (1974), by Gitta Sereny, is one that seems to me to strike a remarkable balance between telling, judging, and understanding. The book is a record of interviews that the author, a British journalist, held in a Düsseldorf prison with Franz Stangl, the former commandant of both Sobibor and Treblinka, and of the further investigations she pursued all over the world in an effort to clarify what she had learned from their conversations.

Sereny's work represents, first of all, a remarkable reconstruction of facts about the two extermination camps. With it comes a judgment, a self-evident one as far as Sereny is concerned. At her very first interview with Stangl, she defines her position: "I told him," she writes, "that he had to know from the start that I abhorred everything the Nazis had stood for and done" (23). For Sereny, however, condemnation is not enough; she will use the opportunity to interrogate a man who not only took an active part in the most extreme evil our century has known but also allows himself to be questioned, the only commandant of a death camp to do so. It is a matter of trying to understand evil, with the willing, if tortuous, collaboration of one of its most accomplished representatives. Sereny's goal is not at all to convert Stangl but simply to uncover the truth of a hitherto incomprehensible world. "I'd give anything to understand," remarks the son of an SS officer at Treblinka (82); Sereny would, too, and she bids us follow her on this quest.

People who have not read Sereny's book tend to be suspicious of her project when I describe it to them. Isn't she guilty of accommodation, of complacency toward this former executioner? Doesn't she do him too much honor by showing such keen interest in the explanations he offers? To understand all is to pardon all, the saying goes; is that what we really want? Such reactions, I believe, reveal the fear one can feel in discovering that evildoers are not radically different from oneself. Sereny's book never lapses into tolerance of evil; to understand an act does not mean to obliterate it, much less to exonerate its perpetrator. There is indeed a danger in what Sereny does, but it is one that threatens the author herself. For in order to carry on an actual discussion with Stangl or any other Nazi, one is obliged to accept a common frame of reference. The danger is not that one might become a Nazi oneself but that one might feel guilty for having agreed to so much complicity with evil. (I myself felt this complicity simply reading Höss's book.) Sereny has this feeling many times, both in her talks with Dieter Allers, an intelligent and utterly unremorseful Nazi functionary of some importance, and at certain moments with Stangl himself. So overpowering is this feeling that at times she has to stop and ask herself if she has the strength to go on listening to their revelations. To talk *with* someone rather than *about* him implies that I recognize a commonality with that person even if my words are incompatible in meaning with his. One must be capable of exceptional detachment to maintain a framework of communication while dissociating oneself from the content of the discussion (and from the acts it evokes).

If Sereny never wavers in her condemnation, she also abstains from using the interviews to chastise her interlocutors or to deny them their dignity and their right to act (in the present) according to their own will. Nothing could be more alien to her than the desire that Lanzmann had "to kill with the camera." Sereny chooses "to question, not to wound"; she seeks to understand the guilty, not to "cause them embarrassment or pain" (15). Stangl's middle daughter, for instance, proved very reticent, but what "the little Renate said, with great effort, she volunteered" (350). When Joseph Oberhauser, a waiter in a café in Munich, refuses to talk, Sereny does not try to force his hand by holding up to him his past as a Nazi executioner. With Franz Suchomel, Sereny has no need for trickery or deception; he collaborates freely.

Sereny's attitude is not only more moral than Lanzmann's but also more productive. People cannot make progress in their search for truth if they know they'll be punished for discoveries that do not please their interlocutors. "My professional interest notwithstanding," Sereny says, "it had been important to me not to persuade or fatigue this man into disclosing more about himself than he wished to. If the sum total of what he could tell, and possibly teach us, was to be valid and of real value, I felt he had to offer it freely, and in full possession of all his faculties" (255). Even as her questions and comparisons clearly made Stangl suffer, she was careful to avoid hurting members of Stangl's family or his victims. At the same time, she never tried to force Stangl to say one thing or another, for she knew that whatever was said under constraint would be of no value. It is for this reason that Sereny's work takes us farther down the path to knowing and understanding evil than Lanzmann's does.

What is the method that Sereny uses to advance our understanding? Right from the start, she brushes aside any talk of self-justification on the part of the former guards: their rationalizations, ever since Nuremberg, have become clichés with nothing more to tell us. Sereny asks instead for a simple personal account and encourages candor. "What I had come for was something quite different," she says. "I wanted him really to talk to me; to tell me about himself as a child, a boy, a youth, a man; to tell me about his father, his mother, his friends, his wife and his children; tell me not what he did or did not do, but what he loved and what he hated" (23). In addition, she brings to her research the qualities one might expect to find in a good historian: a perfect knowledge of her sources and a sense of personal involvement. If Sereny does not rush to judgment, it is because she puts herself in the other's place, whomever it is she is interviewing, and thus can see the complications in what we tend to assume is simple and clear.

Two other aspects of Sereny's method, one passive, so to speak, the other active, are less common. First, Sereny tries to suspend as much as possible any clichés and preconceptions of her own. As a result, like Primo Levi, she avoids both Manicheanism and any tendency to view groups and individuals as uniform and homogeneous. She does not reject out of hand the seemingly paradoxical information that comes her way; nor does she dismiss her subjects' gestures and actions when they do not conform to her expectations. Second, and this is especially important, Sereny refuses to separate the exceptional from the ordinary and the individual from his environment; she refuses to divide human life into two impermeable compartments, one containing important things such as politics and war, the other secondary matters such as relations with family or neighbors, habits, and daily routines. Sereny understands that a division of this sort would compromise her results from the outset, and so instead she asks seemingly absurd or irrelevant questions that nevertheless prompt flashes of insight. She lingers over all the little facts and gestures of Stangl's life, even when they seem extraneous, and questions with great insistence everyone who ever knew Stangl: the individual does not exist outside an intersubjective network. Like Hanna Krall in her later interview with Marek Edelman, Sereny is interested more in memory than in history, more in psychology than in political dictums. As a result, monstrous though his actions were, Stangl himself comes across as a human being. Her methodological choices are therefore already moral choices as well, and even though her book does not articulate abstract conclusions, her thinking is authentically philosophical.

These two traits alone do not allow us to distinguish Sereny's enterprise from Levi's, which is as far from Manicheanism and as attentive to the ordinary as hers is. The difference, a crucial one, lies elsewhere: Sereny is neither a victim of the war nor a Jew herself. Contrary to received wisdom, participants in a situation are not necessarily in the best position to understand it. Victims, whether direct or indirect, are hampered by their partiality, and if they are willing to pursue understanding without reservations, they risk being shattered by it, as Primo Levi ultimately was. Sereny, a woman of Hungarian origin, was a young girl during the war, living in France, where she took care of abandoned children and displaced persons; when the war ended, she went to Germany, where she spent two years engaged in similar work. She therefore has direct knowledge of these events but is not encumbered by too strong an identification with the victims. This kind of middle distance, it seems, must be maintained between evil and the person trying to understand it if that person is to come back and give us an account of his or her descent "into that darkness."

What is it exactly that Sereny brings back to us from her journey? Throughout these pages I have profited from the results of her quest in my own effort to understand as best I can the behavior of the guards (including Stangl) as well as that of their prisoners; for this reason I will refrain from restating her findings yet again. But there is another reason for my reluctance. Sereny offers an account suffused with thoughtfulness and wisdom, not a work of philosophy or a political treatise whose theses might be easily summarized. What she teaches us is how an average human being, Franz Stangl, came to be implicated in one of the most monstrous crimes in all of human history and then how, finding himself thus implicated, he tried to justify himself both in his own eyes and in the eyes of those near to him. Sereny's book, rich in lessons though it is, does not illustrate any particular theory; it practices narrative thought rather than conceptual analysis and in this very gesture proves that it is possible to think and analyze while narrating. This is why one can no more summarize Sereny's book than one can a work of art. One must read it to know what it contains.

EPILOGUE

Notes on Morality

THE SENSE OF MORALITY

There is little reason to conclude this discussion by summarizing the reflections that have brought us to this point, but I do think it necessary to dwell for just a moment on the conceptual framework within which I've situated my analysis. Recall that at the beginning of this book, much taken by my readings on the Warsaw uprisings, I announced that my object of inquiry would be the moral life of the individual and added that what interested me was not the past *per se* but rather the light it cast upon the present. It seems, however, that this conjunction of the terms *moral* and *present* may pose problems, however. Indeed, what characterizes the age we now live in, I expect to be told, is the disappearance of morality. Or, shall I say, the contemporary world seems to favor two supposedly self-evident, if incompatible, propositions on the subject. The first, voiced with either satisfaction or regret, holds that what characterizes Western societies today is the absence of moral life: duty is dead, and in its place we champion something called authenticity. The second proposition tends to be expressed in more imperative tones: it's high time we freed ourselves from the last vestiges of moral oppression, people say. Or: Watch out! Morality is making a comeback! Before turning to the moral lessons of the camps, then, I must ask myself if I haven't been somehow barking up the wrong tree, raising questions that belong to another time and place.

These propositions have their source in two distinct misunderstandings about the meaning and scope of the term *moral*. The first proposition confuses species and genus: from the disappearance of a particular form of morality (the kind rooted in, for lack of a better term, traditional morality), one deduces (falsely) the disappearance of moral life in general. But morality, at least as I understand it, cannot disappear without a veritable mutation of the human race.

Among the variety of ways to classify human activities, one of the most illuminating distinctions is between the teleological and the intersubjective. In the first category are actions that can be defined by their purpose, actions in which one begins with a project and uses various strategies to accomplish it. Whatever the domain to which they belong, whether that of research and scholarship, business and labor, or politics and war, we judge these actions according to their end result—that is, their success or failure. Actions of this kind are served by instrumental thought. The other category comprises actions whose distinguishing feature is that they establish a relationship between two or more individuals. Communicative in the broadest sense, these actions have to do with understanding or emulation, love or power, or the constitution of self or other. Obviously, one can give these two categories different names. Instead of the teleological and the intersubjective, one might speak of the world of things and the world of persons, object and subject relations, cosmos and *anthropos,* I and thou, and so forth. What interests me here, however, is simply the existence of this distinction and the fact that human life is inconceivable without the simultaneous presence of both kinds of activities. On this latter point I think no one would disagree.

Moral life is a constitutive dimension of the intersubjective world, permeating it in its entirety and standing as its crowning achievement. Just as it is impossible to imagine humanity apart from intersubjective relations, so is it impossible to imagine it without a moral dimension. By moral, I mean that which allows us to tell whether an action is good or evil, and when I speak of a "crowning achievement" it is because, no matter what school of philosophy one adheres to, the terms *good* and *evil* define, somewhat tautologically, everything that is most (or least) desirable in the world of human relations. By definition, the most laudable action is the moral action; a world in which morality had no place would be one in which all actions that fell into the category of human relations were equal in value, a nearly unimaginable situation. Conservatives who mourn the passing of the power of tradition cannot deny that, viewed this way, moral judgments continue to exist; similarly, not even the most die-hard individualist can deny the existence of a network of intersubjective relations in which all people are enmeshed. If someone were to ask me why people behave morally, I would have to answer in two ways: first, because we feel profound joy in doing so and, second, because in doing so we conform to the very idea of humanity and so take part in the realization of that idea.

I will go one step further: moral judgments are not arbitrary (they do not depend on the whim of the individual; that is why morality is not reducible to the intensity of a given individual's experience) but rather can be argued rationally. The accounts I have read of life in the camps convince me that the moral action is always one that the individual takes on himself (the moral action is in this sense "subjective") and that is directed toward one or more individuals (it is "personal," for when I act morally I treat the other as a person, which is to say, he becomes the end of my action). The moral action par excellence is "caring." Through caring, the "I" has as its goal the well-being of the "you" (whether singular or multiple). Yet caring is not the only kind of moral act, for there can be other beneficiaries besides the "you." For example, when the moral action is dignity, the beneficiary can be the subject himself, who on such occasions is, as it were, another person to himself. When, on the other hand, the beneficiary is an indeterminate number of other individuals ("my people," "my contemporaries," "my readers"), the moral action belongs to the category I call "the life of the mind." But dignity and mind become moral actions only when they seek the good of specific individuals. The consistent Nazi cannot achieve moral dignity, for by obeying his own dictates he accomplishes no good. Similarly, a scientist does not accomplish a moral act by writing the equation $E=mc^2$ (for there is still no intersubjectivity in that action) unless in doing so he endeavors to make the world more intelligible to others. To sum up: the "disappearance" of morality in the present day is a misunderstanding; morality cannot "disappear" without a radical mutation of the human species.

As for the second proposition, the suggestion that we should forget morality altogether, I believe it proceeds from a misperception, a semantic displacement in which moral action is confused with something related but quite distinct. For instance, we may object—and with good reason—to the moralizing efforts of some of our contemporaries, but moralizing is not the same thing as moral action. And in our dread of notions like the return to a "moral order," we tend to overlook the fact that calls to (moral) order are not moral actions either.

To reiterate: For an action to be moral it must be both subjective—performed by the individual who is the subject of that action—and personal—directed toward other individuals. If either element is missing, what we have is an action that is related to but distinct from the kind of morality with which this book is concerned. If an action is performed by the subject but directed toward some sort of abstraction such as the homeland or liberty or Communism or even humanity, and not toward other individuals, then we are dealing with heroism or one of its derivatives. From a moral standpoint, which is to say, one that takes the interests of individuals into account, heroic acts are in themselves neither good nor bad: they can be either. As we've seen, some heroes care about the effect of their actions on their fellowman, whereas others do not. Without additional information, one cannot know whether a heroic act is morally commendable; if there is no human beneficiary, for instance, heroism becomes something else, an act of bravado, if not pure braggadocio.

If an action is directed toward one or more individuals but not carried out by the subject himself—who may be content just to formulate it or to recommend it to others—then what we have is moralism, that relative of moral action we tend to find so off-putting. The moralistic attitude requires of others that they act in conformity with a code consisting of a body of prohibitions or prescriptions. Morally one can require something only of oneself; to others, one can only give. (Even in the case of dignity, where the "I" is both source and beneficiary of the action, there are still two entities: one part of me gives, the other receives.)

Morality can easily be confused, however, not just with moralism but also with something as desirable as justice. Justice is neither subjective (compliance is obligatory, not meritorious) nor personal (it is directed indifferently to all citizens, even all human beings), but it traces to the same principles as those that guide moral life: concern for the welfare of the individual, respect for his person, and universal application. Morality is thus not to be confused with politics either, which in the best of circumstances consists of actions whose goal is to establish justice (or to increase it) within a given country, something that moral action is incapable of doing. A little like heroism, the political act may or may not serve the people's interests. Finally, morality is not the same thing as reflection on morality, which is a search for truth more than a search for goodness. Even this book, which speaks of morality, is in itself not necessarily a moral act—although, like any activity belonging to the life of the mind, it potentially is.

THE LESSONS OF THE PAST

The notes that follow sum up some of the moral lessons of the camps and of the actions that took place in them, around them, and in response to them. It goes without saying that these are not the only lessons, but any others I prefer to let my readers draw for themselves. A first set of lessons concerns the reasons for the growth of evil in our century. Naturally, it is difficult to compare the evil of one century with that of another, for it is impossible to know both from the inside. Nevertheless, everything we do know suggests that the outbreak of evil that Europe witnessed in the twentieth century was one the likes of which had never (or very rarely) been seen before. It is not simply a question of the number of dead; the suffering inflicted on the victims and the depravity which their tormentors showed themselves capable have few if any historical equivalents. How do we explain this? I don't think that the nature of evil itself has changed: evil has always consisted of denying someone his or her right to be fully human, as the institution of slavery did. Nor do I believe that the human race has undergone a mutation or that a new fanaticism of unprecedented force suddenly exploded onto the world scene. What made this immense evil possible, I believe, are two common, altogether ordinary attributes of our daily lives: the fragmentation of the world we live in and the depersonalization of our relations with others. These came about as a result of a progressive transformation, not exactly of people, but of their societies. Internal fragmentation is the consequence of an increasingly specialized working world and its inevitable compartmentalization; depersonalization comes from a transference of instrumental thought to the realm of human relations. In other words, those qualities appropriate to teleological activities (specialization, efficacity) have also pervaded intersubjective activities, and it is this change that has increased immeasurably a potential for evil probably not so different from that of earlier centuries.

It is in this sense that we can hold our industrial and technological civilization responsible for the camps, not because any spectacular industrial measures were required to carry out the mass murders and bring about suffering of boundless proportions (in Germany, these measures amounted to little more than gunpowder, poison, and fire; a Russia less rich in these simple things killed its people largely by cold, hunger, and disease) but because a technological mentality invaded the human world as well. This development is tragic because one cannot imagine its ever ending; the tendency toward increasing specialization and efficiency has made its indelible mark on our history, and its devastating effect on what is properly the human world cannot be denied. In his time, Rousseau already noticed this development, which is why his vision of humanity is so filled with despair: "Iron and wheat civilized men," he writes, "and ruined the human race" (116). Indeed, the question remains unanswered as to how we might reap the benefits of technology without suffering its repercussions in the way we behave toward one another.

A second group of lessons has to do with the status of good in a century whose emblematic feature is the concentration camp. Unfortunately, the amount of good in the world has not kept up with the growth in evil, but I do not think it has diminished either. Our definition of what is good might change, however, and in this there is reason for optimism: there are many more acts of kindness than those recognized by the traditional moral perspective, which has tended to value the exceptional, even though it is acts of kindness that make up the fabric of our daily lives. The camps confirm the ubiquity of these acts, since even under the most adverse circumstances imaginable, when men and women are faint with hunger, numb with cold, exhausted, beaten, and humiliated, they still go on performing simple acts of kindness—not everyone and not all the time, but enough to reinforce and even augment our faith in goodness. It is up to us, to those of us who live peaceful lives unbeset by the troubles of the world, to recognize and acknowledge these acts of dignity, caring, and creativity, to confirm their value and encourage them more than we habitually do, for while everyone is capable of them, they represent one of the supreme achievements of the human race. In a world as threatened as ours, they are sorely needed. Once again, the lesson gleaned from extremity illuminates our common condition: a code of ordinary moral values and virtues, one commensurate with our times, can indeed be based on the recognition that it is as easy to do good as to do evil. One might go so far as to turn Hannah Arendt's coinage on its head and speak of—and also take heart in—the banality of good. We need not imitate saints. Nor need we fear monsters; both the dangers and the means with which to neutralize them are all around us.

The experience of good in the camps sheds some light on an age-old moral debate as well. In performing a moral act, are we fulfilling our basic nature, conforming, as the ancients argued, to our primary purpose? Or are we, as the modern outlook would have it, submitting to a sense of duty, one that requires that we suppress and transcend our natural desires? This much is certain: acts of goodness performed in the camps were certainly not undertaken out of a sense of duty. Any internal sense of obligation, whether the product of traditional teachings or of reasoned decision, collapsed under the weight of circumstances. If Milena Jesenska insisted on marching out of step to preserve her dignity, if she found a way to slip into a solitary-confinement cell to bolster the spirits of a friend and spoke to her in the shadows of the watchtowers about art and literature, it is not because culture or reason suggested she do these things: she was led to do them by her nature as a human, and therefore social, being and because in doing them she savored an unmitigated joy.

Here again, I am inclined to side with Rousseau. One of the greatest of the moderns and a believer in the perfectibility of humankind, he nevertheless felt that compassion (or pity) was the quality from which "all the social virtues flow." For Rousseau, compassion is "prior to all reflection"; it is not learned from tradition or custom but is a "natural" sentiment. "Despite all their morality," he writes, "men would never have been any better than monsters if nature had not given them pity to support reason" (100–101). Compassion may be natural, but it is not found in all of us, nor do those of us who have it share in it equally. I believe that compassion is something that human beings do not discover in themselves and make an active principle until rather late in life. Children are notoriously merciless, and as for adolescents, they tend to discover justice well before mercy. It is only the adult who accords a special place to sympathy, doubtless because life's circumstances can call for the adult to take care of others— children or parents—and bring him to cherish them, whether in love or friendship, for themselves and not for the pleasure they may afford him.

Moral life in the concentration camp would thus seem to corroborate the "naturalist" thesis about morality, but in fact this experience lies somewhere beyond the opposition between nature and culture. "Natural" though they may be, the moral acts carried out in the concentration camps were not the automatic consequences of animal instinct; they were voluntary acts and therefore free. In other words, sympathy and duty are not necessarily opposed to each other; duty is not only a way of surmounting our natural inclinations but also a way of sublimating them. The fact is that we are inclined in many directions. Sympathy for others, which leads us to desire their well-being, and also for oneself, which helps us act with dignity, is "natural" in a certain sense, but so are our tendencies to fragmentation and depersonalization, which are at the very root of the "ordinary vices" and have made the extreme evil of these times possible. Similarly, just because a given tendency is natural does not mean one ought to give in to it. One has to be able to judge the value of these inclinations from the outside, as it were. Only reason can make such judgments, by determining whether these inclinations are worthy of universal prescription. For if we desire to obey nature alone, then nature is already a normative concept for us, an ideal; yet the highest ideal is the one that can be defended rationally and that all can share. Thus it is not a question of each of us conforming to his or her own dispositions: one inclines to sympathy because it is natural to do so, but it is reason that tells us whether or not to do so is good.

A third group of lessons speaks to the relation between gender and moral values. To account for certain actions and human qualities within the world of the camps but also in the world at large, I drew on a series of oppositions, which I now see as mutually encompassing. At the most abstract level, I distinguished between teleological and inter-subjective activities. I divided the latter into public and private activities, and this division led to yet another division, between politics and morality. The category of moral action itself gave rise to another division, between heroic and ordinary virtues. And, finally, the category of the ordinary virtues called for distinguishing between the morality of principles and that of sympathy. When I spell out these oppositions in this way, several observations seem evident to me.

The first is that each of these oppositions can be cast in terms of a kind of double necessity: even though these are real oppositions that admit of no synthesis, both terms are equally crucial to the life of the individual and to that of society. Work must be efficient *and* human relationships must not be sacrificed to it; it is preferable that society be just *and* that people be good, that heroic virtues manifest themselves in exceptional circumstances *and* that ordinary virtues do so in everyday life. We saw, too, that the actions of the rescuers required both a morality of principle *and* one of sympathy. The question now is whether the tensions created by these pairs of requirements are surmountable.

The second observation, then, concerns the way the societies of Europe (and perhaps elsewhere) have responded to this challenge. It seems that their response has been to distribute on the basis of gender the values attached to each term of the oppositions—not exclusively, of course, but preferentially. To men, the first term is assigned; to women, the second. To men, then, the world of work, politics and public affairs, heroic virtues, and the morality of principles; to women, the domain of human relations, the private sphere, ordinary virtues, and the morality of sympathy. But just as human biological life needs men *and* women to maintain itself, so, too, life in society requires the interaction of "masculine" and "feminine" values.

The opposing terms (and the values attached to them) tend not to be equally appreciated; typically, preference is accorded the masculine values, so much so that at certain times in history these are the only values recognized. Private life, conversation, caring, and compassion, being "left" to women, are treated as though unworthy of philosophical or moral reflection. Thus, as we saw with Etty Hillesum, a woman's emancipation has often been a matter of spurning "feminine" values in favor of "masculine" ones. Things have been changing for some time now, of course, but I fear that the laws have changed more quickly than actual behaviors, and behaviors more quickly than people's consciousness.

What conclusions can we draw? The first is that we must renounce the ideal of unity. (Rousseau came to this same conclusion and it filled him with sadness.) The two terms of each opposition are not contradictory, strictly speaking; yet embodied in concrete actions, they cannot be practiced by the same person at the same time. Both are necessary, however, and this is true whether we are speaking of behavior or of values: it would be disastrous if everyone aligned with the masculine values (or, in a less likely scenario, with the feminine ones). It follows that every individual must accept him- or herself as a heteroclite being, irremediably imperfect with respect to the terms of each set of values, and that we must each in the way we live accept this alternation (or androgyny) along with the necessity of compromise. Finally, we must recognize that the complete moral being may not be the individual but, as we have seen in the case of the rescuers, the couple, which must in turn be built on a compromise between the two types of values, each serving to temper the other. Needless to say, when I speak of the couple I am not speaking of the heterosexual paradigm only or of a relationship that is necessarily stable or permanent.

Furthermore, if traditional societies can be said to have shown a sort of unconscious or intuitive wisdom in maintaining both sets of values, we cannot accept that division today without reorienting it in two basic ways. First, while the duality may be unavoidable, the traditional sex-based division of values is not (gender, a social construct, does not automatically follow from sex, a biological fact). Women go to work and men talk; women hold positions of public responsibilities while men discover the private sphere: the essential thing is that both sets of values be preserved, not that each find expression in one sex rather than the other. At the same time, because those values I have called feminine have been seriously undervalued throughout Western history, it is vital that they now acquire the importance they deserve. Perhaps this book will be a step in that direction.

One last point. While it is true that ordinary virtue can be found everywhere and that we must rejoice in this fact and speak it loud for all to hear, there can come a time in the life of a society, as in that of the individual, when ordinary virtue is not enough. In such moments of anguish and despair, a different virtue is needed. The subject must then not only take upon himself the action he prescribes but accept the risks such action entails both for himself and for those close to him. And not only must he direct his action toward another individual, he must be willing to do so even when the individual is a stranger to him. In short, the heroic virtues, courage and generosity, become as necessary as the ordinary ones. Yet tragically—and this is the final lesson of the camps—the just, those righteous men and women who combine these qualities, are few in number.

There is nothing new in this observation. Traditional moral codes sometimes prescribe giving aid to strangers (charity or alms), but the generosity that results from these injunctions tends to remain external, one of many obligations that the individual hastens to carry out in order to be acquitted of them. In this respect, moreover, we are no worse than our forebears, who had as little taste for risk taking as we do. Should we feel shame or some sort of metaphysical guilt in the face of this reluctance to do for strangers what we would gladly do for those we love—namely, accept risk and thus sacrifice our own tranquillity? I think that that would be a futile gesture of revolt against the human condition. What we can hope for, nevertheless, is that these moments of distress will not go unrecognized and that when appeals are made to us in such times we will hear them. It has been said that during the 1930s and 1940s persecuted Jews had great difficulty passing for non-Jews, regardless of their features or their manner of dress; it was the look of sadness in their eyes that made them recognizable even to someone standing far away. If we should find ourselves unable, when the moment comes, to meet the stranger's gaze—and to be moved by it—then woe to him who is lost, who has wandered far from his people.

Works Cited

Améry, Jean. *At the Mind's Limits.* Trans. Sidney Rosenfeld and Stella P. Rosenfeld. New York: Schocken, 1986.

———. *Radical Humanism.* Trans. Sidney Rosenfeld and Stella P. Rosenfeld. Bloomington: Indiana University Press, 1985.

Antelme, Robert. *The Human Race.* Trans. Jeffrey Haight and Annie Mahler. Marlboro: Marlboro Press, 1992.

Arendt, Hannah. *Eichmann in Jerusalem: A Report on the Banality of Evil.* Harmondsworth: Penguin, 1979.

———. *The Human Condition.* Chicago: University of Chicago Press, 1958.

———. *The Origins of Totalitarianism.* San Diego: Harcourt Brace Jovanovich, 1979.

Au sujet de Shoah. Paris: Belin, 1990.

Berkowitz, Sarah. *Where Are My Brothers?* New York: Helios, 1965.

Bettelheim, Bruno. *The Informed Heart.* Glencoe: Free Press, 1960.

———. *Surviving.* New York: Knopf, 1979.

Blanchot, Maurice. "Les intellectuels en question." *Le débat* 29 (1984): 3–28.

Borowski, Tadeusz. *Le monde de pierre.* Paris: Calmann-Lévy, 1964.

———. *This Way for the Gas, Ladies and Gentlemen.* Trans. Barbara Vedder. New York: Penguin, 1976.

Borwicz, M., ed. *L'insurrection du ghetto de Varsovie.* Paris: Julliard, 1966.

Buber-Neumann, Margarete. *Déportée à Ravensbrück.* Paris: Editions du Seuil, 1988.

———. *Déportée en Sibérie.* Paris: Editions du Seuil, 1949.

———. *Milena.* Trans. Ralph Manheim. New York: Schocken, 1988.

Camon, Ferdinando. *Conversations with Primo Levi.* Trans. John Shepley. Marlboro: Marlboro Press, 1989.

Ciechanowski, Jan M. *The Warsaw Rising of 1944.* New York: Cambridge University Press, 1974.

Conan, Eric. *Sans oublier les enfants.* Paris: Grasset, 1991.

Conquest, Robert. *Kolyma: The Arctic Death Camps.* New York: Viking, 1978.

de Jong, Louis. "The Netherlands and Auschwitz." *Yad Vashem Studies* 7 (1968): 39–55.

Delbo, Charlotte. *Auschwitz and After.* Trans. Rosette C. Lamont. New Haven: Yale University Press, 1995.

———. *Le convoi du 24 janvier.* Paris: Editions de Minuit, 1965.

Des Pres, Terrence. *The Survivor.* New York: Oxford University Press, 1976.

de Voragine, J. *La légende dorée.* Vol. 2. Paris: Garnier-Flammarion, 1967.

Diamant, D. *Héros juifs de la résistance française.* Paris: Editions Renouveau, 1962.

Eichmann par Eichmann. Paris: Grasset, 1970.

Fénelon, Fania. *Playing for Time.* Trans. Judith Landry. New York: Atheneum, 1977. Abr. trans. of *Sursis pour l'orchestre.* Quotations are from English edition where possible and are so noted.

———. *Sursis pour l'orchestre.* Paris: Stock, 1976.

Frank, Hans. *Die Technik des Staates.* Munich: Deutscher Rechtsverlag, 1942.

Frankl, Viktor. *Man's Search for Meaning.* Trans. Ilse Lasch. New York: Pocket, 1963.

Gilbert, G. M. *Nuremberg Diary.* New York: Farrar, Straus and Company, 1947.

———. *The Psychology of Dictatorship.* New York: Ronald Press, 1950.

Ginzburg, Eugenia Semyonovna. *Journey into the Whirlwind.* Trans. Paul Stevenson and Max Hayward. New York: Harcourt, 1967.

———. *Within the Whirlwind.* Trans. Ian Boland. New York: Harcourt, 1982.

Goethe, Wolfgang von. *Faust.* Trans. Walter Arndt. New York: W. W. Norton, 1976.

Grey, John Glenn. *The Warriors.* New York: Harper & Row, 1970.

Grossman, Vasily. *Dobro vam!* Moscow: Sovetskij pisatel', 1967.

———. *Forever Flowing.* Trans. Thomas P. Whitney. New York: Harper & Row, 1972.

———. *Life and Fate.* Trans. Robert Chandler. New York: Harper & Row, 1985.

———. "Memoria" in Dawgava 77. Cited in *Voprosy literatury* (May 1991): 251–54.

Hallie, Philip. *Lest Innocent Blood Be Shed.* New York: Harper & Row, 1979.

Herling, Gustaw. *A World Apart.* Trans. Andrzej Ciozkosz (Joseph Marek). New York: Arbor House, 1986.

Hilberg, Raul, Stanislaw Staron, and Josef Kermisz, eds. *The Warsaw Diary of Adam Czerniakow: Prelude to Doom.* New York: Schocken, 1979.

Hillesum, Etty. *An Interrupted Life: The Diaries of Etty Hillesum.* Trans. Arnold J. Pomerans. New York: Pantheon, 1983.

———. *Letters from Westerbork.* Trans. Arnold J. Pomerans. New York: Pantheon, 1986.

Himmler, Heinrich. *Discours secrets.* Paris: Gallimard, 1978.

Homer. *The Iliad.* Trans. Richmond Lattimore. Chicago: University of Chicago Press, 1951.

Höss, Rudolf. *Le commandant d'Auschwitz parle.* Paris: Maspero, 1979.

Jaspers, Karl. *The Question of German Guilt.* New York: Capricorn, 1962.

Kahler, Erich. *The Tower and the Abyss: An Inquiry into the Transformation of the Individual.* New York: Braziller, 1957.

Kant, Immanuel. *Metaphysics of Ethics.* Trans. J. W. Semple. Edinburgh: T&T Clark, 1871.

Kogon, Eugen. *The Theory and Practice of Hell: The German Concentration Camps and the System behind Them.* New York: Farrar, Straus & Giroux, 1950.

―――. Hermann Langbein, and A. Rückerl. *Les chambres à gaz: Secret d'état.* Paris: Editions du Seuil, 1970.

Krall, Hanna, and Marek Edelman. *Shielding the Flame.* Trans. Joanna Stasinska and Lawrence Weschler. New York: Henry Holt, 1977.

―――. *Mémoires du ghetto de Varsovie.* Paris: Scribe, 1983.

Kremer, J. P. "Diary of Johann Paul Kremer." *KL Auschwitz Seen by the S.S.* Ed. J. Bezwinska and D. Czech. New York: H. Fertig, 1984. 197–280.

Kren, George M., and Leon Rappoport. *The Holocaust and the Crisis of Human Behavior.* New York: Holmes & Meier, 1980.

Kurzman, Dan. *The Bravest Battle.* Los Angeles: Pinnacle, 1978.

Laks, Szymon. *Music of Another World.* Trans. Chester Kisiel. Evanston: Northwestern University Press, 1989.

Laks, Szymon, and R. Coudy. *Musique d'un autre monde.* Paris: Mercure de France, 1948.

Langbein, Hermann. *Hommes et femmes à Auschwitz.* Paris: Fayard, 1975.

Lanzmann, Claude. *Shoah.* New York: Pantheon, 1985.

Laqueur, Walter. *The Terrible Secret.* New York: Penguin, 1982.

Leitner, Isabella. *Fragments of Isabella.* New York: Dell, 1978.

Lengyel, Olga. *Five Chimneys: The Story of Auschwitz.* Trans. Clifford Coch and Paul Weiss. Chicago: Ziff-Davis, 1947.

Levi, Primo. Afterword. Trans. Ruth Feldman. *The Reawakening.* Trans. Stuart Woolf. New York: Collier-Macmillan, 1965. 195–217.

―――. *The Drowned and the Saved.* Trans. Raymond Rosenthal. New York: Vintage, 1989.

―――. *If Not Now, When?* Trans. William Weaver. New York: Penguin, 1986.

―――. *Moments of Reprieve.* Trans. Ruth Feldman. New York: Penguin, 1987.

―――. *The Periodic Table.* Trans. Raymond Rosenthal. New York: Schocken, 1984.

―――. *The Reawakening.* Trans. Stuart Woolf. Collier-Macmillan, 1965.

―――. *Survival in Auschwitz.* Trans. Stuart Woolf. New York: Collier-Macmillan, 1961.

Lifton, Robert Jay. *The Nazi Doctors: Medical Killing and the Psychology of Genocide.* New York: Basic, 1986.

Lingens-Reiner, Ella. *Prisoners of Fear.* London: Victor Gollancz, 1948.

Maier, Charles S. *The Unmasterable Past: History, Holocaust, and German National Identity.* Cambridge: Harvard University Press, 1988.

Marchenko, Anatoly. *My Testimony.* Trans. Michael Scammell. New York: Dutton, 1969.

Marcus Aurelius. *Meditations.* Harvard Classics. Danbury: Grolier, 1980.

Micheels, Louis J. *Doctor 117641.* New Haven: Yale University Press, 1989.

Milosz, Czeslaw. *The Captive Mind.* New York: Vintage, 1981.

Mitscherlich, Alexander, and Fred Mielke. *Doctors of Infamy: The Story of the Nazi Medical Crimes.* New York: Schuman, 1949.

Müller, Filip. *Eyewitness Auschwitz: Three Years in the Gas Chambers.* Trans. Susanne Flatauer. New York: Stein & Day, 1979.

Orwell, George. *The Collected Essays, Journalism, and Letters of George Orwell.* Ed. Sonia Orwell and Ian Angus. Vol. 3. New York: Harcourt, 1968.

Pawelczynska, Anna. *Values and Violence in Auschwitz: A Sociological Analysis.* Trans. Catherine S. Leach. Berkeley: University of California Press, 1979.

Ratushinskaya, Irina. *Grey Is the Color of Hope.* Trans. Alyona Kojevnikov. New York: Knopf, 1988.

Rauschning, Hermann. *Hitler Speaks: The Voice of Destruction.* New York: Putnam, 1940.

Ringelblum, Emmanuel. *Notes from the Warsaw Ghetto.* Ed. and trans. Jacob Sloan. New York: Schocken, 1974.

Roskies, David G., ed. *The Literature of Destruction.* New York: Jewish Publication Society, 1989.

Rousseau, Jean-Jacques. *Discourse on the Origins of Inequality.* Trans. Maurice Cranston. New York: Penguin, 1984.

Rousset, David. *A World Apart.* Trans. Yvonne Moyse and Roger Senhouse. London: Secker & Warburg, 1951.

———. Gerard Rosenthal, and Theo Bernard. *Pour la vérité sur les camps concentrationnaires.* Paris: Ramsay, 1990.

Sartre, Jean-Paul. "Existentialism Is a Humanism." *Existentialism: From Dostoevsky to Sartre.* Ed. Walter Kaufmann. New York: Meridien, 1956. 287–311.

Semprun, Jorge. *The Long Voyage.* Trans. Richard Seaver. London: Weidenfeld & Nicolson, 1963.

Sereny, Gitta. *Into That Darkness.* New York: Vintage, 1893.

Shalamov, Varlam. *Kolyma Tales.* Trans. John Glad. New York: Norton, 1980.

Smith, Bradley F. *Reaching Judgment at Nuremberg.* New York: Basic, 1977.

Solzhenitsyn, Aleksandr. *The Gulag Archipelago.* Vol. 2. Trans. Thomas P. Whitney. New York: Harper & Row, 1975.

Speer, Albert. *Inside the Third Reich.* Trans. Richard Winston and Clara Winston. New York: Collier-Macmillan, 1970.

Stajner, Karlo. *Seven Thousand Days in Siberia.* New York: Farrar, Straus & Giroux, 1988.

Stein, André. *Quiet Heroes: True Stories of the Rescue of Jews by Christians in Nazi-Occupied Holland.* New York: New York University Press, 1988.

Steiner, Jean-François. *Varsovie 44.* Paris: Flammarion, 1975.

Suhl, Yuri, ed. *They Fought Back.* New York: Crown, 1967.

Tec, Nechama. *When Light Pierced the Darkness.* New York: Oxford University Press, 1986.

Tillion, Germaine. *Ravensbrück.* Trans. Gerald Satterwhite. New York: Anchor, 1975.

Trunk, Isaiah. *Jewish Responses to Nazi Persecution*. New York: Stein & Day, 1979.

Vrba, Rudolf, and Alan Bestic. *I Cannot Forgive*. London: Sidgwick & Jackson, 1963.

Wiesel, Elie. *Night*. Trans. Stella Rodway. New York: Hill & Wang, 1960.

Wiesenthal, Simon. *The Sunflower*. New York: Schocken, 1976.

Wieviorka, Annette. *Le procès Eichmann*. Brussels: Complexe, 1989.

Wyman, David S. *The Abandonment of the Jews*. New York: Pantheon, 1984.

Zawodny, J. K. *Nothing but Honour*. Palo Alto: Hoover Institution Press, 1978.

Index

Abel, 139
Achilles, 47–48, 50, 52
Aeneas, 110
Alberto, 34
Allers, Dieter, 279
Améry, Jean, 26, 32, 52, 59–60, 61, 62, 94, 108, 130, 181, 182, 216, 229, 240, 261, 262, 263, 264, 278
Andersen, Hans Christian, 51
Andromache, 109
Anielewicz, Mordechai, 14, 15, 17, 19, 20–22, 25, 110, 211
Antelme, Robert, 35, 74, 83, 88, 135
Antigone, 50
Arendt, Hannah, 28, 115, 124–25, 137, 149, 163, 166, 218, 291
Aristotle, 273
Ascanius, 110
Astyanax, 109
Aurelius, Marcus, 114, 198

Bach, Johann Sebastian, 95, 98, 143
Bartoszewski, Wladislaw, 276
Bataille, Georges, 181
Beauvoir, Simone de, 81
Beckett, Samuel, 50
Beethoven, Ludwig van, 106
Benn, Gottfried, 233
Beria, Lavrenti Pavlovitch, 124

Berkowitz, Sarah, 255
Bettelheim, Bruno, 27, 60–61, 63, 68, 69, 104, 106, 122, 130, 137, 138, 159, 215–16, 238, 239, 246, 255, 262
Blady Szwajger, Adina, 19
Blanchot, Maurice, 115–16
Boehm, Arno, 144
Boger, Wilhelm, 142
Bomba, Abraham, 272
Bool, Jan, 199
Boris N., 94
Bor–Komorowski, Tadeusz, 6, 8, 9, 10
Borowski, Tadeusz, 31, 33, 34, 38, 62, 71, 97, 98, 143–44, 197, 217, 221, 262
Borwicz, M., 21, 106
Bostramer, 100
Bovary, Emma, 50
Bradbury, Ray, 92
Bradfisch, Otto, 149
Braun, Wernher von, 101
Brecht, Bertolt, 54
Brinker, Hans, 48
Broad, Pery, 143
Brueghel, Pieter, 95
Buber–Neumann, Margarete, 37, 57–58, 64–65, 73, 74–75, 76, 80, 88–89, 90, 95, 111, 133, 134, 138, 156, 239, 245
Bulawko, Henry, 148

Cain, 139
Camus, Albert, 59, 233, 251, 252
Cavani, Liliana, 137
Chamberlain, Neville, 53
Chaplin, Charlie, 50
Churchill, Winston, 53, 54
Ciechanowski, Jan M., 6, 7, 8, 9
Conan, Eric, 248, 274
Conquest, Robert, 182
Constant de Rebecque, Benjamin, 92
Coudy, R., 33, 35, 95
Creusa, 110
Czerniakow, Adam, 16, 19, 210, 214

Daladier, Édouard, 53
Daniel, Yuli, 77
Dante, Alighieri, 93, 98, 262
de Gaulle, Charles, 53, 54
de Jong, Louis, 245
Delbo, Charlotte, 56, 86, 87, 92, 98,
    228, 267
Des Pres, Terrence, 37, 39
de Voragine, Jacques, 49
Diamant, David, 57
Doentiz, Karl. See Dönitz, Karl
Doiret, Madeleine, 267
Dönitz, Karl, 151, 152
Dostoevsky, Feodor, 92
Drexler, Frau, 181
Duprat, François, 219

Edelman, Marek, 13–19, 21, 22–23, 31,
    92, 97, 200, 211, 247, 276, 281
Eichmann, Adolf, 100, 124, 137, 138,
    143, 152, 153, 154, 161–62, 164, 166,
    169, 171, 172–76, 177–78, 185, 189,
    218, 234, 249
Eicke, Theodor, 127, 164, 166, 171, 239
Eleazar, 48–49, 58

Fanon, Franz, 60
Faust, 99
Fénelon, Fania, 58, 69, 74, 78–79, 95,
    100, 105, 145, 146, 150, 181, 217
Flaubert, Gustave, 92

Frank, Anne, 215
Frank, Hans, 166, 236, 237
Frank, Willi, 142
Frankl, Viktor, 43, 61, 88, 91, 102, 106,
    156–57, 216–17
Freud, Sigmund, 180
Fuchrer, Mira, 21
Führer. See Hitler, Adolf
Fyodorovna, Eugenia, 66

Gajowniczek, Franciszek, 55
Galilée, Galileo, 54
Gawkowski, Henrik, 272
Gedaleh, 220
Gepner, Abraham, 18
Gilbert, G. M., 125, 164, 191, 236
Gildenman, Misha, 214
Ginzburg, Eugenia, 32, 35, 42, 63, 72–
    73, 74, 77, 80, 83, 84, 85, 89, 91, 92–
    93, 95, 96, 98, 111, 122, 156, 159,
    167, 175, 201, 213, 243, 244, 246
Glazar, Richard, 33, 86, 230, 245, 272,
    275
Goebbels, Josef, 123
Goering, Hermann. See Göring,
    Hermann
Goethe, Johann Wolfgang von, 112
Goliborska, Tosia, 18
Göring, Hermann, 69, 164, 190, 236,
    237, 238
Gradowski, Zalmen, 62, 76, 96, 214
Graf, Maria, 89
Graff, 138
Grey, John Glenn, 85, 86, 144, 238
Grossman, Vasily, 26, 28, 112–13, 117,
    118, 124, 130, 139, 142, 147–48, 183,
    231–32
Grot-Rowecki, Stefan, 9

Hallie, Philip, 82, 115, 138, 221, 222,
    226
Hanke, Karl, 235
Hector, 48, 109, 110
Heidegger, Martin, 116, 150, 233
Heine, Heinrich, 50

Heisenberg, Werner, 101
Hempel, Ella, 57–58
Hercules, 51, 188
Herling, Gustaw, 39, 62, 66, 92, 94, 135, 251
Heydrich, Reinhard, 123, 153
Hilberg, Raul, 16, 130, 272
Hillesum, Etty, 81, 95, 98, 102, 136, 138, 198–201, 202–9, 213, 214, 220, 238, 265, 266, 294
Himmler, Heinrich, 69, 122, 123, 158, 161–62, 169, 175, 189, 191, 192
Hirsch, Fredy, 209–11
Hitler, Adolf, 20, 25, 53, 57, 83, 99, 101, 113, 116, 123, 128, 132–33, 134, 142, 151, 153, 157, 158, 163–64, 168, 172, 175, 176, 177, 183, 188, 189, 190–91, 192, 201, 202, 203, 207, 208, 214, 234, 236, 237, 239, 250, 254, 257
Hobbes, Thomas, 39, 139
Hölderlin, Friedrich, 94
Homer, 48, 110
Horace, 28
Höss, Rudolf, 68, 69, 108, 125, 127, 134, 145, 152, 153, 154, 158, 160, 161, 162, 164, 166, 168, 169–72, 174, 175, 177–78, 185, 189, 190, 233, 279

Ikonnikov, 112
Irena, 248
Ivan the Terrible, 207

Jaspers, Karl, 231, 238, 265
Jean the Pikolo, 34, 93, 94
Jesenska, Milena, 64–65, 74–75, 89, 90, 95, 102, 156, 291
Jo, 74
Jodl, Alfred, 236
Judas, 232
Jünger, Ernst, 233
Juszek, 60

Kafka, Franz, 64, 94
Kahler, Erich, 101, 162
Kaltenbrunner, Ernst, 236

Kant, Immanuel, 59, 104, 114, 158, 166
Karl, 202
Karski, Jan, 272, 273
Kastner, Rudolf, 107
Katznelson, Yitzhak, 106
Kautsky, Benedikt, 122
Kesten, Hermann, 233
Ketlinskaya, Vera, 188
Kiš, Danilo, 87
Klaas, 199, 201
Klein, Fritz, 168
Klepfisz, Michal, 15, 24, 56
Koenig, Hans, 138
Kogon, Eugen, 161, 197
Kolbe, Maximilian, 55–56, 58, 86
Korczak, Janusz, 18
Kosciuszkowa, J., 71
Kostylev, Mikhaïl, 92
Krall, Hanna, 13, 14, 16, 22–23, 31, 97, 281
Kramer, Josef, 100, 143, 144, 145
Kremer, Johann Paul, 141–42
Kren, George M., 154
Krug, Else, 64
Kurzman, Dan, 21, 24

Laks, Szymon, 33, 35, 95, 100
Langbein, Hermann, 64, 71, 148, 161, 168, 184, 202, 230, 263, 266
Lanzmann, Claude, 160, 243, 245, 248, 260, 271–78, 279, 280
Laqueur, Walter, 248, 250
Lederer, Vitezslav, 201
Lengyel, Olga, 41, 63, 72, 88
Lenin, Vladimir Illich, 127, 147–48, 158, 183
Less, Avner, 152
Levi, Primo, 29, 30, 32, 34, 66, 67, 69, 73, 82, 93, 94, 95, 98, 106–7, 123, 126, 135, 136, 137, 138–39, 141, 182, 183, 201, 219, 220, 229, 230, 238, 243, 244, 246, 256, 260–65, 267–71, 277, 281
Lifszyc, Pola, 17, 18, 20, 23, 26, 71, 72, 90, 147, 211

Lifton, Robert Jay, 145–46, 155, 162
Lingens-Reiner, Ella, 35–36, 89, 111, 230
Lorenzo, 67, 73, 265
Lubetkin, Tzivia, 106
Luther, Martin, 149

MacDonald, Dwight, 123
Maier, Charles, 117
Mandel, Maria, 100, 143, 145
Marchenko, Anatoly, 33, 39, 40–41, 77, 78, 79
Marie, 79
Marx, Karl, 37, 150
Massarek, Rudi, 55–56
Mauriac, François, 233
Mayer, Hans. See Améry, Jean
Mendel, 138, 219–20
Mengele, Josef, 69, 100, 124, 142, 143
Mephistopheles, 99, 112
Metzger, 226
Micheels, Louis, 89, 95, 100, 245
Mikolajczyk, Stanislaw, 7, 13
Milgram, Stanley, 167
Miller, Alice, 163
Milosz, Czeslaw, 38, 252
Mischka, 95
Mitscherlich, Alexander, 137, 234
Monter, Antoni, 6, 10
Morgenthau, Henry, Jr., 217–18
Morozov, Pavlik, 164
Moshe, 148
Moshe the Beadle, 244
Müller, Dr., 243, 269–70
Müller, Filip, 62, 63, 76, 210, 214, 245, 272
Munk, Alice, 210

Napoleon Bonaparte, 249
Neumeier, Hiasl, 64
Nietzsche, Friedrich, 37

Oberhauser, Joseph, 279
Odysseus, 49, 50, 55, 93
Ohlendorf, Otto, 149

Okulicki, Colonel, 5–7, 8–10, 11, 12, 15, 20, 21, 24, 110, 193
Orwell, George, 67, 106

Pascal, Blaise, 59, 85
Pasternak, Boris, 92, 255
Paulhan, Jean, 233
Pawelczynska, Anna, 36, 87, 181
Pechersky, Sacha, 54–55, 56, 73
Pelczynski, Tadeusz, 6, 7, 9, 10, 12, 14
Perpetua, Saint, 49, 57
Pestek, Viktor, 201–2
Pétain, Philippe, 83
Petrov, Vladimir, 182
Pikolo. See Jean the Pikolo
Pindar, 98
Plato, 103
Popieluszko, Father, 3
Porsche, Ferdinand, 68
Presserova, Maria, 89
Puccini, Giacomo, 100
Pushkin, Aleksandr, 92, 143

Raiman, Marcel, 56–57
Rappoport, Leon, 154
Ratushinskaya, Irina, 41, 42, 64, 67, 73, 74, 78, 88, 201
Rauschning, Hermann, 158
Renan, Ernest, 50
Ringelblum, Emmanuel, 16, 21, 22, 24, 25, 211
Rodman, David, 73
Rose, Alma, 69, 105, 143, 145, 150
Rosenberg, Alfred, 236, 237
Roskies, David, 62, 97, 214
Rousseau, Jean-Jacques, 39, 101, 139, 290, 291–92
Rousset, David, 126, 133–34, 251
Rückerl, A., 161
Rumkowski, Chaim, 183
Russell, Bertrand, 251

Salus, Grete, 266
Sartre, Jean-Paul, 108–9, 110–11, 251

Schmitt, Carl, 233
Schumann, Robert, 100, 143
Schwarzhuber, Johann, 142, 144
Semprun, Jorge, 40, 41, 42, 167, 269
Sereny, Gitta, 33, 56, 68, 86, 146, 147,
    153, 160, 161, 171, 230, 235, 240,
    241–42, 244, 245, 260, 272, 275, 278–
    82
Seyss-Inquart, Arthur, 125, 172
Shakespeare, William, 103, 106
Shalamov, Varlam, 32, 34–35
Siedlecki, Joe, 230, 231
Sinyavski, Andrei, 77
Smith, Bradley F., 218
Socrates, 48
Solzhenitsyn, Aleksandr, 28, 35, 41, 42,
    56, 66, 67, 136, 199, 251
Sorel, Julien, 50
Sosnkowski, Kazimierz, 7, 8, 17
Speer, Albert, 68, 87–88, 98–99, 124,
    142, 151, 152, 154, 157, 163, 164,
    169, 171, 175–78, 183, 184, 188, 190,
    234, 235, 269
Staf, Leon, 95
Stajner, Karlo, 87
Stalin, Joseph, 25, 57, 62, 116, 128, 131,
    132–33, 134, 143, 147, 153, 158, 167,
    188, 189, 190, 201, 237, 246, 252,
    254
Stangl, Franz, 68, 99, 110, 146–47, 148,
    152, 153, 160, 161, 171, 231, 233,
    235, 240, 241, 278–80, 281, 282
Stangl, Renate, 147, 280
Stangl, Theresa, 146–47, 231, 241
Stein, André, 105, 221, 223, 224, 228
Steiner, Jean-François, 5–7, 9–12, 14,
    18, 19
Steinlauf, 66
Suchomel, Franz, 272, 275, 277, 280
Suhl, Yuri, 20, 21, 22, 24, 25, 64, 71, 74,
    95, 215
Szmajzner, Stanislaw, 231

Tec, Nechama, 73, 224, 248
Tenenbaum, Mrs. and Miss, 18, 19
Teresa, Mother, 50
Thilo, 141
Tillion, Germaine, 36, 37, 73, 77, 86, 90,
    97, 122, 126, 131, 143, 184, 197, 198,
    201, 202, 251
Tocqueville, Alexis de, 50
Trocmé, André, 138, 225–26
Trocmé, Magda, 221–22, 225–26
Trunk, Isaiah, 71, 267

Ulysses. See Odysseus

Vaillant-Couturier, Marie-Claude, 251
Valéry, Paul, 115–16
van der Bergh, Lily, 55
Velikanova, Tatyana Mikhailovna, 74
Vercors, 233
Vidal-Naquet, Pierre, 256
Vincent de Paul, Saint, 50
Virgil, 110
Vrba, Rudolf, 73, 76, 138, 209, 210, 211,
    218, 265, 269, 272

Wagner, Richard, 143
Walser, Martin, 263
Walter, Anton, 74
Weber, Max, 11
Weiss, Ena, 35
Werfel, Franz, 117
Wiesel, Elie, 33, 90, 244
Wiesenthal, Simon, 229, 233
Wieviorka, Annette, 174
Wilner, Aryeh, 21
Wirths, Eduard, 145–46, 147, 148
Wittenberg, Isaac, 36
Wyman, David S., 250

Zawodny, J. K., 6, 10, 12
Zimetbaum, Mala, 63, 74
Zimmerman, 111